Essential Formal Semantics

Essential Formal Semantics

DONALD NUTE

ROWMAN AND LITTLEFIELD
Totowa, New Jersey

First published in the United States 1981 by
Rowman and Littlefield, 81 Adams Drive, Totowa, New Jersey 07512.

Distributed in the U.K. and Commonwealth by
George Prior Associated Publishers Limited
37-41 Bedford Row
London WC1R 4JH, England

Library of Congress Cataloging in Publication Data

Nute, Donald, 1947-
Essential formal semantics.

Bibliography: p.
1. Semantics (Philosophy) 2. Logic. I. Title.
B840.N87 160 81-12114
ISBN 0-8476-7026-0 AACR2

Printed in the United States of America

A person who will let himself be persuaded by a fallacious argument is ripe for the picking. This book is dedicated to my daughter Achsa who at the age of three recognized this fact and gleefully pressed her advantage whenever she could.

Analytical Table of Contents

Preface

The concepts and methods of that area of scholarship known as formal semantics are widely recognized as powerful tools to be employed in the investigation of a variety of problems in philosophy, linguistics, and other areas. This recognition is reflected in the scholarly literature in these disciplines where these concepts and methods are frequently used. Consequently the serious student in these areas is well advised to become familiar with at least the most essential content and techniques of formal semantics.

The material included in this book covers various aspects of axiomatic set theory, the philosophy of logic, formal semantics for sentential and predicate logic, modal logic, and the logic of conditionals. There are many excellent books which cover one or another of these topics in far greater detail than they are covered here, and I have mentioned some of my favorites in the Select Bibliography at the end of this volume. Why, then, do we need another book on these topics? Many students who want and need advanced training in formal methods will for various reasons be unwilling to complete a program of four or five courses to obtain this training. Indeed, such a series of courses may well involve more than many of these students actually need. In particular they may not need to study all of the special results which a really good text in any single one of the areas included here will present. Many of these results are of interest primarily to the student who wishes to specialize in logic. What these students do need is a rigorous introduction to the basic results in formal semantics. They need to see how formal semantics is built upon set theory, how formal systems and their interpretations are tailored to fit each other, and how formalization can play an important role in achieving greater understanding of other questions which may be of more immediate concern to them. They need to study several systems with applications in several areas of philosophy and language so they can see the wide range of problems which can be approached through formal semantics, learn how similar techniques may be used repeatedly to produce new results in these diverse areas, and get a feel for semantics as a field of lively innovation rather than a static body of theory. No one book can provide everything which such students might need, but I have attempted to collect the most basic and essential ideas and techniques and to present them together in a way which recognizes the need for breadth and relevance but does not sacrifice rigor.

This text was developed in courses which I taught for the Department of Philosophy and Religion and the Linguistics Program at the University of Georgia. Typically both graduates and advanced undergraduates in philosophy, linguistics, psychology, mathematics, and computer science enroll in these courses. The only prerequisite is familiarity with natural deduction systems for sentential and predicate logic such as those developed in the elementary logic texts mentioned in the Select Bibliography. The text provides material for an accelerated course lasting one term or a more leisurely course lasting two terms. The book is organized into many short sections each of which introduces only a few new concepts or techniques. Most sections include exercises, and answers to some of the more difficult exercises are collected in a section at the end of the book. Many of the exercises are very simple, a feature which has contributed to the effectiveness of the book as a text for use with undergraduates and other students with limited backgrounds in mathematics. Also, many exercises in later chapters resemble those in earlier chapters. This provides opportunities for students to review techniques they have learned earlier and thus improves retention. I have made every effort to make the material accessible to a wide range of students without sacrificing rigor.

I am very grateful to my teachers, particularly Nino Cocchiarella and Michael Dunn who have had the greatest influence upon the contents of this book. I am indebted to the University of Georgia for giving me the opportunity to teach this material and for providing financial support during the summer of 1979 when I began the task of putting this material together into its present form. I thank Beverly Chandler and Ellen Johnson for their secretarial help, and Jim Feather at Rowman & Littlefield for helping me bring this project to completeion. I sincerely appreciate the patience and the help of the many students who have used various early versions of this text in my courses, and I particularly thank my friend and student Clyde Melton who helped with the final proof-reading. Finally and always, I thank my wife Jane for her proof-reading and her many helpful suggestions and, more than that, for sharing and helping in every part of all I do.

CHAPTER 1

Preliminaries

§1. Metalanguage and Object Language. We are going to be studying certain kinds of languages. One kind of language that can be studied is a language like English, French, or German. Languages of this sort which people use to conduct their day-to-day lives are called natural languages. These are languages which have evolved naturally over the course of many years. The languages we will be studying will not be natural. They will be languages which we make up as we go along. They are called artificial or formal languages. These formal languages are intended to be similar to natural languages in certain respects, but we will consider these similarities only as they become apparent.

Suppose we were studying some natural language like German. We would use a German textbook of the sort that is familiar to many readers. If we were to look inside that textbook, we would find not only German words and phrases, but also English words and phrases. If we were asked in what language the textbook was written, we would probably say that it was written in English. Yet the book is about German, and many German words appear in it. The language which is being studied, in this case German, is called the *object language*; the language which is used to say things about the object language, in this case English, is called the *metalanguage*.

The object language and the metalanguage may be either the same or different when we are engaged in talk about a language. If we were to study English grammar or composition, our textbook would be written in English about English.

To talk about a language, we must have some way of referring to the words and expressions of that language. In a German textbook, we accomplish this by the simple expedient of using the German words and expressions themselves to indicate what we are talking about. In a manner of speaking, no German words occur in the main text of our textbook at all. Instead we can think of ourselves as having a number of English words which look just like certain German words and which we use in English for no other purpose than to refer to the German words like which they look. For example, when we see the word 'drei' in our German textbook we can think of this as an English word which we use to refer to the German word which looks just like it. The special English word 'drei', which we add to English simply to have a way of referring to the German word, does not mean the same thing as does the English word 'three'; instead we think of it as a name of the German word which does mean the same thing as the English word 'three'. This is not quite all there is to the story since our textbook will also contain long passages which really are in German and which we are to translate into English as exercises. Nevertheless, in order to talk about German we must have a way to refer to German words and expressions, and this is usually accomplished simply by adding words which look like German words to our metalanguage, English, and using these new English words as names for the original German words which they resemble.

It is very important to keep our object language and our metalanguage distinct when they are different. Otherwise we can end up trying to say things by using the words and expressions of the one in combination with the words and expressions of the other. The result of this is nonsense since we have said nothing in any language. But the real danger is that sometimes the resulting gibberish may seem to make sense, and when it does it can lead us into error. Here we will be using English as our metalanguage, where we interpret English as including the logical symbols necessary for predicate logic with identity and that part of mathematics known as set theory. As we go along, we will add special expressions to our metalanguage which will enable us to refer to the items of the various object languages about which we wish to talk.

QUESTIONS

1.1 Suppose a textbook of the usual kind were written to help people whose native language is German to read French. What would the metalanguage of this textbook be? What would be the object language?

1.2 What are the metalanguage and the object language of _Webster's New Collegiate Dictionary_?

§2. Syntax and Semantics. Looking once again at our German textbook, we find two different kinds of statements in this book. For example, the textbook might tell us that 'drei' is an adjective. It might also tell us that 'drei' means _three_. The first of these statements tells us something about the way in which the German word can be used along with other words to form acceptable German sentences. It tells us the grammatical category of the German word. The second statement tells us what the word means. In fact the German textbook is a combination of what we would call a German _grammar_ and what we would call a German _dictionary_. The functions of a grammar and of a dictionary are quite different.

We can learn German grammar without ever learning what any German word means. Grammars are concerned with the ways the expressions of a language can be put together to form more complex expressions. Grammars give us the accepted rules of formation for the language. They are ultimately concerned only with certain relations between the words and expressions themselves without any reference to anything beyond the linguistic items such as meanings. A more general term than 'grammar' for the study of relations between the items in a language is the term '_syntax_'. Grammar is primarily concerned with formation rules, with which compound expressions in the language satisfy the conditions for being grammatical or well-formed. Syntax involves this and more. Syntax is the study of all kinds of relations between linguistic items, including such relations as those involved in the answers to questions about whether a certain sentence in the language _follows from_ certain other sentences.

We can also learn the meanings of German words without learning German grammar. If we knew the German counterparts for all English words, we might try to translate the English sentence 'They had gone to work early' simply by replacing each English word in the sentence with its German equivalent. But if we were to do this, we would not produce a German sentence since German grammar demands a different word order from that required by English grammar. Of course meaning really involves more than what a dictionary or a textbook vocabulary list gives. _Semantics_, which is the study of meaning, is also concerned with the way in which the meanings of complex expressions in the language are determined by the structures of the expressions together with the meanings of the simple components occurring in the expressions. Without syntax, we would not know whether the semantics we provided for a language took adequate account of the contribution which form makes to meaning.

The kind of semantics we will be studying is called _formal semantics_. As was suggested in the last paragraph, the meaning of a complex expression is determined both by the meanings of its simple components and by its structure or form. We will be concentrating on that part of meaning which is due to the form of the expression. We will not even attempt to give specific meanings for most of the simple components of the formal languages we study beyond saying that they have meanings of a certain kind due to the kinds of positions they can occupy within the structure of complex expressions.

Besides studying formal syntax and semantics separately, we will also be looking at the relations between syntax and semantics for each language we study and at the ways in which these resemble the syntax and semantics of a natural language like English.

QUESTIONS

2.1 Do punctuation rules belong to syntax or semantics?

2.2 Do the postulates of Euclidean geometry belong to syntax or semantics?

§3. Sets and Set Membership. We will develop the languages which we wish to examine as mathematical structures of certain sorts. When we begin to interpret these languages, we will do so in terms of other mathematical structures. The mathematical background we will need for this work comes from that branch of mathematics known as set theory. Besides the work we do here, set theory has been suggested as a foundation for much other work which is done in modern mathematics.

In order to do set theory, we need to add two new, primitive symbols to the symbols we already have available for predicate logic with identity. These two new symbols are the constant symbol '$\emptyset$' which is read 'the empty set' and the two-place predicate symbol 'ε' which is read 'is a member of', 'is in', or 'belongs to'. To say that these two symbols are primitive means that we will not provide definitions for them.

While we do not define '$\emptyset$' and 'ε', we can still convey their meanings in two ways. The first way is by analogy, comparing them to other expressions which we understand and which have meanings which are in some way similar. The other way is to list certain basic truths involving essential use of these symbols. These basic truths are called the axioms of set theory. This axiomatic approach to developing the meanings of our two primitive set-theoretic symbols will be pursued in the next several sections.

To get some idea of what 'ε' means, let's consider some other kinds of membership, "being-in", and "belonging-to" relations. One such relation is that of spatial containment. Some coins are placed in a wallet and the wallet is placed in a purse. Both the wallet and the purse are kinds of things which can have things "in" them, while the coins are not. Of course, any coin which is in the wallet is also in the purse. This means that spatial containment is a transitive relation. Set membership is something like spatial containment, but it is not spatial containment. One important difference is that set membership is not transitive. We can have three things x, y, and z such that $x \varepsilon y$ and $y \varepsilon z$, but $\sim(x \varepsilon z)$. (We often write '$\sim(x \varepsilon z)$' as '$x \notin z$'.)

Let's consider another example. Georgia is in the United States and the United States is in the United Nations. However, Georgia is not in the United Nations. The membership relation we are talking about here is more like the set membership relation than is spatial containment because it is transitive.

We use the notion of set membership to define the notion of a set. Basically a set is something which has members in the appropriate way. There is a problem with thinking of sets in this way, however, and that problem is the empty set. The empty set is supposed to be a set which doesn't have any member, which is of course why it is called "empty". To get at something like the notion of the empty set, let's consider an example. Suppose I have developed a new recipe for making fried chicken. I decide to start a chain of restaurants in which this new fried chicken is to be sold. I incorporate and I begin to look for people who will buy franchises in my new restaurant chain. Any restaurant built and operated under one of my franchises will be a member of the Better Fried Chicken chain. But right now there are no such restaurants. We could say that as of this moment I own an empty restaurant chain. We might balk at talking about a chain of restaurants until some restaurants belonged to that chain, but it is sometimes very convenient to talk about such a chain. For example, I might go public and sell shares in my chain even though there aren't yet any restaurants in the chain. Just so, we will wish to speak of $\emptyset$ and say that it is a set even though it has no members.

Combining all of this, we can now say what it is for something to be a set. Something is a set just in case it either has some members or is the empty set, i.e., $(x)(x \text{ is a set} \leftrightarrow ((\exists y)y \in x \vee x = \emptyset))$. We will use this statement as a definition of what it is to be a set. In making general statements like definitions in mathematics, we frequently omit the universal quantifier at the beginning of the statement. Following this practice, we have our first definition.

<u>DEFINITION 1.</u> x is a set $\leftrightarrow ((\exists y)y \in x \vee x = \emptyset)$.

We will be able to use Definition 1 whenever we wish to justify a claim in an argument, just as we will be able to use any of the definitions, axioms, and theorems yet to be developed. Thus whenever we already have one side of the equivalence in Definition 1 as a line in an argument or proof, we will be able to write down the other side as a conclusion using Definition 1 as our reason.

One important difference between set membership and other relations which are in some way similar to set membership is that you can't have two different sets with exactly the same members. By this I do not mean that $x \varepsilon y$ and $x \varepsilon z$ and $y \neq z$ can't all hold. For contrast, suppose we have two lodges in a particular town, the Octopus Lodge and the Roundfellows Lodge. It is quite possible that these two lodges have exactly the same members, yet this wouldn't lead us to say that the Octopus Lodge and the Roundfellows Lodge were really the same lodge. Yet if we were talking about sets instead of lodges and about set membership instead of lodge membership, we would be entitled to draw exactly this conclusion. Once you know the members of a set, there is a sense in which there is nothing more to know about that set.

§4. Special Variables. So far, we have used only one kind of variable. We have been using 'x', 'y', etc., as general variables which range over everything. Thus Definition 1 implies that Thales is a set $\leftrightarrow$ $((\exists y) y \varepsilon \text{ Thales} \vee \text{Thales} = \emptyset)$ and that General Motors is a set $\leftrightarrow$ $((\exists y)(y \varepsilon \text{ General Motors} \vee \text{General Motors} = \emptyset)$. Of course Thales and General Motors are not sets. (Anything which is not a set is an individual.) Sometimes it is convenient to use special variables which range over only things of a certain kind. We might sometimes want to restrict the range of a variable on a particular occasion just to persons or just to numbers. When we want to restrict all of the variables we use on a particular occasion to one specific kind of thing, we usually continue to use general variables with the understanding that those variables are now being used with a restricted range. When we do this, we say we are limiting the universe of discourse. We might symbolize 'Everyone who is a Φ is also a Ψ' as '$(x)((x \text{ is a person} \ \& \ \Phi(x)) \rightarrow \Psi(x))$' or we might shorten our symbolization by restricting the range of our variables to persons so that we need only write '(x)(Φ(x) → Ψ(x))'. Sometimes though we want to restrict the range of some of our variables while leaving the ranges of other variables unrestricted, or we may want to restrict some variables to things of one kind and restrict other variables to things of another kind. In such cases the technique of limiting the universe of discourse is inadequate for our needs. Instead we must use special symbols for each of the different kinds of things to which we wish to restrict our variables.

Suppose on a certain occasion we wish to restrict certain of our variables to only those things which have some property Φ. We can use '@' as a special variable which ranges only over Φ's. In any formula in which '@' occurs, it will be possible to eliminate all occurrences of '@' and replace them with a combination of occurrences of general variables and the predicate 'Φ'. The way we do this in a particular case depends on whether the occurrence of '@' we are eliminating is bound by a universal or an existential quantifier. For example, '(@)(∃x)@ ε x' is equivalent to '(y)(Φ(y) → (∃x)y ε x)', while '(x)(∃@)@ ε x' is equivalent to '(x)(∃y)(Φ(y) & y ε x)'. While special variables are often convenient, they are not essential and they can always be eliminated whenever they occur.

We will introduce two kinds of special variables at this time. For set variables we will use the capital letters 'A', 'B', 'C', etc., at the beginning of the alphabet. For variables which range over positive integers (whole numbers greater than zero) we will use the letters 'i', 'j', 'k', etc., in the middle of the alphabet. We shall be introducing additional special variables as the need arises.

EXERCISES

4.1 Eliminate the set variables in '(A)(B)(∃C)(x)(x ε C

$\leftrightarrow$ (x ε A $\vee$ x ε B)'.

4.2* Eliminate the special variables in '(i)(j)(i + (j + 1) = (i + j) + 1)'.

4.3* Show that A $\neq \emptyset \rightarrow (\exists x)(x \ \varepsilon \ A)$.

4.4 Rewrite '(x)(x is a positive integer $\rightarrow$ ($\exists$y)(y is a set & x ε y))' using special variables for positive integers and sets.

§5. The Unit Set Axiom and the Extensionality Axiom. So far we know what a set is, at least in terms of set membership and the empty set, but we have not said yet whether there are any sets. We haven't even said that $\emptyset$ exists. Just because we have a name doesn't mean that there exists anything to which the name refers; otherwise Pegasus and Dracula would exist to name but two. Now we come to our first basic truth about sets, an axiom which tells us that certain sets exist. One kind of set is the kind of set which has only one member. We call such a set a unit set or a singleton. Our first axiom tells us that each and every thing that exists is the unique member of some unit set.

THE UNIT SET AXIOM. $(\exists A)(y)(y \ \varepsilon \ A \leftrightarrow y = x)$.

The Unit Set Axiom tells us that for each object x there is a set A which has x as its only member.

Our next axiom gives us the conditions under which we can conclude that two sets are not really distinct sets at all but are instead one and the same set. The identity criterion for sets is membership and sets with exactly the same membership are identical.

THE EXTENSIONALITY AXIOM. $(x)(x \ \varepsilon \ A \leftrightarrow x \ \varepsilon \ B) \rightarrow A = B$.

Using both of these axioms, we can show that each object belongs to exactly one unit set.

(1)	$(\exists A)(y)(y \in A \leftrightarrow y = x)$	Unit Set Axiom
(2)	$(y)(y \in A \leftrightarrow y = x)$	(1), EI
(3)	$(y)(y \in B \leftrightarrow y = x)$	Assumed Premise
(4)	$y \in A \leftrightarrow y = x$	(2), UI
(5)	$y \in B \leftrightarrow y = x$	(3), UI
(6)	$y \in A \leftrightarrow y \in B$	(4), (5), several rules combined
(7)	$(x)(x \in A \leftrightarrow x \in B)$	(6), UG
(8)	$(y)(y \in B \leftrightarrow y = x) \rightarrow (x)(x \in A \leftrightarrow x \in B)$	(3)-(7), Conditional Proof
(9)	$(x)(x \in A \leftrightarrow x \in B) \rightarrow A = B$	Extensionality Axiom
(10)	$(y)(y \in B \leftrightarrow y = x) \rightarrow A = B$	(8), (9), HS
(11)	$(B)((y)(y \in B \leftrightarrow y = x) \rightarrow A = B)$	(10), UG
(12)	$(y)(y \in A \leftrightarrow y = x)$ & $(B)((y)(y \in B \leftrightarrow y = x) \rightarrow A = B)$	(2), (11), Conj.
(13)	$(\exists A)((y)(y \in A \leftrightarrow y = x)$ & $(B)((y)(y \in B \leftrightarrow y = x) \rightarrow A = B))$	(12), EG

Line (13) is the desired result. This argument also shows us how we may use axioms in proving various results.

Mathematicians do not usually formulate their arguments as we have done here. Their proofs are briefer and are written in a style much closer to that of ordinary prose. One of our goals is to develop a mathematical prose style as we progress. Let's look at the way a mathematician might reformulate our argument.

> To see that every object belongs to exactly one unit set, we first let x be any object. By the Unit Set Axiom, we can let A be a set such that for any object y, $y \in A$ if and only if $y = x$. Now suppose B is a set such that for any y, $y \in B$ if and only if $y = x$. Then for all y, $y \in A$ if and only if $y \in B$, and by the Extensionality Axiom $A = B$. Thus x belongs to exactly one unit set.

We now define a new notation which we will use to refer to the unique unit set corresponding to any object.

DEFINITION 2. $\{x\} = y \leftrightarrow (z)(z \in y \leftrightarrow z = x)$.

EXERCISES

5.1* Show that $y \in \{x\} \leftrightarrow y = x$.

5.2 Show that $x \in \{x\}$.

5.3* Show that $\{x\} = \{y\} \rightarrow x = y$.

§6. The Union Axiom and n-tuplet Sets. Sometimes we want to talk about all the members of two possibly distinct sets A and B. It would be convenient if there were a set which had as its members exactly those things which are in A and B. Our next axiom tells us that this is in fact the case.

THE UNION AXIOM. $(\exists C)(x)(x \in C \leftrightarrow (x \in A \vee x \in B))$.

We call such a set C a union of the sets A and B. It turns out that two sets A and B have exactly one union. Suppose C and D are both unions of A and B. Suppose, that is, that $(x)(x \in C \leftrightarrow (x \in A \vee x \in B))$ and $(x)(x \in D \leftrightarrow (x \in A \vee x \in B))$. Then $(x)(x \in C \leftrightarrow x \in D)$, and $C = D$ by the Extensionality Axiom. Since every pair of sets has a unique union, we can introduce new notation to use in referring to the union of two sets.

DEFINITION 3. $A \cup B = x \leftrightarrow (y)(y \in x \leftrightarrow (y \in A \vee y \in B))$.

We read '$A \cup B$' as 'the union of A and B' or as 'A union B'.

Substituting '$\{x\}$' and '$\{y\}$' for 'A' and 'B' in the Union Axiom, we find that $(\exists C)(z)(z \in C \leftrightarrow (z \in \{x\} \vee z \in \{y\}))$. But we saw in Exercise 5.1 that $z \in \{x\} \leftrightarrow z = x$, so $(\exists C)(z)(z \in C \leftrightarrow (z = x \vee z = y))$. We can easily show that the set we have shown to exist here is unique. Where $x = y$, the set we have shown to exist is just $\{x\}$. But where $x \neq y$, we have a new kind of set which has exactly two members. We call such a set a doubleton or a pair. We find in fact that $(z)(z \varepsilon \{x\} \cup \{y\} \leftrightarrow (z = x \vee z = y))$. Continuing in this manner, we can show that $(w)(w \varepsilon (\{x\} \cup \{y\}) \cup \{z\} \leftrightarrow (w = x \vee w = y \vee w = z))$, etc. Thus for any positive integer n and n-many distinct objects $x_1,\ldots,x_n$, there is a unique set C such that $(y)(y \varepsilon C \leftrightarrow (y = x_1 \vee \ldots \vee y = x_n))$. We call such a set an n-tuplet. '$((\{x\} \cup \{y\}) \cup \{z\}) \cup \{w\}$' is a very cumbersome way to represent the unique four-tuplet which has all and only x, y, z, and w as members, so we introduce new notation which is more convenient.

DEFINITION 4. $\{x,y\} = \{x\} \cup \{y\}$;
$\{x,y,z\} = \{x,y\} \cup \{z\}$;
etc.

We end this section with a warning. '$\cup$' is neither a sentence connective like '&' and '$\vee$' nor a predicate like '=' and 'ε'. A sentence connective combines with one or more sentences to produce a new sentence, e.g., 'x is a set & y is a set'. A predicate expression combines with one or more referring expressions to form a sentence, e.g., 'x = y'. But '$\cup$' combines with two referring expressions to form a new referring expression, e.g., '$\emptyset \cup$ {Frege}'. For this reason we should never have something like 'Suppose A $\cup$ B' or 'Therefore A $\cup$ B' occur as a separate line in a proof or argument. This would be like saying 'Suppose Descartes' or 'Therefore Kant'. These are not complete sentences. This warning will apply as well to other "term forming" operators which we will introduce later.

EXERCISES

6.1 Show that $x \varepsilon A \cup B \leftrightarrow (x \varepsilon A \vee x \varepsilon B)$.

6.2 Show that $A \cup B = B \cup A$.

6.3* Show that $\{x,y,x\} = \{x,y\}$.

6.4 Show that $\{x,y\} \cup \{z,w\} = \{x,z\} \cup \{y,w\}$.

§7. Russell's Paradox and the Axiom Schema of Separation.

Think of some property and all those things which have that property. We may wonder whether there is a set which has as its members all and only those things which have the property about which we are thinking. We will not attempt to answer this question, but we will look instead at a closely related question. Think of some open sentence like 'x is red' or 'x is square'. By an open sentence I mean a sentence containing a free variable. Let's consider only open sentences containing a single free variable. '$x \varepsilon x$' is an open sentence of the sort I mean, but '$x \varepsilon y$' is not. Let '$\Phi(x)$' be the open sentence we have in mind. We will say of any object y that '$\Phi(x)$' is true of y just in case the sentence we get by substituting some name for y for every occurrence of 'x' in '$\Phi(x)$' is true. Is there a set which has as its members all and only those things for which '$\Phi(x)$' is true? Early in the development of set theory it was thought that the answer to this question should be affirmative. Because of this belief a certain general claim about sets was adopted.

PRINCIPLE OF ABSTRACTION. $(\exists A)(x)(x \varepsilon A \leftrightarrow \Phi(x))$.

Actually there is not a single Principle of Abstraction but a different principle for each open sentence '$\Phi(x)$'. We now know that for at least some open sentences the corresponding Principle of Abstraction is false.

Bertrand Russell proved that the Principle of Abstraction was not reliable and hence could not be accepted as an axiom schema of set theory. To accept such an axiom schema would be to reduce set theory to inconsistency. Consider the open sentence '$x \not\varepsilon x$'. The corresponding Principle of Abstraction claims that $(\exists A)(x)(x \varepsilon A \leftrightarrow x \not\varepsilon x)$. By EI we have $(x)(x \varepsilon A \leftrightarrow x \not\varepsilon x)$, and by UI we have $A \varepsilon A \leftrightarrow A \not\varepsilon A$, a contradiction.

So for at least some open sentences the corresponding Principle of Abstraction must be rejected. This result is called Russell's Paradox.

Perhaps not every open sentence gives us a Principle of Abstraction which we can accept, but surely some do. Both the Unit Set Axiom and the Union Axiom have such formulas as their instantiations. For example, the Unit Set Axiom tells us that the Principle of Abstraction corresponding to the open sentence 'x = the Empire State Building' is true, and the Union Axiom tells us that the Principle of Abstraction corresponding to the open sentence '$x \varepsilon \{4,57,21\} \vee x \varepsilon \emptyset$' is true. What we need, then, is some other principle which allows us to abstract in certain cases but which does not lead to contradiction. Both the Unit Set Axiom and the Union Axiom are such principles, but we seek a more general principle.

It was discovered that if we began with something which we knew to be a set and then limited the new set which we formed by abstraction to those members of the original set of which the open sentence upon which we based our abstraction was true, then no contradiction arose. The problem with the Principle of Abstraction is that it allows us to abstract with regard to the fundamental notions of set theory in such a way as to lead to contradiction. But if we begin with something which is already a set, there appears to be no problem in assuming that we can separate from it as a possibly different set all of its members for which some open sentence is true. This leads to a very powerful axiom schema.

> THE AXIOM SCHEMA OF SEPARATION. $(\exists B)(x)(x \varepsilon B \leftrightarrow (x \varepsilon A \& \Phi(x)))$.

A restriction on this axiom schema is that 'B' not occur free in '$\Phi(x)$'. We call this an axiom schema rather than simply an axiom because it gives us the pattern of an axiom, a pattern which is only completed when we provide an appropriate open sentence with which to replace '$\Phi(x)$' and a name of a set with which to replace 'A'. Thus we have a different Axiom of Separation for each open sentence and set. For a fuller discussion of this axiom schema (and for a more detailed development of set theory generally), see Patrick Suppes, Axiomatic Set Theory, Dover, 1972. I will show that $(\exists x)x = \emptyset$ and that $(x)x \notin \emptyset$ using the Axiom Schema of Separation. Beginning with the set {Plato} and the open sentence '$x \neq x$', we have it by the Axiom Schema of Separation that $(\exists A)(x)(x \in A \leftrightarrow (x \in \{Plato\} \,\&\, x \neq x))$. But since $(x)x = x$, $(x)x \notin A$ and $(\exists A)(x)x \notin A$. When we eliminate set variables we have $(\exists y)(y$ is a set $\&$ $(x)x \notin y)$. Let y be such a set. Then by Definition 1, $y = \emptyset$. So $(\exists x)x = \emptyset$. But since $y = \emptyset$ and $(x)x \notin y$, $(x)x \notin \emptyset$.

EXERCISES

7.1 Show that $(\exists C)(x)(x \in C \leftrightarrow (x \in A \,\&\, x \in B))$.

7.2 Show that $(\exists C)(x)(x \in C \leftrightarrow (x \in A \,\&\, x \notin B))$.

§8. Containment, Set Intersection, and Set Difference.

When all of the members of one set A are also members of another set B we say that A is contained in B. We introduce a new symbol to represent this relation between sets.

DEFINITION 5. $A \subseteq B \leftrightarrow (x)(x \in A \rightarrow x \in B)$.

It follows from the Extensionality Axiom and Definition 5 that $(A \subseteq B \,\&\, B \subseteq A) \rightarrow A = B$. Sometimes we wish to say that A is contained in B and yet B is larger than A in the sense that B has some members which A does not have. Then we say that A is properly contained in B and we represent this relation with another symbol.

DEFINITION 6. $A \subset B \leftrightarrow (A \subseteq B \,\&\, A \neq B)$.

Containment and set membership are different relations

with different properties. Notice for example that {Chomsky} $\subseteq$ {Chomsky} but that {Chomsky} $\notin$ {Chomsky}. On the other hand, $\{\emptyset\} \in \{\{\emptyset\}\}$ but $\{\emptyset\} \not\subseteq \{\{\emptyset\}\}$. However, $\emptyset \in \{\emptyset\}$ and $\emptyset \subseteq \{\emptyset\}$. So neither relation implies the other and neither relation excludes the other. Also containment is transitive unlike set membership, i.e., $(A)(B)(C)(A \subseteq B \mathbin{\&} B \subseteq C \rightarrow A \subseteq C)$.

The Union Axiom tells us that for any two sets A and B there is a set $A \cup B$ such that something is a member of $A \cup B$ just in case it is a member of either A or B. Is there also a set which has as its members all and only those things which are members of both A and B? Or a set which has as its members exactly those things which are members of A but not of B? Do we need additional axioms to insure that such sets exist? We do have sets like this, but we don't need any new axioms to prove that we do. In fact, we already proved that there are such sets in Exercises 7.1 and 7.2. It is also easy enough to prove that such sets are unique for any A and B. (The proofs are left to the reader.) Thus we have two new symbols to define.

DEFINITION 7. $A \cap B = y \leftrightarrow ((x)(x \in y \leftrightarrow (x \in A \mathbin{\&} x \in B)) \mathbin{\&} y \text{ is a set})$.

DEFINITION 8. $A - B = y \leftrightarrow ((x)(x \in y \leftrightarrow (x \in A \mathbin{\&} x \notin B)) \mathbin{\&} y \text{ is a set})$.

We read '$A \cap B$' as 'the intersection of A and B' or as 'A intersect B', and we read '$A - B$' as 'the difference between A and B' or as 'A less B'. We should notice that $A - B$ may not be the same thing as $B - A$. For example, $\{\emptyset\} - \emptyset = \{\emptyset\}$, but $\emptyset - \{\emptyset\} = \emptyset$. We should also notice that like '$\cup$', '$\cap$' and '$-$' are not sentence connectives; rather they are symbols which combine with referring expressions to form new referring expressions.

EXERCISES

8.1 Show that $x \varepsilon A \cap B \leftrightarrow (x \varepsilon A \ \& \ x \varepsilon B)$.

8.2 Show that $x \varepsilon A - B \leftrightarrow (x \varepsilon A \ \& \ x \not\varepsilon B)$.

8.3 Show that $A \cap B = B \cap A$.

8.4 Show that $A \cap (B \cup C) = (A \cap B) \cup (A \cap C)$.

8.5 Show that $(A - B) \cup (B - A) = (A \cup B) - (A \cap B)$.

8.6 Show that $A \cup \emptyset = A$.

8.7 Show that $A \cap \emptyset = \emptyset$.

8.8* Show that $A \subseteq B \leftrightarrow A \cap B = A$.

8.9 Show that $A \subseteq B \leftrightarrow A \cup B = B$.

8.10 Identify some other sets which, like $\{\emptyset\}$, contain some of their members. Can you find any other sets which contain all of their members?

§9. Defining Sets by Abstraction. In Section 7 we saw that for an open sentence '$\Phi(x)$' there may or may not exist a set whose members are all and only those things for which '$\Phi(x)$' is true. Nevertheless we will use open sentences to define sets. We will simply take precautions for those cases in which there is no set of all those things for which the open sentence is true.

DEFINITION SCHEMA 9. $\{x: \Phi(x)\} = y \leftrightarrow (((x)(x \varepsilon y \leftrightarrow \Phi(x)) \ \& \ y \text{ is a set}) \lor (y = \emptyset \ \& \ \sim(\exists A)(x)(x \varepsilon A \leftrightarrow \Phi(x))))$.

We read '$\{x: \Phi(x)\}$' as 'the set of all x such that $\Phi(x)$' or as 'the set of all Φ's'. Where there is a set whose members are exactly those things for which '$\Phi(x)$' is true, we let '$\{x: \Phi(x)\}$' denote that set. Where there is no such set, we let '$\{x: \Phi(x)\}$' denote $\emptyset$.

Notice that in the right hand side of Definition Schema 9 'x' does not occur free. This means that 'x' does not occur free in '$\{x: \Phi(x)\}$' either. In other words, '{-:---}' is a variable binding notation much like the notations '(-)' and

'(∃-)' which we use in the universal and existential quantifiers.

In later chapters we will often use definition by abstraction without addressing the problem whether or not there is actually a set whose members are exactly those things for which the open sentence we use in our abstraction is true. In such cases it will be possible to show that such sets exist, but the details of such proofs would divert us too far from our main line of development. It would be a gross oversimplification to pass over Russell's Paradox and the difficulties hidden in defining sets by abstraction without comment, but for the most part we can ignore these difficulties in what follows.

EXERCISES

9.1* Show that $\{x: x \notin x\} = \emptyset$.

9.2 Show that $\{x: x = x\} = \emptyset$.

9.3 Show that $A = \{x: x \in A\}$.

9.4 Show that $y \in \{x: \Phi(x)\} \rightarrow \Phi(y)$.

9.5 Give a counterexample to show that $\Phi(y) \rightarrow y \in \{x: \Phi(x)\}$ is false.

§10. Ordered Pairs and Relations. Normally we think of a relation as a way in which two or more things might be connected. Familiar examples of two-place relations are 'is the father of', 'is married to', and 'is larger than'. We need a set-theoretic notion which corresponds to our ordinary notion of a relation.

The order in which we mention things which are related is important. The sun is larger than the earth, but the earth is not larger than the sun. Speaking of the sun and the earth, we say that the former is larger than the latter. In order to speak of the "former" and the "latter", we first have to have the two items presented together with some order. In this case the order is that in which the two items are mentioned. We can form the set {sun,earth} whose members are exactly the two things about which we are speaking, but this set does not convey any order in which the two things are presented. We could form the set $\{x: (\exists y)(\exists z)(x = \{y,z\}\ \&\ y$ is larger than $z)\}$, and in some sense this set corresponds to the ordinary relation represented by 'is larger than'. But since $\{y,z\} = \{z,y\}$, the essential element of order is missing. What we need are not just pairs but pairs with an order.

DEFINITION 10. $\langle x,y\rangle = \{\{x\},\{x,y\}\}$.

We call $\langle x,y\rangle$ the *ordered pair* whose *first member* is x and whose *second member* is y. Typographically we distinguish the first and second members of an ordered pair by the order in which we write down the symbols standing for these members, but set-theoretically the first and second members of an ordered pair are distinguished in quite a different way. The first member of an ordered pair is always the unique member of the intersection of the members of the ordered pair. Thus $z \in \{x\} \cap \{x,y\} \leftrightarrow z = x$. The second member of the ordered pair is the unique member of the union of the differences of the members of the ordered pair. Thus $z \in (\{x\} - \{x,y\}) \cup (\{x,y\} - \{x\}) \leftrightarrow z = y$. These two operations upon the members of an ordered pair always allow us to recover the first and second members of the ordered pair. Notice however that $x \notin \langle x,y\rangle$ and $y \notin \langle x,y\rangle$. The first and second "members" of an ordered pair are not members *simpliciter* of the ordered pair. Being the first or second member of an ordered pair is quite a different relation from the relation of set membership.

Ordered pairs provide the essential ingredient of order which mere pairs do not. We find that while we always have $\{x,y\} = \{y,x\}$, we have $\langle x,y\rangle = \langle y,x\rangle$ only if $x = y$. To see this suppose that $\langle x,y\rangle = \langle y,x\rangle$, i.e., that $\{\{x\},\{x,y\}\} =$

$\{\{y\},\{y,x\}\}$. Then since $\{x\} \in \langle x,y\rangle$, $\{x\} \in \langle y,x\rangle$, i.e., $\{x\} \in \{\{y\},\{y,x\}\}$ and either $\{x\} = \{y\}$ or $\{x\} = \{y,x\}$. But in either of these cases $x = y$. Since ordered pairs are indeed ordered we might say, for example, that the ordered pair <sun,earth> exemplifies the *larger than* relation while the ordered pair <earth, sun> does not. Mathematically, a relation is nothing more than a set of ordered pairs.

DEFINITION 11. A is a relation $\leftrightarrow (x)(x \in A \leftrightarrow (\exists y)(\exists z)(x = \langle y,z\rangle))$.

We can define relations by abstraction in much the same way as we do other sets. For example the relation $\{x: (\exists y)(\exists z)(x = \langle y,z\rangle$ & y is larger than z)$\}$ corresponds in an obvious way to the ordinary relation *larger than*. Of course the same set-theoretic relation might correspond to two or more different ordinary relations. It could become the case, for example, that x was the legal guardian of y if and only if x was the parent of y. This is not the case now but it is only an accident of history that it is not. Should it someday become the case, then the mathematical relations corresponding to these quite different ordinary relations would be one and the same.

There is an easier way of writing down expressions for relations using abstraction than that which we have used so far. Where 'Φ' is a two-place predicate expression, we will abbreviate '$\{x: (\exists y)(\exists z)(x = \langle y,z\rangle \;\&\; \Phi(y,z))\}$' as '$\{\langle y,z\rangle: \Phi(y,z)\}$'. So we will normally represent the relation corresponding to our ordinary *larger than* relation, for example, as '$\{\langle x,y\rangle$: x is larger than y$\}$'.

Some properties are of a sort we call relational. For example, in order to be a parent one must stand in the relationship of parenthood to something else. Mathematically the set of parents will be identical to the set of all first members of ordered pairs in the relation corresponding to parenthood. This example shows that it may sometimes be convenient to have a convention for referring to all the first members of a relation, or to all second members of a relation, or even to all members whether first or second.

DEFINITION 12. A is a relation $\rightarrow$ (Domain(A) = $\{x\colon (\exists y)(\langle x,y\rangle \in A)\}$).

DEFINITION 13. A is a relation $\rightarrow$ (Range(A) = $\{x\colon (\exists y)(\langle y,x\rangle \in A)\}$).

DEFINITION 14. A is a relation $\rightarrow$ (Field(A) = Domain(A) $\cup$ Range(A)).

EXERCISES

10.1* Show that $\langle w,x\rangle = \langle y,z\rangle \rightarrow (w = y \;\&\; x = z)$.

10.2 Show that $\emptyset$ is a relation.

10.3 How many members does $\{\langle x,y\rangle\colon x \in \{1,2\} \;\&\; y \in \{1,2\} \;\&\; x \geq y\}$ have?

10.4 Show that (A is a relation & B is a relation) $\rightarrow$ A $\cup$ B is a relation.

10.5 What is the domain of $\{\langle x,y\rangle\colon (\exists z)$(x is the brother of z and z is the parent of y)$\}$?

§11. Functions. Some ordinary relations have the rather interesting property that something can only stand in such a relation to one object. For example, each of us has a single natural mother, each of us has at most (in the United States) one lawfully wedded spouse, each of us has at most one firstborn, etc. In mathematics there is for each positive integer n exactly one positive integer m such that $n^2 = m$, exactly one integer k such that $n = k + 1$, etc. Linguistically we find corresponding to such relations expressions which employ the determiner 'the' such as 'the mother of', 'the spouse of', 'the firstborn of', 'the square of', 'the successor of', etc. The use of the definite article 'the' in each of these cases is appropriate because each object stands in such a relation to at most one thing. Corresponding to relations which lack this feature we find expressions using the indefinite article 'a(n)' such as 'a parent of', 'a child of', etc. The set-theoretic counterpart of an ordinary relation of this sort is a set of ordered pairs such that nothing appears as the first member of more than one pair in that set. We call such a relation a function.

DEFINITION 15. A is a function $\leftrightarrow$ (A is a relation & $(x)(y)(z)((\langle x,y\rangle \varepsilon A \& \langle x,z\rangle \varepsilon A) \rightarrow y = z))$.

We will use the small letters 'f', 'g', and 'h' as special variables which range over functions.

We see that if f is a function and x ε Domain(f), then there is a unique y such that $\langle x,y\rangle \varepsilon f$. We call this unique item associated with x in f the image of x under f or the value of f at x.

DEFINITION 16. $f(x) = y \leftrightarrow \langle x,y\rangle \varepsilon f$.

Another way to think of a function is as a way of assigning to each member of one set, the domain of the function, a unique member of another set, the range of the function. Each member of the domain can be thought of as being sent to a member of the range. For example, consider the function f = $\{\langle 1,7\rangle,\langle 2,8\rangle,\langle 3,8\rangle\}$. Domain(f) = {1,2,3} and Range(f) = {7,8}. Pictorially, we can represent this function as follows:

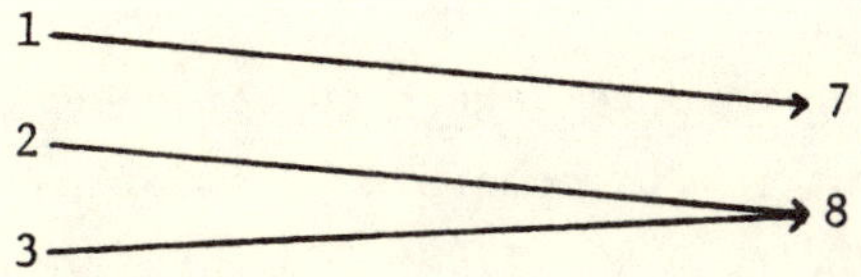

Each arrow in our diagram represents one of the ordered pairs in f. Notice that we can have two different arrows going <u>to</u> the same thing (something can be the second member of more than one pair in the function), but two different arrows can not come <u>from</u> the same thing (nothing can be the first member of more than one pair in the function). Several of us may have the same mother, but none of us can have more than one (natural) mother.

Sometimes we will want to talk about a function when we don't know exactly what its range is. We may, though, know a set which contains its range. For example, the range of the squaring function as performed on the set of positive integers is itself contained in the set of positive integers, i.e., whenever we square a positive integer the result is another positive integer. Thus we say that squaring is a function from the set of positive integers <u>into</u> the set of positive integers.

<u>DEFINITION 17.</u> $f:A \longrightarrow B \leftrightarrow (\mathrm{Domain}(f) = A \ \& \ \mathrm{Range}(f) \subseteq B)$.

<u>DEFINITION 18.</u> $f:A \xrightarrow{\text{onto}} B \leftrightarrow (f:A \longrightarrow B \ \& \ \mathrm{Range}(f) = B)$.

Of course every function is a function from its domain <u>onto</u> its range. Finally we notice that some functions do not assign any item in their ranges to more than one item in their domains. Such a function is said to be <u>one-to-one</u>.

<u>DEFINITION 19.</u> $f:A \xrightarrow{1\text{-}1} B \leftrightarrow (f:A \longrightarrow B \ \& \ (x)(y)(f(x) = f(y) \rightarrow x = y))$.

Sometimes we need to take a function and change its value at a single point in its domain. Consider for example the function f = {<1,7>,<2,8>,<3,8>} for which we drew a diagram earlier. Suppose we want to consider the function which we get by beginning with f, sending 2 to 7 instead of 8, and leaving all the other assignments made by f alone. Call this function f* for the moment. Then we can draw a diagram for f* as follows:

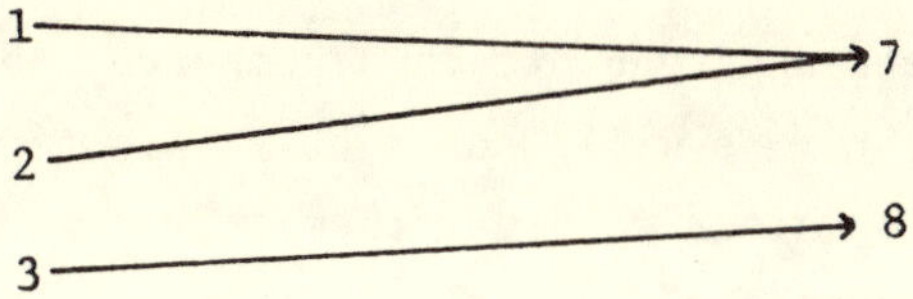

f* is the result of changing the value f takes at 2 from 8 to 7. What we have done is to delete the ordered pair <2,8> from f and put the ordered pair <2,7> in its place. To show this, we will represent f* as $f(x|y)$.

DEFINITION 20. $x \varepsilon \text{Domain}(f) \rightarrow (f(x|y) = (f - \{\langle x,f(x)\rangle\}) \cup \{\langle x,y\rangle\})$.

EXERCISES

11.1 Define a function from {Descartes,Leibniz,Spinoza} onto {1,2}.

11.2 Define a 1-1 function from {1,2} into {Descartes, Leibniz,Spinoza}.

11.3 Can you define a function from {1,2} onto {Descartes, Leibniz,Spinoza}?

11.4 Can you define a 1-1 function from {Descartes, Leibniz, Spinoza} into {1,2}?

11.5 Let N be the set of positive integers. Define a 1-1 function from N into N which is not onto.

11.6 Define a function from N onto N which is not 1-1.

11.7 Show that (f is a function & $x \varepsilon \text{Domain}(f)) \rightarrow f(x|y)$ is a function.

11.8 Show that $x \varepsilon \text{Domain}(f) \rightarrow f(x|y)(x) = y$.

§12. Sequences. Ordered pairs give us a way of thinking

of two things in order, but we sometimes need to keep more than two things in order. Suppose for example we are removing several vacuum tubes from a radio and we need to keep track of which tube goes in which socket. One way to do this is to number the sockets and then attach a numbered label to each tube as we remove it. We will use exactly this technique of assigning numbers to things to order them. Then we can use the order of the numbers as the order of the things numbered. Another way to think of this procedure is as making a numbered list of the items. Thinking in these terms, we will also sometimes find it convenient to talk about a blank list just as we have been talking before about an empty set. We will call such lists <u>sequences</u>.

<u>DEFINITION 21.</u> f is an <u>x-place</u> <u>sequence</u> $\leftrightarrow (x \in N \cup \{0\}$ & $\mathrm{Domain}(f) = \{n: n \leq x\})$.

Technically a sequence assigns items to numbers rather than assigning numbers to items. We can think of our sequence as the result we get when we start with a piece of paper with numbers written on it and then write items down beside the numbers. The number of places of the sequence is the number of items on the final list. Obviously an empty list will have 0 many items on it.

Since Domain(f) = {k: k ≤ 3} where f is the function {<1,Napoleon>,<2,Josephine>,<3,Napoleon>}, f is a 3-place sequence. A more convenient way to represent such a short sequence is to list the <u>values</u> of the sequence in order: <Napoleon;Josephine;Napoleon>. This tells us what the function f is because we already know f's domain. We will use this notation extensively.

<u>DEFINITION 22.</u> $\langle x_1;\ldots;x_n\rangle = \{\langle 1,x_1\rangle,\ldots,\langle n,x_n\rangle\}$.

Notice that it doesn't matter if the same item appears more than once on a list since we don't ask that sequences be 1-1.

Where f is an n-place sequence and $k \leq n$ we call f(k) the $\underline{k^{th}}$ member of f. We often write the kth member of a sequence f as 'f_k' rather than 'f(k)'. Notice that in Definition 22 we use semicolons rather than commas to separate the members of a sequence. We do this to avoid an ambiguity. If we did not do this, we would be unable to distinguish the ordered pair <x,y> from the 2-place sequence <x;y>. The reader should be warned that this is not a standard convention and there are other ways to develop the notion of a sequence. We choose this way because Definition 22 is very simple and straightforward. As with ordered pairs we must notice that the kth member of an n-place sequence is not a member simpliciter of the sequence. Being a kth member of a sequence is a different relation from set membership.

Suppose you and someone else put together two separate lists of items you need to buy for a picnic. Tape the two lists together and you have a new list. There may be repetitions, but that doesn't matter. We can "tape" together sequences just as we can shopping lists. This process is called concatenation. Before defining concatenation precisely, it will be convenient to adopt some new special symbols. We will use the Greek letters 'σ', 'τ', 'ρ', and 'π' as special variables which range over sequences of some number of places. Our task will also be easier if we first define the notion of the length of a sequence as the number of places the sequence has.

DEFINITION 23. $\ell(\sigma) = x \leftrightarrow \sigma$ is an x-place sequence.

Now we can define the concatenation of two sequences.

DEFINITION 24. $\sigma * \tau = \rho \leftrightarrow (\ell(\rho) = \ell(\sigma) + \ell(\tau)$ & $(k)(k \leq \ell(\sigma) \rightarrow \rho_k = \sigma_k)$ & $(k)(\ell(\sigma) < k \leq \ell(\sigma) + \ell(\tau) \rightarrow \rho_k = \tau_{k - \ell(\sigma)}))$.

This definition is rather complicated but the idea behind it is simple. Let's consider two short sequences σ = <a;b> and

$\tau = \langle c;d;c \rangle$. If we thought of these as lists which we taped together, we would expect the resulting new list $\sigma * \tau$ to be $\rho = \langle a;b;c;d;c \rangle$. Let's see whether this sequence satisfies the conditions set down in Definition 24. First we see that $\ell(\rho) = 5 = 2 + 3 = \ell(\sigma) + \ell(\tau)$ satisfying the first part of Definition 24. Next $\rho_1 = a = \sigma_1$ and $\rho_2 = b = \sigma_2$ satisfying the second part of the definition. Finally we see that each of 3, 4, and 5 is greater than $\ell(\sigma) = 2$ but less than or equal to $\ell(\sigma) + \ell(\tau) = 2 + 3 = 5$; but $\rho_3 = c = \tau_1$, $\rho_4 = d = \tau_2$, and $\rho_5 = c = \tau_3$ satisfying the last part of the definition. So $\sigma * \tau = \rho$ just as it should.

One question prompted by Definition 24 is the following: Can we be sure that there is only one sequence which satisfies this definition for a given σ and τ? If not, then $\sigma * \tau$ is not well-defined. The proof of this necessary result is included as an exercise at the end of this section. The reader will also be asked to prove that for any two sequences σ and τ there exist a sequence ρ which satisfies Definition 24. These two results together assure us that any two sequences have a unique concatenation.

The notion of a sequence is absolutely essential to everything we will do from now on. It is easy to see why this is so. We wish to study languages, and in a language we use sentences to say things. How do we reduce the notion of a sentence to some mathematical object which we may be able to manipulate in some helpful way? What is a sentence? It is a string of sounds or written marks which satisfies certain rules of grammar. But a string of this sort is just a group of linguistic items ordered by either a temporal (for oral speech) or spatial (for written speech) relation. If we substitute the mathematical order of positive integers for the temporal or spatial order of such a string of linguistic items, we have a sequence. So we can think of a sentence like 'It is raining' as corresponding to the 3-place sequence <'it';'is';'raining'>.

In the languages we develop later this correspondence will be even closer since we will define sentences in these languages as sequences of certain sorts. Of course not every string of words is a sentence. For example, 'Bread toadstool verily' is not a sentence of English. When the time comes we will have to lay down some rules which determine which sequences of symbols will count as sentences of the formal languages we are examining and which will not.

Not only sentences but also proofs can be thought of as sequences. When you learned to do proofs or derivations in earlier logic courses, you learned to write down numbered lines of sentences with justifications to one side. You were taught to number the lines as you wrote them down since this made it easier to refer back to a line by number when you wanted to cite that line as part of the justification for a later line. A proof with n many lines is nothing more than an n-place sequence of formulas every member of which has a justification of some sort. So we will also be able to reduce the notion of a proof or derivation to that of certain kinds of sequences.

Our discussion of proofs raises an interesting point. If a sentence or formula is just a sequence of symbols and a proof is just a sequence of formulas, then some sequences must be sequences of sequences. Take for example the two sequences $\sigma = \langle a;b \rangle$ and $\tau = \langle c;d;c \rangle$ once again. Now $\sigma * \tau$ is a sequence of letters just as are σ and τ, but we can also combine σ and τ in another way. We can also form the sequence $\langle \sigma;\tau \rangle = \langle\langle a;b\rangle;\langle c;d;c\rangle\rangle$ which is not a sequence of letters but is instead a sequence of sequences. $\sigma * \tau$ is a 5-place sequence, but $\langle \sigma;\tau \rangle$ is only a 2-place sequence. The third member of $\sigma * \tau$ is c, but $\langle \sigma;\tau \rangle$ doesn't even have a third member. And *no* member of $\langle \sigma;\tau \rangle$ is a letter.

EXERCISES

In all of the following, let σ = <Socrates;Plato;Aristotle> and let τ = <Sapir;Whorf>.

12.1 What is Domain(τ)?

12.2 What is $\ell(\sigma)$?

12.3 What is Range(σ)?

12.4 What is $(\sigma*\tau)_2$?

12.5 What is $(\sigma*\tau)_4$?

12.6 What is τ_3?

12.7 What is $(<\sigma;\tau>)_2$?

12.8 What is $((<\sigma;\tau>)_2)_1$?

12.9 What is $((<\sigma;\tau>)_1)_2$?

12.10 If $\ell(\rho) = 8$ and $\ell(\pi) = 17$, what is $(\rho*\pi)_{19}$? What is $\ell(\rho*\pi)$?

12.11 If $\ell(\rho) = m$ and $\ell(\pi) = n$, what is $(\rho*\pi)_1$? What is $(\rho*\pi)_m$? What is $(\rho*\pi)_{m+1}$? What is $(\rho*\pi)_{m+n}$? What is $(\rho*\pi)_{m+3}$?

12.12 Show that $(\exists\rho)(\ell(\rho) = \ell(\pi) + \ell(\mu)\ \&\ (k)(k \leq \ell(\pi) \rightarrow \rho_k = \pi_k)\ \&\ (k)(\ell(\pi) < k \leq \ell(\pi) + \ell(\mu) \rightarrow \rho_k = \mu_{k - \ell(\pi)})$.

12.13 Show that $(\ell(\rho) = \ell(\pi) + \ell(\mu)\ \&\ (k)(k \leq \ell(\pi) \rightarrow \rho_k = \pi_k)\ \&\ (k)(\ell(\pi) < k \leq \ell(\pi) + \ell(\mu) \rightarrow \rho_k = \mu_{k - \ell(\pi)})\ \&\ \ell(\nu) = \ell(\pi) + \ell(\mu)\ \&\ (k)(k \leq \ell(\pi) \rightarrow \nu_k = \pi_k)\ \&\ (k)(\ell(\pi) < k \leq \ell(\pi) + \ell(\mu) \rightarrow \nu_k = \mu_{k - \ell(\pi)})) \rightarrow \rho = \nu$. This shows that π and μ have a unique concatenation. Don't use Definition 24.

12.14 Show that $\sigma*\emptyset = \sigma$.

12.15 Show that $\emptyset*\sigma = \sigma$.

12.16 Show that $\sigma*\emptyset*\tau = \sigma*\tau$.

§13. Mathematical Induction. We will use many of the familiar properties of the positive integers throughout the rest of this work. For example, we know that $n < n + 1$, that $n < m \rightarrow n - 1 < m$, and that $n \leq m \rightarrow (n - k \leq m - k\ \&\ n + k \leq m + k)$. We also know that $\{n\colon n \leq k\} = \{1,2,3,\ldots,k\}$. We will often use such facts and we will not attempt to review all of them at this time. Although many of us may lack a background in set theory, we should all have a foundation in basic arithmetic and the properties of the positive integers. There is, however, one interesting property of positive integers with which you may not be familiar. This is the property which is incorporated into the Principle of Mathematical Induction.

We will continue to use the convention adopted in an earlier exercise of using 'N' to stand for the set of all positive integers. The positive integers have a property called the Well Ordering Property which insures that $A \subseteq N \rightarrow (A = \emptyset \vee (\exists n)(n \in A \,\&\, (k)(k \in A \rightarrow n \leq k)))$. In other words, every nonempty set of positive integers has a smallest member. Of course it is not true that every set of positive integers has a largest member. N itself, for example, has no largest member. We shall see that there is a connection between the Well Ordering Property and the Principle of Mathematical Induction which we will introduce in this section. The Principle of Mathematical Induction may seem difficult when you first see it, but the Well Ordering Principle should seem simple and obvious to you.

Let '$\Phi(x)$' be some open sentence which can be true of positive integers. Suppose we show that $\Phi(1)$ and suppose we also show that $(n)(n < k \rightarrow \Phi(n)) \rightarrow \Phi(k)$. That is, suppose we show that the number 1 has the property denoted by 'Φ' and we also show that for any number k, if every positive integer smaller than k has the property denoted by 'Φ', then k must have it too. By instantiating this second claim, we have $(n)(n < 2 \rightarrow \Phi(n)) \rightarrow \Phi(2)$. But we know that 1 is the only positive integer less than 2, and we know that $\Phi(1)$, so we may conclude that $(n)(n < 2 \rightarrow \Phi(n))$. Then by *modus ponens*, $\Phi(2)$. Now we can instantiate again to get $(n)(n < 3 \rightarrow \Phi(n)) \rightarrow \Phi(3)$. But the only positive integers less than 3 are 1 and 2 and we know that $\Phi(1)$ and $\Phi(2)$, so $(n)(n < 3 \rightarrow \Phi(n))$ and by *modus ponens* once again,

$\Phi(3)$. We can continue in this way to show that $\Phi(4)$, $\Phi(5)$, $\Phi(6)$, etc. If we go on in this way indefinitely, we will eventually show for each positive integer n that $\Phi(n)$. But of course we can't go on indefinitely and that is why we need the Principle of Mathematical Induction. It tells us that once we establish the two things we supposed at the beginning of this paragraph, then we can conclude that $(n)\Phi(n)$.

PRINCIPLE OF MATHEMATICAL INDUCTION. $(\Phi(1)\ \&\ (k)((n)(n < k \rightarrow \Phi(n)) \rightarrow \Phi(k))) \rightarrow (n)\Phi(n)$.

Learn this principle well since we will use it repeatedly.

Before we see how mathematical induction can be used in a proof, let's see how the principle follows from the more obvious Well Ordering Property of the positive integers. We will do this using an indirect proof. (Indirect proofs are very common in mathematics.) First suppose that the Principle of Mathematical Induction is false. For it to be false, there must be a predicate 'Φ' for which the antecedent of the principle is true and the consequent is false, that is, we can pick a 'Φ' such that $\Phi(1)\ \&\ (k)((n)(n < k \rightarrow \Phi(n)) \rightarrow \Phi(k))\ \&\ \sim(n)\Phi(n)$. So $(\exists n)\sim\Phi(n)$ and $\{n: \sim\Phi(n)\} \neq \emptyset$. Then by the Well Ordering Property $\{n: \sim\Phi(n)\}$ has a smallest member m. Then $\sim\Phi(m)\ \&\ (k)(k < m \rightarrow \Phi(k))$. But by instantiation $(n)(n < m \rightarrow \Phi(n)) \rightarrow \Phi(m)$, and by *modus ponens* $\Phi(m)$. This is a contradiction since we can't have both $\Phi(m)$ and $\sim\Phi(m)$. Therefore our original assumption that the Principle of Mathematical Induction is false must itself be false, i.e., the principle is true for every predicate 'Φ'.

How do we use mathematical induction? Notice that the antecedent of the principle is a conjunction of two conditions. If we want to prove for some predicate 'Φ' that $(n)\Phi(n)$, we must prove that both of these conditions are satisfied. First we need to show that $\Phi(1)$. The part of our argument where we do this is called the *basis step*. Then we need to show that

$(k)((n)(n < k \rightarrow \Phi(n)) \rightarrow \Phi(k))$. The part of our argument where we show this is called the induction step. The reason for these names should be obvious. 1 is the starting point or basis of the string of arguments we first looked at to see how we could show that each positive integer in its turn has the property we have in mind. Once we know that 1 has the property we use the conclusion of the induction step to show that 2 has the property. Once we know that both 1 and 2 have the property we use the induction step to show that 3 has the property. And so on. The basis step gives us a starting point and the induction step lets us add on all the rest of the integers one at a time. The principle itself just says that we eventually get all of the positive integers by doing this infinitely many times.

Now let's take a closer look at the induction step. What we want to show is a universal generalization of a material conditional. We can proceed by doing a conditional proof to establish the conditional and then simply using universal generalization to get the desired result. Our proof would then have the following form:

→ $(n)(n < k \rightarrow \Phi(n))$	Assumed Premise
.	
.	
.	
$\Phi(k)$	
$(n)(n < k \rightarrow \Phi(n)) \rightarrow \Phi(k)$	Conditional Proof
$(k)((n)(n < k \rightarrow \Phi(n)) \rightarrow \Phi(k))$	UG

So our induction step always begins with an assumed premise. We give this assumed premise a special name, calling it our inductive hypothesis. Once we have stated our inductive hypothesis, $(n)(n < k \rightarrow \Phi(n))$, and then used it and anything else we may have available to show that $\Phi(k)$, the remaining steps of the argument always look the same. Because it always looks the same from this point on, mathematicians usually leave this part of the argument unstated. After we show $\Phi(k)$ in our induction step, the next and final line in our inductive argument always runs, 'So by mathematical induction, $(n)\Phi(n)$'.

Let's take a specific example to see how we use mathematical induction in a proof. Let's show that $(n)(1 + 2 + 3 + \ldots + n = n(n + 1)/2)$. In the left hand side of this equation '$1 + 2 + 3 + \ldots + n$' represents the result of adding together all positive integers less than or equal to n. For example, where $n = 2$, '$1 + 2 + 3 + \ldots + n$' actually represents $1 + 2$, i.e., 3. Having clarified what it is we are to prove, let's proceed.

Basis step. Where $n = 1$, $1 + 2 + 3 + \ldots + n = 1$. But $1(1 + 1)/2 = 1(2)/2 = 2/2 = 1$. So our equation holds for $n = 1$.

Induction step. Let k be any positive integer and suppose $(n)(n < k \rightarrow 1 + 2 + 3 + \ldots + n = n(n + 1)/2)$. Then since $k - 1 < k$, $1 + 2 + 3 + \ldots + (k - 1) = (k - 1)((k - 1) + 1)/2$. (We are assuming that $k > 1$ since we already know that the equation holds for $n = 1$. Then we are instantiating our inductive hypothesis to $k - 1$, using the arithmetical fact that $k - 1 < k$, and using modus ponens.) So $1 + 2 + 3 + \ldots + (k - 1) + k = (k - 1)((k - 1) + 1)/2 + k$. (Here we add the same quantity, k, to both sides of the equation.) But $(k - 1)((k - 1) + 1)/2 + k = (k - 1)k/2 + 2k/2 = (k^2 - k + 2k)/2 = (k^2 + k)/2 = k(k + 1)/2$ and our equations holds for k. (This is the end of our induction step.)

Therefore by mathematical induction $(n)(1 + 2 + 3 + \ldots + n = n(n + 1)/2)$.

EXERCISES

13.1 Show that $(n)(1^2 + 2^2 + 3^2 + \ldots + n^2 = n(n + 1)(2n + 1)/6)$.

13.2* Show that $(n)(3 + 3^2 + 3^3 + \ldots + 3^n = 3(3^n - 1)/2)$.

Reminder: You multiply powers of the same number by adding together the exponents. For example, $3^4(3^5) = 3^{4 + 5} =$

3^9, not 3^{20}.

§14. Power Sets, Infinite Sets, Finite Sets, and Countability. We add one last set-theoretic axiom to our list.

THE POWER SET AXIOM. $(\exists B)(x)(x \varepsilon B \leftrightarrow x \subseteq A)$.

The Power Set Axiom tells us that for any set A there exists another set B which has as its members all and only the subsets of A, that is , all and only those sets which are contained in A. Such a set B is called a power set of A. We can easily see that each set has only one power set, so we are also able to add a new definition to our list.

DEFINITION 25. $\text{Power}(A) = B \leftrightarrow (x)(x \varepsilon B \leftrightarrow x \subseteq A)$.

As an illustrative example, consider the set $A = \{1,2\}$. $\text{Power}(A) = \{\emptyset,\{1\},\{2\},A\}$. While A has only two members, Power(A) has four or 2^2 members. In general if A has n members, then Power(A) has 2^n members and therefore is bigger than A. One might think that the claim that Power(A) is bigger than A is only true when A is finite, for how could any set be bigger than an infinite set? It turns out, though, that some infinite sets are in a certain sense larger than others. We will say that a set A is at least as large as a set B if there is a function from A onto B. For some infinite sets A and B there is a function from A onto B but there is no function from B onto A. This means that there are so many members of A that no matter how we assign members of A to members of B, we always have some members of A left over when we are done. In a case like this it seems reasonable to say that the infinite set A is larger than the infinite set B.

But how do we know that some infinite sets are larger than others in this sense? Consider the two sets N and Power(N). We can easily see that there are functions from Power(N) onto N, for we can assign to every singleton $\{n\}$ in Power(N) the positive integer n and assign to every member of Power(N) that is not a singleton the integer 1. But we can't define a function from N onto Power(N). We will show this by indirect proof, supposing first that $g{:}N \xrightarrow{\text{onto}} \text{Power}(N)$. Let $A = \{n: n \notin g(n)\}$. Since g is onto Power(N) and $A \in \text{Power}(N)$, we let $m \in N$ such that $g(m) = A$. Then $m \in g(m) \leftrightarrow m \in \{n: n \notin g(n)\} \leftrightarrow m \notin g(m)$, which is a contradiction. Therefore there is no function $g{:}N \xrightarrow{\text{onto}} \text{Power}(N)$.

We have been using undefined notions of finite and infinite sets. Our next definition makes these notions and a special notion of a countably infinite set precise.

> DEFINITION 26. a. A is infinite $\leftrightarrow (x)(x \in A \rightarrow (\exists f)(f{:}A - \{x\} \xrightarrow{\text{onto}} A))$. b. A is finite $\leftrightarrow$ A is not infinite. c. A is countable (or countably infinite) $\leftrightarrow (\exists f)(f{:}N \xrightarrow{\text{onto}} A$ & A is infinite).

Essentially, a set is finite if you can't throw away any of its members without producing a smaller set, and a set is countable if it's the same size as N. A function f such that Domain(f) = N is sometimes called an infinite sequence, as opposed to the finite sequences of the last section. The notion of countability and the associated notion of an infinite sequence are very important for what we will be doing later. When an infinite set is countable, we can use mathematical induction to prove things about its members. What we do is arrange its members in an infinite sequence, prove that the first member of the infinite sequence has some property, and then prove that whenever the first several members of the sequence have that property, then the next member has it. (We can also use something called transfinite induction to prove things about uncountably infinite sets, but such techniques require set-theoretic axioms which for the sake of simplicity we will not discuss. Certain of our later results can be made more general by allowing certain sets to be uncountably infinite which we will have restricted to countable infinity. When we come to such results they will be identified.)

There is an important result concerning countability which we will need later. I state it here without proof since the proof is rather long and complicated. The result simply says that if A is countable, then {σ: σ is a finite sequence of members of A} is also countable.

EXERCISES

14.1 What is Power({1,2,3})?

14.2 Show that Power(A) ≠ ∅.

14.3 Show that the set of even positive integers is countable.

14.4 Show that (A is countable & B is countable) → A ∪ B is countable.

14.5 Show that (A is countable & B is infinite & B ⊆ A) → B is countable.

§15. Formal Languages. We have developed all the set-theoretic machinery we need. Now we will use it to define the notion of a formal language.

> DEFINITION 27. L is a formal language ↔ (∃S)(∃T)(∃F)(S is a recursive set & T is a recursive set & F is a recursive set & L = <S;T;F> & S ≠ ∅ & (x)(x ε T ∪ F → x is a finite sequence of members of S)).

We will not try to formulate a precise definition of the notion of a recursive set, but we do at least need an intuitive notion of what makes a set recursive. To say that a set is recursive is first and foremost to say that there is an effective way of determining whether or not something is a member of that set. One way to define a set which will guarantee that it is recursive is by first designating some other set which we know to be recursive and then specifying certain operations which, applied finitely many times to the members of the original recursive set, will produce all of the other members of the new set. As an example we consider N. The set {1} is obviously recursive. In fact any finite set is recursive since we can easily tell whether something is a member of it just by looking. We can then generate any other member of N by beginning with 1 and then add 1's finitely many times. 4, for example, is just (((1 + 1) + 1) + 1).

> DEFINITION 28. L = <S;T;F> is a formal language → (σ is an L-expression ↔ σ is a finite sequence of members of S).

Where L = <S;T;F> is a formal language, we call S the set of symbols of L and members of S L-symbols, we call T the set of terms of L and members of T L-terms, and we call F the set of formulas of L and members of F L-formulas. So L-terms and L-formulas are all L-expressions.

Intuitively L-symbols are the simplest items in a language, the basic building blocks out of which all expressions in the language are constructed. Examples of symbols in English include words like 'red' and 'is', prefixes like 'un-', and suffixes like '-ing'. The notion of a symbol for a formal language corresponds to the notion of a morpheme for a natural language. The simplest expressions in any formal language will be the 1-place sequences whose first (and only) member is a symbol of that language. Of course the 0-place sequence ∅ will be an expression of every formal language. The terms of a language are to be thought of as the referring expressions of the language. These are the expressions which we use to mention the things about which we wish to talk. Examples of terms in English include 'George Washington' and 'the first President of the United States of America'. The formulas of a formal language correspond to the sentences of a natural language. A sentence is one of those expressions which can be used to make a statement, ask a question, or perform one of the many other kinds of action which we perform through the use of language. It is possible to devise formal languages such that the formulas of that language correspond in some important respect to the questions, commands, etc., of a natural language, but we will only look at formal languages which are devised with the intention that the formulas should correspond in some important respects to the declarative sentences of natural languages as they are used to make statements.

Where we know that L is a formal language, we will sometimes denote the symbols of L as S_L, the terms of L as TM_L, and the formulas of L as FM_L. We will use the Greek letters 'ϕ', 'ψ', 'χ', and 'θ' as special variables which range over the formulas of the language about which we are talking.

QUESTIONS

Let $L = \langle N;\emptyset;\{\sigma\colon (k)(k < \ell(\sigma) \rightarrow \sigma_k \leq \sigma_{k+1})\}\rangle$.

15.1 Is L a formal language?

15.2 Is <2;5;65;0;23> an L-formula? Is it an L-expression? Explain.

15.3 Is <7;68;5;7> an L-formula? Is it an L-expression? Explain.

15.4 Is <5;6;8;8;10> an L-formula? Explain.

15.5 Suppose σ and τ are both L-formulas. Is $\sigma * \tau$ an L-formula? Is $\sigma * \tau$ an L-expression? Explain.

§16. Formal Systems.

DEFINITION 29. Σ is a formal system $\leftrightarrow$ $(\exists S)(\exists T)(\exists F)(\exists A)(\exists D)(\Sigma = \langle S;T;F;A;D\rangle$ &

1. <S;T;F> is a formal language &
2. $A \subseteq F$ &
3. D is a relation between subsets of F and members of F, i.e., $D \subseteq \{\langle\Gamma,\phi\rangle\colon \Gamma \cup \{\phi\} \subseteq F\}$, such that if we let $D(\Gamma) = \{\phi\colon \langle\Gamma,\phi\rangle \in D\}$ for each $\Gamma \subseteq F$, then for

every $K \subseteq F$,

a. $K \subseteq D(K)$ &

b. $D(K) = D(D(K))$ &

c. $K \subseteq \Gamma \subseteq F \rightarrow D(K) \subseteq D(\Gamma)$ &

d. $\phi \in D(K) \rightarrow (\exists\Gamma)(\Gamma \subseteq K$ & Γ is finite & $\phi \in D(\Gamma)))$.

Where $\Sigma = \langle S;T;F;A;D\rangle$ is a formal system, we call A the set of <u>axioms</u> of Σ and members of A <u>Σ-axioms</u>, and we call D the <u>derivability relation</u> of Σ. The derivability relation of a formal system is to be thought of as a relation between sets of formulas of the system considered as premises and individual formulas of the system considered as conclusions which are derivable or deducible from the sets of premises. Where K is a set of formulas of a system, D(K) is the set of all formulas of the system which are derivable from K. The four conditions which the derivability relation must satisfy are not too difficult to understand. The first says that any premise can be derived from any set of premises which includes it. The second says that anything can be derived from a set of premises if and only if it can be derived from those things which can be derived from that same set of premises. The third says that anything that can be derived from a set of premises can still be derived if we add more premises to the set. And the fourth says that even if we should begin with infinitely many premises and derive something, we never actually need more than finitely many of the premises we have available for our derivation.

Where Σ is a formal system, we sometimes denote the set of symbols of Σ as S_Σ, the set of terms of Σ as TM_Σ, the set of formulas of Σ as FM_Σ, the set of axioms of Σ as AX_Σ, and the derivability relation of Σ as $\vdash_\Sigma$. We write $K \vdash_\Sigma \phi$ if $\langle K,\phi\rangle \in \vdash_\Sigma$.

EXERCISES

Let $S = \{1,2\}$, $T = \emptyset$, $F = \{\langle 1\rangle,\langle 2\rangle\}$, $A = \{\langle 1\rangle\}$, and $D =$

{<∅;<1>>,<{<1>};<1>>,<{<2>};<1>>,<{<2>};<2>>,<F;<1>>,<F;<2>>}. Let Σ = <S;T;F;A;D>.

16.1 Show that <S;T;F> is a formal language.

16.2 Show that Σ is a formal system.

16.3* Let D' = D - {<{<2>};<1>>} and let Σ' = <S;T;F;A;D'>. Show that Σ' is not a formal system.

16.4 Let D* = D ∪ {<{<1>};<2>>} and let Σ* = <S;T;F;A;D*>. Show that Σ* is a formal system.

§17. Natural Deduction Systems and Axiomatic Systems. A primary reason for studying logic is because we are interested in arguments. An argument of the sort we encounter in informal discourse is simply a group of sentences which are presented together with the implicit claim that some one of these sentences, called the *conclusion* of the argument, is related to the rest of the sentences, called the *premises* of the argument, in a certain way. Typically we say that the conclusion of the argument is represented as *following from* the premises. If the set of premises of the argument actually is related to the conclusion in the manner implicitly claimed, then we say that the argument is *valid*.

One explanation of what it is for a conclusion to follow from a set of premises says that this happens just in case it is *impossible* for the premises all to be true and the conclusion to be false. This is a much stronger requirement than merely demanding that it *not be the case* that all the premises are true and the conclusion is false, and unpacking this notion is a chief motive for developing formal systems. Yet some philosophers think that an even stronger requirement is involved in our intuitive notion of validity. If we have a conclusion which *must* be true and thus is necessarily the case, such as '2 + 2 = 4', then this conclusion follows from any set of premises whatever. This is so because it is *impossible* for '2 + 2 = 4' to be false, and so it is impossible for all the members of any set of premises to be true and '2 + 2 = 4' to be false. But, say these philosophers, surely '2 + 2 = 4' does not follow from anything whatever. For example, it does not follow from 'There is life on the moon'. It might, however, follow from '2 + 1 = 3' and '3 + 1 = 4' taken together. The additional requirement that these philosophers suggest is a requirement of relevancy. '2 + 2 = 4' is not supposed to follow from 'There is no life on the moon' because whether there is life on the moon simply is not relevant to whether 2 + 2 = 4.

Relevancy is not the only sort of additional requirement philosophers have claimed to be involved in our intuitive notion of what it is for the conclusion of an argument to follow from the premises of the argument. But however philosophers have wished to strengthen our account of the following from relation, they have always agreed that something very much like the requirement that it be impossible for the premises all to be true and the conclusion to be false is a necessary condition for the conclusion to follow from the premises. The controversy has been over whether this necessary condition is also a sufficient condition. In this condition, then, we seem to have a minimal notion of what it is for an informal argument to be valid.

In the usual introductory course in symbolic logic, the student learns to "move around" in what is called a natural deduction system. The goal is to develop a technique for showing the validity of those informal arguments which are in fact valid. This is accomplished by first representing the informal argument by a list of formulas in the symbolism of the deduction system and then showing that the symbolic counterpart of the conclusion of the informal argument can be derived from the symbolic counterparts of the premises of the informal argument. The assumption is that the informal argument will be intuitively valid just in case the symbolization of its conclusion can be derived from the symbolizations of its premises.

Besides its symbolism (which really amounts to a formal language) and its machinery for pairing off sentences of a natural language with formulas in the symbolism, a natural deduction system consists of rules of inference. These rules tell us that when we have written down certain things in constructing a derivation, we can then write down certain other things. The derivations themselves, then, are simply lists or sequences of formulas of the system. Every line we write down in the derivation must either be a symbolization of a premise of the informal argument with which we started or follow from earlier lines in the derivation by one of the inference rules. If we can write down a list of formulas of the system which satisfies this condition and the last line of which is the symbolization of the conclusion of our original informal argument, then we say that the symbolization of the conclusion is derivable from the symbolizations of the premises, and we call the list of formulas which satisfies these two conditions a derivation of the symbolization of the conclusion from the symbolizations of the premises.

How are the rules of inference for a natural deduction system chosen? Surely we would have little hope of paralleling our intuitive notion of validity for informal arguments if we simply pick our rules at random. What we do is look for rather short, simple informal arguments which seem to us to be valid. Then we pattern an inference rule after this short informal argument. For example, 'If kangaroos hopped, they would have legs. Kangaroos do hop. So kangaroos have legs.' seems to satisfy our needs. Surely it is impossible for the first two sentences of this simple argument to be true and the third to be false. Suppose we abbreviate 'Kangaroos hop' by 'H' and we abbreviate 'Kangaroos have legs' by 'L'. Then our argument becomes 'If H, then L. H. So L.' Next we replace 'H' and 'L' by place-holders, perhaps 'ϕ' and 'ψ'. Now 'ϕ' and 'ψ' are not to be taken as the abbreviations of any particular sentences; instead each marks the place where a sentence could go. Thus we have 'If ϕ, then ψ. ϕ. So ψ.' To complete our transformation of the informal argument into an inference rule we put this last stage of our transformation into the form of a rule. The rule might run something like this: "If 'If ϕ, then ψ' and 'ϕ' are already lines in your derivation, then you may write down 'ψ' as the next line in your derivation." But we are not yet finished. We need to test this rule to see if it is completely dependable. To do this we try to think of sentences which we could stick in for 'ϕ' and 'ψ' which would make 'If ϕ, then ψ' and 'ϕ' true and make 'ψ' false. In other words we need a true sentence 'T' and a false sentence 'F' such that 'If T, then F' is true. If we decide there are no sentences which satisfy these conditions, then we accept the rule as *sound*, and we may make it an explicit rule in our natural deduction system. When we feel we have enough rules to get everything we are likely to want, we stop. Knowing what to add and knowing when to stop are both difficult problems.

Notice that in the rule discussed in the last paragraph, which may be familiar to you as *modus ponens*, we are allowed to write down a line of a certain form only provided that we already have written down two other lines of related forms. Most rules in natural deduction systems are of a similar sort, only allowing us to write down a new line provided we already have one or more other lines of a certain sort. This should not be too surprising since we get our rules by taking simple, intuitively valid informal arguments as our models. The premises of the arguments we start with are transformed into a specification of previous lines which must be present before we can write down the new line; the conclusion of the original argument gives us the form of the new line which we are allowed to write down next. Yet some rules in some natural deduction systems are not like this. They tell us that we can write down a certain kind of line regardless of what we have or have not already written. For example, if we are working within a natural deduction system for the predicate logic with identity, we may have a rule which says that for any variable or constant 'α', we may write down '$\alpha = \alpha$' at any time as the next line in our derivation. Such rules may seem a bit strange if we take for our model of rule-formation the process just described in which a simple, intuitively valid informal argument is transformed into a rule of inference. Since informal arguments always have premises, rules of inference would seem always to require that we already have lines of a certain kind written down before we can write down anything new. So why do we have rules of the sort we are now discussing? It turns out that many informal arguments involve hidden premises of a special sort. One such premise which we are always entitled to assume but which we are unlikely ever to mention is that everything is identical with itself. We are entitled to assume this in any context whatsoever because it is necessary; it couldn't possibly be false. But when we are doing a derivation in our natural deduction system our inference rules don't allow us to write down new lines just because we have them in our heads and everyone knows that they are true. This would undermine the entire program of devising a natural deduction system which is intended to make precise the kinds of moves we can make in an argument. In order to make use of this common knowledge which everyone knows _must_ be the case we have to make it explicit that we can use it whenever we need it. These strange rules which make no requirements concerning what is already written down, which tell us that we can write down something regardless of what our earlier lines may be, serve this purpose. They allow us to invoke those special premises which we all know to be necessarily true but which we never mention in the course of an informal argument.

The formal systems which we will be studying are both

like and unlike the natural deduction systems studied in introductory logic courses. These new systems are usually called axiomatic systems. Besides rules of inference they also involve special kinds of formulas which we call axioms. These axioms can be written down at any time in a derivation regardless of what the earlier lines in the derivation may be. They correspond, then, to those unusual rules in natural deduction systems which do not require that we already have written down lines of a certain sort before we can write down a new line. But there is another way to think of these axioms. They are also those necessary truths which we all implicitly assume and which we could therefore make explicit and include among the explicit premises of our argument if we wished to do so. Axioms, then, serve as special kinds of inference rules or as special formulas which are always to be included implicitly among the premises of any derivation which we may construct.

By adding axioms to our deduction system we are able in most cases to shorten the list of rules of inference we need. In fact all of the formal systems at which we will look will initially sanction only one kind of inference from previous lines. This one rule is modus ponens. We will be able to show that many other rules are acceptable for these systems, but the only rule we will actually use in our derivations, apart from the axioms themselves if we think of them as rules, will be modus ponens.

This is not to imply that all formal systems of the sort we defined in the last section are axiomatic systems and that natural deduction systems are therefore not formal systems of this kind. Indeed, all of the natural deduction systems you have studied can be fit into the form of the formal systems with which we are concerned. When we cast one of these systems into this form, though, the set of axioms of the system turns out to be $\emptyset$. A formula in the system will be derivable from a set of formulas in the system just in case there is a derivation of the individual formula from some members of the set. The difference between a natural deduction system and an axiomatic system, then, is not so very great. A natural deduction system involves no axioms but may involve many rules of inference, while an axiomatic system reduces the number of rules of inference through the expedient of adopting a number of axioms. We can have a natural deductive system and an axiomatic system which share exactly the same formal language and exactly the same derivability relation. The difference between the two will lie in the fact that one has no axioms and in the differences in the processes by which we determine whether a particular set of formulas and a particular formula of the systems stand in the derivability relation to each other.

Natural deduction systems resemble our informal patterns of argument in a more obvious manner than do axiomatic systems. We typically assert conclusions on the basis of premises; we rarely assert that something is necessarily true without preamble. Rules of inference are in a way more "natural" than are axioms. This is why natural deduction systems are usually taught in introductory courses. But when we begin to want to prove things _about_ our formal systems rather than merely to _use_ these systems, we naturally prefer systems which take very simple forms. The advantage of axiomatic systems from our point of view is that they can be developed much more simply in most cases than can natural deduction systems which share the same formal languages and derivability relations. Since the analysis of informal arguments, and hence the formal notion of a derivability relation, is of primary concern we should not balk at confining our examination to those systems which can be described most simply so long as the derivability relation remains unchanged. This is why we look at axiomatic systems here. We hope the "unnaturalness" of such systems will be overcome by these remarks.

CHAPTER 2

Sentential Logic

§18. The Symbols of Sentential Logic. The first formal system we will discuss is sentential logic. In order to talk about this system we need to add special constants to our metalanguage which we can use to refer to the symbols of the language of the sentential logic. First we add '$\underline{n}$' which we read as 'the negation symbol'. Next we add '$\underline{i}$' which we read as 'the implication symbol'. Finally for each positive integer k we add 'P_k' which we read as 'the kth sentence letter'.

DEFINITION 30. $S_{SL} = \{\underline{n},\underline{i}\} \cup \{P_k: k \in N\}$.

The members of S_{SL} are called SL-symbols. We assume that $\underline{n} \neq \underline{i}$ and that neither $\underline{n}$ nor $\underline{i}$ is a sentence letter. We further assume that $k \neq m \rightarrow P_k \neq P_m$. Finally we assume that no SL-symbol is a sequence of SL-symbols. We call these our distinctness assumptions. It follows from these distinctness assumptions that S_{SL} is countably infinite.

DEFINITION 31. σ is an SL-expression $\leftrightarrow$ σ is a finite sequence of SL-symbols.

Where σ and τ are SL-expressions, we have the following definition.

DEFINITION 32. $\sim\sigma = \langle\underline{n}\rangle * \sigma$.

$\sigma \supset \tau = \langle\underline{i}\rangle * \sigma * \tau$.

$$\sigma \wedge \tau = \sim(\sigma \supset \sim\tau).$$

$$\sigma \vee \tau = \sim\sigma \supset \tau.$$

$$\sigma \equiv \tau = (\sigma \supset \tau) \wedge (\tau \supset \sigma).$$

Notice particularly the definition of '⊃'. We write '⊃' between the names of two SL-expressions, but in doing this we represent an SL-expression in which the implication symbol comes in front of the symbols flanking the '⊃'. Intuitively this means that in the object language we place the implication symbol in front of the two expressions it connects rather than between them. This system for writing complex expressions was devised by Polish logicians and is called _Polish notation._ The advantage of Polish notation is that we do not require punctuation (parentheses, brackets, etc.) to distinguish one expression from another similar expression. The other way of writing complex expressions, which we will use in our metalanguage and which places the '⊃' between the expressions it connects, is called _algebraic notation._ In algebraic notation we can not distinguish between $\sim<P_1> \supset <P_2>$ and $\sim(<P_1> \supset <P_2>)$ except by using parentheses. In Polish notation these two expressions are distinguished by the order in which the symbols occur: $<\underline{i};\underline{n};P_1;P_2>$ and $<\underline{n};\underline{i};P_1;P_2>$ respectively. By adopting Polish notation for our object language, we do not have to include parentheses, etc., as SL-symbols. However most of us are more familiar with algebraic notation, so this is what we will use in our metalanguage to refer to expressions in the object language. We will use punctuation as needed in the metalanguage without providing explicit conventions for its use.

You should also notice that none of '~', '⊃', '∧', '∨', and '≡' stand for SL-symbols. We use these symbols in the metalanguage to refer to expressions in the object language, but by themselves they do not refer to anything in the object language. They are only meaningful in combination with other expressions in the metalanguage. They are only defined in context.

EXERCISES

Rewrite the following SL-expressions without using '~', '⊃', '∧', '∨', or '≡'.

18.1 $<P_1;\underline{n};P_5> \wedge <\underline{i}>$.

18.2 $\sim((<P_6> \vee \sim<P_{12}>) \supset <P_6>)$.

Which of the following stand for SL-expressions? Explain your answers.

18.3* $\sim P_1 \supset (<P_2> \supset <P_3>)$.

18.4 $<P_4> \supset \sim<P_5>$.

18.5 $\sim\sim<P_6>$.

18.6 $\sim \supset <P_7>$.

§19. SL-sentences.

DEFINITION 33. $AT_{SL} = \{<P_k>: k \in N\}$.

We call the members of AT_{SL} atomic SL-sentences. Beginning with the atomic SL-sentences, we build up other SL-sentences using n and i, our two logical constants.

> DEFINITION 34. σ is an SL-construction $\leftrightarrow$ $(n)(n \leq \ell(\sigma) \rightarrow (\sigma_n \in AT_{SL} \vee (\exists i)(i < n \,\&\, \sigma_n = \sim\sigma_i) \vee (\exists i)(\exists j)(i < n \,\&\, j < n \,\&\, \sigma_n = \sigma_i \supset \sigma_j)))$.
>
> DEFINITION 35. $ST_{SL} = \{\phi: (\exists\sigma)(\sigma$ is an SL-construction $\& \ \sigma_{\ell(\sigma)} = \phi)\}$.

The members of ST_{SL} are called SL-sentences. Definition 35 tells us that something is an SL-sentence just in case it is the last member of some SL-construction. Definition 34 tells us what an SL-construction is: it is a sequence every member of which is either an atomic SL-sentence or a negation of an earlier member or a conditional formed from earlier members. An example of an SL-construction is $\sigma = <<P_1>;\sim<P_1>;<P_1> \supset <P_1>;\sim(<P_1> \supset <P_1>);\sim(<P_1> \supset <P_1>) \supset \sim<P_1>>$. We see that σ is a 5-place sequence such that $\sigma_1 \in AT_{SL}$, $\sigma_2 = {\sim}\sigma_1$, $\sigma_3 = \sigma_1 \supset \sigma_1$, $\sigma_4 = {\sim}\sigma_3$, and $\sigma_5 = \sigma_4 \supset \sigma_2$. Since σ is an SL-construction, σ_5 ($= \sigma_{\ell(\sigma)}$) is an SL-sentence. To show that some ϕ is an SL-sentence, we produce a construction which has ϕ as its last member.

We can also show that something is not an SL-sentence by showing that it is not the last member of any SL-construction. This is not as difficult as it may first sound. Let's show that $\phi = {\sim}(\langle P_1\rangle \supset \langle P_2;P_3\rangle)$ is not an SL-sentence. We will use an indirect proof. Suppose $\phi \in ST_{SL}$. Then by Definition 35 we can let σ be an SL-construction such that $\sigma_{\ell(\sigma)} = \phi$. Since σ is an SL-construction, $\phi \in AT_{SL} \vee (\exists i)(i < \ell(\sigma) \,\&\, \phi = {\sim}\sigma_i) \vee (\exists i)(\exists j)(i < \ell(\sigma) \,\&\, j < \ell(\sigma) \,\&\, \phi = \sigma_i \supset \sigma_j)$. Clearly $\phi \notin AT_{SL}$ since by our distinctness assumptions no sentence letter is a sequence of SL-symbols. Since the first member of ϕ is $\underline{n}$ (by Definition 32), and since $\underline{n} \neq \underline{i}$ and $\underline{n}$ is not a sequence of SL-symbols and $\underline{i}$ is not a sequence of SL-symbols by our distinctness assumptions, ${\sim}(\exists i)(\exists j)(i < \ell(\sigma) \,\&\, j < \ell(\sigma) \,\&\, \phi = \sigma_i \supset \sigma_j)$. So $(\exists i)(i < \ell(\sigma) \,\&\, \phi = {\sim}\sigma_i)$ and we can let i be a positive integer such that $i < \ell(\sigma)$ and $\sigma_i = \langle P_1\rangle \supset \langle P_2;P_3\rangle$. By reasoning similar to that we just used, we can let j and k be positive integers such that $j < i \,\&\, k < i \,\&\, \sigma_j = \langle P_1\rangle \,\&\, \sigma_k = \langle P_2;P_3\rangle$. But then since σ is an SL-construction, $\langle P_2;P_3\rangle \in AT_{SL} \vee (\exists m)(m < k \,\&\, \langle P_2;P_3\rangle = {\sim}\sigma_m) \vee (\exists m)(\exists n)(m < k \,\&\, n < k \,\&\, \langle P_1;P_2\rangle = \sigma_m \supset \sigma_n)$. But it is clear that $\langle P_2;P_3\rangle \notin AT_{SL}$, and our distinctness assumptions make our other alternatives impossible. Therefore our original assumption is false and ${\sim}(\langle P_1\rangle \supset \langle P_2;P_3\rangle) \notin ST_{SL}$.

The 3-place sequence $\langle S_{SL};\emptyset;ST_{SL}\rangle$ satisfies the conditions of Definition 27 and is therefore a formal language. We will call this 3-place sequence the language of sentential logic.

In the remainder of this chapter we will adopt the convention of using 'K' and 'Γ' as special variables which range over subsets of ST_{SL}.

EXERCISES

19.1 Show that $(\langle \underline{n}; P_1\rangle \vee \langle P_6\rangle) \supset (\langle P_3\rangle \equiv \langle P_1\rangle) \in ST_{SL}$.

19.2* Show that $\langle \underline{i}; \underline{n}; \underline{i}; P_1; P_2; \underline{i}; P_3; \underline{n}; P_4; \underline{n}\rangle \notin ST_{SL}$.

19.3 Show that $\phi \in ST_{SL} \rightarrow {\sim}\phi \in ST_{SL}$. Hint: Use the construction of ϕ as the starting point for building a construction of ${\sim}\phi$.

19.4 Show that $(\phi \in ST_{SL} \mathbin{\&} \psi \in ST_{SL}) \rightarrow \phi \supset \psi \in ST_{SL}$.

19.5 Show that $AT_{SL} \subseteq ST_{SL}$. Hint: Let $\phi \in AT_{SL}$ and build a construction of ϕ.

§20. An Induction Principle for ST_{SL}. In this section we will establish an induction principle for ST_{SL} which allows us to prove things about SL-sentences in a fashion similar to that in which mathematical induction allows us to prove things about positive integers. This principle is given in the following theorem.

THEOREM 1. (Induction Principle for ST_{SL}.) $(AT_{SL} \subseteq A \mathbin{\&} (\phi)(\phi \in A \rightarrow {\sim}\phi \in A) \mathbin{\&} (\phi)(\psi)((\phi \in A \mathbin{\&} \psi \in A) \rightarrow \phi \supset \psi \in A)) \rightarrow ST_{SL} \subseteq A$.

This principle is stated in terms of membership in some set A instead of in terms of the possession of some property, but this doesn't really distinguish Theorem 1 from the Principle of Mathematical Induction since we are only going to be interested in properties which can be used to define non-empty sets by abstraction. Before we see how we can use Theorem 1, we should determine that Theorem 1 is true.

Proof. (Since our theorem is a conditional, we will use a conditional proof.) Assume that $AT_{SL} \subseteq A \mathbin{\&} (\phi)(\phi \in A \rightarrow {\sim}\phi \in A) \mathbin{\&} (\phi)(\psi)((\phi \in A \mathbin{\&} \psi \in A) \rightarrow \phi \supset \psi \in A)$. (By Definition 5, we need to show that $(\phi)(\phi \in ST_{SL} \rightarrow \phi \in A)$. We will also use a conditional proof to show this.) Assume that $\phi \in ST_{SL}$. Then by Definition 35 we can let σ be an SL-construction of

ϕ, i.e., an SL-construction whose last member is ϕ. If we can show that every member of σ is also a member of A, then we can conclude that $\phi \in A$ since ϕ is the last member of σ. To show that every member of σ is also a member of A, we will use mathematical induction. What we want to show is that $(n)(n \leq \ell(\sigma) \to \sigma_n \in A)$. That is, we want to show that for every positive integer n, if σ has an nth member, then the nth member of σ is a member of A.

Basis step. By Definition 34, $\sigma_1 \in AT_{SL} \vee (\exists i)(i < 1 \mathbin{\&} \sigma_1 = {\sim}\sigma_i) \vee (\exists i)(\exists j)(i < 1 \mathbin{\&} j < 1 \mathbin{\&} \sigma_1 = \sigma_i \supset \sigma_j)$. But there is no positive integer i such that $i < 1$, so $\sigma_1 \in AT_{SL}$. Since by our original assumption $AT_{SL} \subseteq A$, we can conclude that $\sigma_1 \in A$.

Induction step. Assume that k is a positive integer and that $(n)(n < k \to (n \leq \ell(\sigma) \to \sigma_n \in A))$. Either $k \leq \ell(\sigma)$ or not. If not, then ${\sim}(k \leq \ell(\sigma)) \vee \sigma_k \in A$, and thus $k \leq \ell(\sigma) \to \sigma_k \in A$. Now let's consider the case where $k \leq \ell(\sigma)$. Then σ has a kth member σ_k and by Definition 34 we know that $\sigma_k \in AT_{SL} \vee (\exists i)(i < k \mathbin{\&} \sigma_k = {\sim}\sigma_i) \vee (\exists i)(\exists j)(i < k \mathbin{\&} j < k \mathbin{\&} \sigma_k = \sigma_i \supset \sigma_j)$. We need to show that whichever of these three cases holds, $\sigma_k \in A$.

Case 1. $\sigma_k \in AT_{SL}$. But $AT_{SL} \subseteq A$ by our original assumption, so $\sigma_k \in AT_{SL}$.

Case 2. $i < k \mathbin{\&} \sigma_k = {\sim}\sigma_i$. Since $i < k$, $i \leq \ell(\sigma) \to \sigma_i \in A$ by our inductive hypothesis. But $k \leq \ell(\sigma)$, so $i < \ell(\sigma)$ and hence $\sigma_i \in A$. By our original assumption that $(\phi)(\phi \in A \to {\sim}\phi \in A)$, ${\sim}\sigma_i \in A$. So since $\sigma_k = {\sim}\sigma_i$, $\sigma_k \in A$.

Case 3. $i < k \mathbin{\&} j < k \mathbin{\&} \sigma_k = \sigma_i \supset \sigma_j$. By our inductive hypothesis, $(i < \ell(\sigma) \to \sigma_i \in A) \mathbin{\&} (j < \ell(\sigma) \to \sigma_j \in A)$. But since $k \leq \ell(\sigma)$, $i < \ell(\sigma) \mathbin{\&} j < \ell(\sigma)$. By our original assumption that $(\phi)(\psi)((\phi \in A \mathbin{\&} \psi \in A) \to \phi \supset \psi \in A)$, $\sigma_i \supset \sigma_j \in A$. Since $\sigma_k = \sigma_i \supset \sigma_j$, $\sigma_k \in A$.

In any of our three cases, $\sigma_k \in A$. So $k \leq \ell(\sigma) \to \sigma_k \in A$. Then by mathematical induction $(n)(n \leq \ell(\sigma) \to \sigma_n \in A)$. So

$\ell(\sigma) \leq \ell(\sigma) \rightarrow \sigma_{\ell(\sigma)} \in A$. But of course $\ell(\sigma) \leq \ell(\sigma)$, so $\sigma_{\ell(\sigma)} \in A$. And since $\phi = \sigma_{\ell(\sigma)}$, $\phi \in A$.

Therefore, $ST_{SL} \subseteq A$ and our proof is complete.

When we count we begin with the number 1. When we have counted all of the numbers before k, the next number must be k. That's why in the basis step for mathematical induction we prove something about the number 1, and why in the induction step for mathematical induction we prove something about k after having assumed that that something is true for all the numbers before k. The situation is a little different for SL-sentences. When we start building SL-sentences we can begin with any atomic SL-sentence. There is exactly one starting point for counting, but there are countably many starting points for building an SL-sentence. Our basis step for doing an induction on ST_{SL}, then, will consist in showing for every atomic SL-sentence that it is a member of the set A at which we are looking or, what amounts to much the same thing, showing that every atomic SL-sentence has some property. Once we have constructed several SL-sentences, we have two ways of constructing additional ones (since we have already "constructed" all of the atomic SL-sentences in our basis step). We can either form the negation of some sentence we have already constructed or we can form a conditional from sentences we have already constructed. Unlike in the case of counting, there are two different ways we may proceed. So there are two different things we must show in our induction step when we do an induction on ST_{SL}. First we must show that if ϕ belongs to the set (or has the property) with which we are concerned, then $\sim\phi$ must also belong (have the property). Second we must show that if ϕ and ψ both belong (have the property), then so does $\phi \supset \psi$. Once we have shown all of this, we can use Theorem 1 to conclude that every SL-sentence belongs to the set (has the property) in question.

Let's see how we can use induction on ST_{SL} (Theorem 1) to prove something. You will use Theorem 1 in an exercise at the end of this section to show that every SL-sentence is an SL-expression. Remember that every SL-expression is a finite sequence of SL-symbols, so we can talk about the last member, $\phi_{\ell(\phi)}$, of an SL-sentence ϕ. Let's prove that $(\exists n)(\phi_{\ell(\phi)} = P_n)$, i.e., that the last member of an SL-sentence is always a sentence letter. Let $A = \{\phi\colon (\exists n)(\phi_{\ell(\phi)} = P_n)\}$.

Basis step. Let $\phi \in AT_{SL}$. By Definition 33 $(\exists n)(\phi = \langle P_n\rangle)$. But then $\ell(\phi) = 1$ & $\phi_1 = P_n$, so $(\exists n)(\phi_{\ell(\phi)} = P_n)$ and $\phi \in A$.

Induction step. Let σ and τ be SL-expressions such that $\sigma \in A$ & $\tau \in A$. Then $\sim\sigma_{\ell(\sim\sigma)} = \sigma_{\ell(\sim\sigma) - 1} = \sigma_{\ell(\sigma)}$, and $(\sigma \supset \tau)_{\ell(\sigma \supset \tau)} = \tau_{\ell(\sigma \supset \tau) - \ell(\sigma) - 1} = \tau_{\ell(\tau)}$. So $(\exists n)(\sim\sigma_{\ell(\sim\sigma)} = \sigma_{\ell(\sigma)} = P_n)$, $(\exists n)((\sigma \supset \tau)_{\ell(\sigma \supset \tau)} = \tau_{\ell(\tau)} = P_n)$, $\sim\sigma \in A$, and $\sigma \supset \tau \in A$.

So by Theorem 1 $ST_{SL} \subseteq A$, i.e., the last member of every SL-sentence is a sentence letter.

EXERCISES

20.1 Show that every SL-sentence is an SL-expression.

20.2 Show that $ST_{SL} \subseteq \{\sigma\colon \sigma \in AT_{SL} \vee \sigma_1 = \underline{n} \vee \sigma_1 = \underline{i}\}$.

20.3 Show that $\phi_{\ell(\phi)} \neq \underline{i}$.

20.4* Show that $\phi * \sigma \in ST_{SL} \rightarrow \sigma = \emptyset$. Hint: Do a mathematical induction on the length of ϕ.

20.5* Show that $\sigma * \langle\underline{i}\rangle * \tau \in ST_{SL} \rightarrow (\exists\phi)(\exists\psi)(\exists\rho)(\tau = \phi * \psi * \rho)$. Don't forget that we are using 'ϕ' and 'ψ' as special variables which range over SL-sentences.

20.6 Show that $(\phi)(\sigma)(\tau)(\rho)((\sigma * \tau \in ST_{SL}$ & $\phi = \tau * \rho) \rightarrow (\sigma = \emptyset \vee \tau = \emptyset \vee \rho = \emptyset))$.

§21. The Truth-functional Interpretation of the Language of Sentential Logic.

We could interpret the sentences of the sentential logic in a number of ways, but the standard way of interpreting them is truth-functionally. This is the sort of interpretation which is provided for natural deduction system versions of the sentential logic in introductory logic texts. Each atomic SL-sentence is thought of as bearing one or the other of two truth values. The logical constants are then interpreted as representing functions of these truth values. These functions are defined by the familiar truth tables. We will interpret the sentential logic in essentially the same way.

DEFINITION 36. v is a valuation $\leftrightarrow$ $v{:}AT_{SL} \longrightarrow \{0,1\}$.

Intuitively a valuation assigns 1 to each true atomic SL-sentence and assigns 0 to each false atomic SL-sentence. Of course there is nothing about a sentence letter which tells us whether the atomic SL-sentence containing it must be true or false. Any assignment of truth values to atomic SL-sentences must be arbitrary given no more information about what the sentence letters are than we have available to us. So there are infinitely many, in fact uncountably many, different valuations. We will use 'v', 'v*', etc., as special variables to range over valuations.

Once we have assigned values to the atomic SL-sentences, we define derivative values for all SL-sentences.

DEFINITION 37. For each valuation v we define a function $I_v{:}ST_{SL} \longrightarrow \{0,1\}$ as follows:

1. $\phi \in AT_{SL} \rightarrow I_v(\phi) = v(\phi)$;

2. $I_v(\sim\phi) = \begin{Bmatrix} 1 \text{ if } I_v(\phi) = 0 \\ 0 \text{ if } I_v(\phi) = 1 \end{Bmatrix}$;

3. $I_v(\phi \supset \psi) = \begin{Bmatrix} 1 \text{ if } I_v(\phi) = 0 \text{ or } I_v(\psi) = 1 \\ 0 \text{ if } I_v(\phi) = 1 \text{ and } I_v(\psi) = 0 \end{Bmatrix}$.

Given a valuation v, the function I_v tells us for each SL-sentence whether that SL-sentence is true of false.

We remarked in the last chapter that the intuitive notion of validity has usually been thought to require at least the impossibility of all the premises of the valid argument being true while the conclusion of the argument is false. This condition for validity is captured formally in the notion of tautological implication. A set K of premises tautologically implies an SL-sentence ϕ just in case there is no way to assign truth values to the atomic SL-sentences so as to make all of the members of K true without also making ϕ true.

DEFINITION 38. $K \models \phi \leftrightarrow (v)((\psi)(\psi \in K \to I_v(\psi) = 1) \to I_v(\phi) = 1)$.

We read '$K \models \phi$' as 'K tautologically implies ϕ'.

DEFINITION 39. $\models \phi \leftrightarrow \emptyset \models \phi$.

We read '$\models \phi$' as 'ϕ is a tautology'. Of course any valuation will result in 1 being assigned to every member of $\emptyset$. So $\models \phi \leftrightarrow (v)(I_v(\phi) = 1)$, i.e., ϕ is a tautology if and only if ϕ is true regardless of how we assign values to the atomic SL-sentences. This corresponds exactly to the account of tautologies found in introductory logic texts.

EXERCISES

21.1 Show that $K \models \phi \wedge \psi \to (K \models \phi \ \& \ K \models \psi)$.

21.2 Define a valuation v such that $I_v(\langle P_1 \rangle \supset {\sim}\langle P_2 \rangle) = 0$. (To define a valuation, you must specify the value that valuation assigns to each atomic SL-sentence.)

21.3 Show that $\sim(\phi)(\psi)(\{\phi \supset \psi, \psi\} \models \phi)$.

§22. Semantical Consistency. Intuitively a set of statements is consistent if it is possible for all of them to be true at once. All of the statements in the set need not be true in order for the set to be consistent, but there must at least be the possibility of their all being true. This is exactly the notion we wish to capture in our definition of semantical consistency for sets of SL-sentences.

DEFINITION 40. K is semantically consistent $\leftrightarrow$ $(\exists v)(\phi)(\phi \in K \rightarrow I_v(\phi) = 1)$.

If K is not semantically consistent, we say that K is semantically inconsistent. So K is semantically inconsistent if and only if $(v)(\exists\phi)(\phi \in K \ \& \ I_v(\phi) = 0)$, i.e., if and only if it is impossible for the members of K to be all true.

There are a number of other ways we might have defined semantical consistency all of which are equivalent to Definition 40, but each of them is less natural than Definition 40. It will be convenient, though, to have these alternative criteria of semantical consistency available.

THEOREM 2. K is semantically consistent $\leftrightarrow$ $(\exists\phi)\sim(K \models \phi)$.

THEOREM 3. K is semantically consistent $\leftrightarrow$ $\sim(\exists\phi)(K \models \phi \ \& \ K \models \sim\phi)$.

Proof. First assume that K is semantically consistent. Then by Definition 40 we let v be a valuation such that $(\phi)(\phi \in K \rightarrow I_v(\phi) = 1)$. If $K \models \phi \ \& \ K \models \sim\phi$, then by Definition 38, $I_v(\phi) = 1 \ \& \ I_v(\sim\phi) = 1$. But if $I_v(\phi) = 1$, then by Definition 37.2, $I_v(\sim\phi) = 0$. Since $0 \neq 1$, $\sim(K \models \phi \ \& \ K \models \sim\phi)$, $(\phi)\sim(K \models \phi \ \& \ K \models \sim\phi)$, and $\sim(\exists\phi)(K \models \phi \ \& \ K \models \sim\phi)$.

Now assume that $\sim(\exists\phi)(K \models \phi \ \& \ K \models \sim\phi)$. If K were semantically inconsistent, then $K \models \langle P_1 \rangle \ \& \ K \models \sim\langle P_1 \rangle$ by Theorem 2, contradicting our assumption. Therefore K is semantically consistent and our proof is complete.

THEOREM 4. K is semantically consistent $\leftrightarrow$ $\sim(\exists\phi)(K \models \sim(\phi \supset \phi))$.

THEOREM 5. $K \models \phi \leftrightarrow K \cup \{\sim\phi\}$ is semantically inconsistent.

THEOREM 6. (K is semantically consistent $\& \ K \models \phi) \rightarrow$

$K \cup \{\phi\}$ is semantically consistent.

EXERCISES

22.1* Prove Theorems 2, 4, 5, and 6.

§23. SL-axioms and SL-derivations. Now that we have defined the language of the sentential logic, we need only augment this with a specification of the axioms and the derivability relation of the sentential logic to complete our definition of this formal system.

DEFINITION 41. $\phi \in AX_{SL} \leftrightarrow (\exists\psi)(\exists\chi)(\exists\theta)(\phi = \psi \supset (\chi \supset \psi) \vee \phi = (\psi \supset (\chi \supset \theta)) \supset ((\psi \supset \chi) \supset (\psi \supset \theta)) \vee \phi = (\sim\psi \supset \sim\chi) \supset (\chi \supset \psi))$.

The members of AX_{SL} are called SL-axioms. Remember that the intuitive idea behind axioms is that these are sentences which may be written down at any time as the next line in a derivation. Of course we have yet to define the notion of an SL-derivation. Informally a derivation in the sentential logic of some sentence ϕ from some set of premises K will be a list of sentences ending with ϕ. Each line we write down in this list will be a premise (a member of K), an SL-axiom, or something which follows from earlier lines by our one inference rule modus ponens. Of course the set-theoretic counterpart of a list is a sequence, so the set-theoretic counterpart of a derivation is a sequence satisfying certain conditions.

DEFINITION 42. σ is an SL-derivation of ϕ from K $\leftrightarrow$ $(\sigma_{\ell(\sigma)} = \phi \;\&\; (n)(n \leq \ell(\sigma) \rightarrow (\sigma_n \in K \vee \sigma_n \in AX_{SL} \vee (\exists i)(\exists j)(i < n \;\&\; j < n \;\&\; \sigma_i = \sigma_j \supset \sigma_n))))$.

DEFINITION 43. $K \vdash_{SL} \phi \leftrightarrow (\exists\sigma)(\sigma$ is an SL-derivation of ϕ from K).

Notice that every member of an SL-derivation from K is either a member of K or an SL-axiom or a modus ponens consequence of earlier members. This last alternative may not be immediately obvious. One of the conditions which a member, say the nth member, of an SL-derivation σ may satisfy is that $(\exists i)(\exists j)(i < n \;\&\; j < n \;\&\; \sigma_i = \sigma_j \supset \sigma_n)$. Since σ_j comes earlier than σ_n in the derivation, and since σ_i $(= \sigma_j \supset \sigma_n)$ also comes earlier than σ_n, we see that σ_n is after all a modus ponens consequence of two earlier members σ_i and σ_j.

Since the only rule of inference we have for the sentential logic is modus ponens (which is built into the definition of an SL-derivation), the many other rules we find listed for most natural deduction systems must somehow be replaced by the SL-axioms. It is clear how this is accomplished in some cases. For example, the rule of Transposition or Contraposition is replaced at least in part by all of those axioms of the form $(\sim\phi \supset \sim\psi) \supset (\psi \supset \phi)$. And the rule of Addition is replaced by all of those axioms of the form $\phi \supset (\sim\psi \supset \phi)$, which by Definition 32 is just $\phi \supset (\psi \vee \phi)$. We will see how the roles of some of the other rules are played by other SL-sentences we can derive from the SL-axioms as we go along.

Let's look at some examples of SL-derivations. $\sigma = \langle\phi; \phi \supset (\psi \supset \phi); \psi \supset \phi\rangle$ is a derivation of $\psi \supset \phi$ from $\{\phi\}$, so we have $\{\phi\} \vdash_{SL} \psi \supset \phi$. $\tau = \langle\sim\phi; \sim\phi \supset (\sim\psi \supset \sim\phi); \sim\psi \supset \sim\phi; (\sim\psi \supset \sim\phi) \supset (\phi \supset \psi); \phi \supset \psi\rangle$ is an SL-derivation of $\phi \supset \psi$ from $\{\sim\phi\}$, so we have $\{\sim\phi\} \vdash_{SL} \phi \supset \psi$. Looking at this last derivation more closely we might write it down with justifications as follows.

$\tau_1 = \sim\phi$	premise
$\tau_2 = \sim\phi \supset (\sim\psi \supset \sim\phi)$	AX1 (i.e., an SL-axiom of the first of the three forms specified in Definition 41)
$\tau_3 = \sim\psi \supset \sim\phi$	τ_1, τ_2, modus ponens
$\tau_4 = (\sim\psi \supset \sim\phi) \supset (\phi \supset \psi)$	AX3
$\tau_5 = \phi \supset \psi$	τ_3, τ_4, modus ponens

So the sequence σ is simply this derivation without the justifications.

Suppose we have an SL-derivation σ such that $(n)(n \leq \ell(\sigma) \rightarrow (\sigma_n \in AX_{SL} \vee (\exists i)(\exists j)(i < n \,\&\, j < n \,\&\, \sigma_i = \sigma_j \supset \sigma_n)))$. Then we could say that the last member of σ was derivable from <u>no premises at all</u>.

<u>DEFINITION 44.</u> $\vdash_{SL}\phi \leftrightarrow \emptyset\vdash_{SL}\phi$.

If $\vdash_{SL}\phi$, then we call ϕ an <u>SL-theorem.</u>

Now that we have the language and the axioms, all we need to complete the definition of this first formal system is the derivability relation for sentential logic.

<u>DEFINITION 45.</u> $\vdash_{SL} = \{\langle K,\phi\rangle: K\vdash_{SL}\phi\}$.

By Definition 45 we see that $K\vdash_{SL}\phi \leftrightarrow \langle K,\phi\rangle \in \vdash_{SL}$.

<u>DEFINITION 46.</u> $SL = \langle S_{SL};\emptyset;ST_{SL};AX_{SL};\vdash_{SL}\rangle$.

EXERCISES

23.1* Show that $\{\phi,\phi \supset (\psi \supset \chi),\phi \supset \psi\}\vdash_{SL}\chi$.

23.2 Show that $\{\phi \supset \psi,\psi \supset \chi\}\vdash_{SL}\phi \supset \chi$. (This result should be familiar to you as the rule Hypothetical Syllogism.)

23.3 Show that $\vdash_{SL}\phi \supset \phi$.

§24. Some Basic Results Concerning SL-derivability.

<u>THEOREM 7.</u> $\phi \in K \rightarrow K\vdash_{SL}\phi$.

Proof. Suppose $\phi \in K$. Then $\sigma = \langle\phi\rangle$ is a 1-place sequence such that $\sigma_{\ell(\sigma)} = \sigma_1 = \phi$, and $(n)(n \leq 1 \rightarrow \sigma_n \in K)$. So σ is an SL-derivation by Definition 42 and $K\vdash_{SL}\phi$ by Definition 43.

<u>THEOREM 8.</u> $\phi \in AX_{SL} \rightarrow (K\vdash_{SL}\phi \,\&\, \vdash_{SL}\phi)$.

<u>THEOREM 9.</u> $(K\vdash_{SL}\phi \,\&\, K\vdash_{SL}\phi \supset \psi) \rightarrow K\vdash_{SL}\psi$.

Proof. Suppose that $K\vdash_{SL}\phi \,\&\, K\vdash_{SL}\phi \supset \psi$. Then by Definition 43 we can let σ be an SL-derivation of ϕ from K and let τ be an SL-derivation of $\phi \supset \psi$ from K. We will show that $\rho = \sigma*\tau*\langle\psi\rangle$ is an SL-derivation of ψ from K. We already know that

$\rho_{\ell(\rho)} = \psi$, so by Definition 42 all we need to show is that $(n)(n \leq \ell(\rho) \rightarrow (\rho_n \in K \vee \rho_n \in AX_{SL} \vee (\exists i)(\exists j)(i < n \,\&\, j < n \,\&\, \rho_i = \rho_j \supset \rho_n)))$. Suppose $n \leq \ell(\rho)$. Then since $\ell(\rho) = \ell(\sigma) + \ell(\tau) + 1$, $n \leq \ell(\sigma) \vee \ell(\sigma) < n \leq \ell(\sigma) + \ell(\tau) \vee n = \ell(\sigma) + \ell(\tau) + 1$. We will consider each of these three possibilities separately.

Case 1. $n \leq \ell(\sigma)$. Then $\rho_n = \sigma_n$. But σ is an SL-derivation of ϕ from K, so $\sigma_n \in K \vee \sigma_n \in AX_{SL} \vee (\exists i)(\exists j)(i < n \,\&\, j < n \,\&\, \sigma_i = \sigma_j \supset \sigma_n)$. Now $(i)(i < n \rightarrow i < \ell(\sigma))$ and hence $(i)(i < n \rightarrow \rho_i = \sigma_i)$. So $\rho_n \in K \vee \rho_n \in AX_{SL} \vee (\exists i)(\exists j)(i < n \,\&\, j < n \,\&\, \rho_i = \rho_j \supset \rho_n)$ (since $\rho_i = \sigma_i$, $\rho_j = \sigma_j$, and $\rho_n = \sigma_n$).

Case 2. $\ell(\sigma) < n \leq \ell(\sigma) + \ell(\tau)$. Then $\rho_n = \tau_{n - \ell(\sigma)}$. But τ is an SL-derivation of $\phi \supset \psi$ from K, so $\tau_{n - \ell(\sigma)} \in K \vee \tau_{n - \ell(\sigma)} \in AX_{SL} \vee (\exists i)(\exists j)(i < n - \ell(\sigma) \,\&\, j < n - \ell(\sigma) \,\&\, \tau_i = \tau_j \supset \tau_{n - \ell(\sigma)})$. Now $(i)(i < n - \ell(\sigma) \rightarrow \ell(\sigma) < i + \ell(\sigma) < \ell(\sigma) + \ell(\tau))$ and hence $(i)(i < n - \ell(\sigma) \rightarrow \rho_{i + \ell(\sigma)} = \tau_i)$. So $\rho_n \in K \vee \rho_n \in AX_{SL} \vee (\exists k)(\exists m)(k < n \,\&\, m < n \,\&\, \rho_k = \rho_m \supset \rho_n)$ (where $k = i + \ell(\sigma)$ and $m = j + \ell(\sigma)$).

Case 3. $n = \ell(\sigma) + \ell(\tau) + 1$. Then $\ell(\sigma) < n \,\&\, \ell(\sigma) + \ell(\tau) < n$. Since $\ell(\sigma) \leq \ell(\sigma)$ and since σ is an SL-derivation of ϕ, $\rho_{\ell(\sigma)} = \sigma_{\ell(\sigma)} = \phi$. Since $\ell(\sigma) < \ell(\sigma) + \ell(\tau) \leq \ell(\sigma) + \ell(\tau)$ and since τ is an SL-derivation of $\phi \supset \psi$, $\rho_{\ell(\sigma) + \ell(\tau)} = \tau_{\ell(\sigma) + \ell(\tau) - \ell(\sigma)} = \tau_{\ell(\tau)} = \phi \supset \psi$. Finally, $\rho_n = \psi$. So $\ell(\sigma) < n \,\&\, \ell(\sigma) + \ell(\tau) < n \,\&\, \rho_{\ell(\sigma) + \ell(\tau)} = \rho_{\ell(\sigma)} \supset \rho_n$.

In each of our three cases $\rho_n \in K \vee \rho_n \in AX_{SL} \vee (\exists i)(\exists j)(i < n \,\&\, j < n \,\&\, \rho_i = \rho_j \supset \rho_n)$, and so ρ is an SL-derivation of ψ from K by Definition 42. Thus $K \vdash_{SL} \psi$ by Definition 43 and our proof is complete.

<u>THEOREM 10.</u> $(K \vdash_{SL} \phi \,\&\, K \subseteq \Gamma) \rightarrow \Gamma \vdash_{SL} \phi$.

<u>THEOREM 11.</u> $K \vdash_{SL} \phi \rightarrow (\exists \Gamma)(\Gamma \subseteq K \,\&\, \Gamma \text{ is finite } \&\, \Gamma \vdash_{SL} \phi)$.

Proof. Suppose $K \vdash_{SL} \phi$. We can let σ be an SL-derivation of ϕ from K by Definition 43. Let $\Gamma = \{\sigma_n : n \leq \ell(\sigma) \,\&\, \sigma_n \in K\}$. Since σ is a finite sequence, Γ must be finite. It is easy to see that σ is an SL-derivation of ϕ from Γ. So $\Gamma \vdash_{SL} \phi$ by Definition 43, completing our proof.

EXERCISES

24.1 Prove Theorem 8.

24.2 Prove Theorem 10.

24.3 Show that $\vdash_{SL} \phi \rightarrow K \vdash_{SL} \phi$.

24.4 Show that $\vdash_{SL}$ satisfies all the conditions listed for a derivability relation in Definition 29. This is all that remains to show that SL is a formal system.

§25. The SL-consequences of a Set of SL-sentences.

DEFINITION 47. $CN_{SL}(K) = \{\phi: K \vdash_{SL} \phi\}$.

Sometimes we want to show that something is true of everything that can be derived from some set of premises. For any set K of SL-sentences we call the set $CN_{SL}(K)$ of all those things which we can derive from K in sentential logic the set of SL-consequences of K. So ϕ is an SL-consequence of K if and only if $K \vdash_{SL} \phi$. We have an induction principle for $CN_{SL}(K)$ just as we do for N (mathematical induction) and for ST_{SL} (Theorem 1).

THEOREM 12. (Induction Principle for $CN_{SL}(K)$.)
$(K \subseteq A \mathbin{\&} AX_{SL} \subseteq A \mathbin{\&} (\phi)(\psi)((\phi \in A \mathbin{\&} \phi \supset \psi \in A) \rightarrow \psi \in A))$
$\rightarrow CN_{SL}(K) \subseteq A$.

We say that a set A such that $(\phi)(\psi)((\phi \in A \mathbin{\&} \phi \supset \psi \in A) \rightarrow \psi \in A)$ is closed under modus ponens. Theorem 12 tells us that any set which contains both K and AX_{SL} and which is closed under modus ponens must also contain everything which can be derived from K in sentential logic.

Proof. Assume that $K \subseteq A \mathbin{\&} AX_{SL} \subseteq A \mathbin{\&} (\phi)(\psi)((\phi \in A \mathbin{\&} \phi \supset \psi \in A) \rightarrow \psi \in A)$. We want to show that $CN_{SL}(K) \subseteq A$, i.e., that $(\phi)(\phi \in CN_{SL}(K) \rightarrow \phi \in A)$. Suppose $\phi \in CN_{SL}(K)$. Then $K \vdash_{SL} \phi$ by Definition 47, and by Definition 43 we can let σ be an

SL-derivation of ϕ from K. By Definition 42, the last member of σ is ϕ. If we could show that every member of σ was also a member of A, we could conclude that $\phi \in A$ and we would be through. We will use mathematical induction to show that every member of σ is a member of A. What we want to show is that $(n)(n \leq \ell(\sigma) \rightarrow \sigma_n \in A)$.

Basis step. Since σ is an SL-derivation, and by Definition 42, $\sigma_1 \in K \vee \sigma_1 \in AX_{SL} \vee (\exists i)(\exists j)(i < 1 \ \& \ j < 1 \ \& \ \sigma_i = \sigma_j \supset \sigma_1)$. But $\sim(\exists i)(i < 1)$, so $\sigma_1 \in K \vee \sigma_1 \in AX_{SL}$. $K \subseteq A \ \& \ AX_{SL} \subseteq A$ by our original assumption, so $\sigma_1 \in A$ and $1 \leq \ell(\sigma) \rightarrow \sigma_1 \in A$.

Induction step. Assume that $(n)(n < k \rightarrow (n \leq \ell(\sigma) \rightarrow \sigma_n \in A))$. If $\sim(k \leq \ell(\sigma))$, then $k \leq \ell(\sigma) \rightarrow \sigma_k \in A$. So suppose $k \leq \ell(\sigma)$. Since σ is an SL-derivation from K, $\sigma_k \in K \vee \sigma_k \in AX_{SL} \vee (\exists i)(\exists j)(i < k \ \& \ j < k \ \& \ \sigma_i = \sigma_j \supset \sigma_k)$. If $\sigma_k \in K \vee \sigma_k \in AX_{SL}$, then $\sigma_k \in A$ since by our original assumption $K \subseteq A \ \& \ AX_{SL} \subseteq A$. Suppose, however, that $i < k \ \& \ j < k \ \& \ \sigma_i = \sigma_j \supset \sigma_k$. By our inductive hypothesis, $\sigma_i \in A$ and $\sigma_j \in A$, i.e., $\sigma_j \supset \sigma_k \in A \ \& \ \sigma_j \in A$. But A is closed under <u>modus ponens</u> according to our original assumption, so $\sigma_k \in A$. So in any case, $\sigma_k \in A$.

Then by mathematical induction, $(n)(n \leq \ell(\sigma) \rightarrow \sigma_n \in A)$. Since $\ell(\sigma) \leq \ell(\sigma)$, $\sigma_{\ell(\sigma)} \in A$. But $\sigma_{\ell(\sigma)} = \phi$, so $\phi \in A$. Thus $CN_{SL}(K) \subseteq A$. Once again, we have used mathematical induction to establish another induction principle.

Let's consider what the basis step and the induction step will be when we do an induction on $CN_{SL}(K)$. The first line of an SL-derivation must be either a premise or an SL-axiom. So in our basis step we must show that every premise (every member of K) and every SL-axiom belongs to the set (has the property) with which we are concerned. Once we have several lines in our derivation, the next line must be either a premise or an SL-axiom or a <u>modus ponens</u> consequence of earlier lines. Since we already took care of all our premises and SL-axioms in our basis step, we need only concern ourselves with the modus ponens consequences of earlier lines. So in our induction step we need only show that if ϕ and $\phi \supset \psi$ belong to the relevant set (have the relevant property), then so does ψ.

For an example of how we use Theorem 12, see the proof of Theorem 13 in the next section.

EXERCISES

25.1 Use Theorem 12 to show that $CN_{SL}(AX_{SL}) \subseteq CN_{SL}(\emptyset)$.

25.2 Show that $\vdash_{SL}\phi \leftrightarrow AX_{SL} \vdash_{SL}\phi$.

25.3 Use Theorem 12 to show that $CN_{SL}(K) \subseteq ST_{SL}$.

§26. The Deduction Theorem for SL.

THEOREM 13. (Deduction Theorem for SL.)
$K \cup \{\phi\} \vdash_{SL}\psi \leftrightarrow K \vdash_{SL}\phi \supset \psi$.

Proof. We will use the Induction Principle for $CN_{SL}(K)$ (Theorem 12). Let $\Gamma = \{\psi\colon K \vdash_{SL}\phi \supset \psi\}$.

Basis step. We need to show that $K \cup \{\phi\} \subseteq \Gamma$ & $AX_{SL} \subseteq \Gamma$. $\emptyset \vdash_{SL}\phi \supset \phi$ by Exercise 23.3, $K \vdash_{SL}\phi \supset \phi$ by Theorem 10, and thus $\phi \in \Gamma$ by the definition of Γ. Suppose $\psi \in K$. Then $<\psi;\psi \supset (\phi \supset \psi);\phi \supset \psi>$ is an SL-derivation of $\phi \supset \psi$ from K, $K \vdash_{SL}\phi \supset \psi$, and $\psi \in \Gamma$. So $K \cup \{\phi\} \subseteq \Gamma$. By Exercise 26.1 below, $AX_{SL} \subseteq \Gamma$.

Induction step. See Exercise 26.2 below.

So $CN_{SL}(K \cup \{\phi\}) \subseteq \Gamma$ by Theorem 12. But $\Gamma \subseteq CN_{SL}(K \cup \{\phi\})$ by Exercise 26.3 below. So $K \cup \{\phi\} \vdash_{SL}\psi \leftrightarrow K \vdash_{SL}\phi \supset \psi$. This completes our proof.

The Deduction Theorem for SL corresponds to the rule of Conditional Proof in a natural deduction system. Suppose we want to show that $K \vdash_{SL}\phi \supset \psi$. We begin by writing down ϕ as an assumed premise. This amounts to adding ϕ to our original set K of premises to produce a new set of premises $K \cup \{\phi\}$. Then we derive ψ from this new set of premises; that is, we show

$K \cup \{\phi\} \vdash_{SL} \psi$. Once we have done this, we discharge our assumed premise by removing it from our set of premises and concluding that $\phi \supset \psi$ follows from our original set of premises, i.e., that $K \vdash_{SL} \phi \supset \psi$. This last step in which we apply the rule of Conditional Proof amounts to an application of Theorem 13, the Deduction Theorem for SL.

To get an idea of how useful the Deduction Theorem can be, let's use it to show that $\vdash_{SL} {\sim}\phi \supset (\phi \supset \psi)$. We showed in Section 23 that $\{{\sim}\phi\} \vdash_{SL} \phi \supset \psi$. But $\{{\sim}\phi\} = \emptyset \cup \{{\sim}\phi\}$, so $\emptyset \cup \{{\sim}\phi\} \vdash_{SL} \phi \supset \psi$, $\emptyset \vdash_{SL} {\sim}\phi \supset (\phi \supset \psi)$ by Theorem 13, and $\vdash_{SL} {\sim}\phi \supset (\phi \supset \psi)$ by Definition 44.

EXERCISES

26.1 Show that $AX_{SL} \subseteq \{\psi: K \vdash_{SL} \phi \supset \psi\}$.

26.2 Show that $\{\psi: K \vdash_{SL} \phi \supset \psi\}$ is closed under <u>modus ponens</u>.

26.3 Show that $K \vdash_{SL} \phi \supset \psi \rightarrow K \cup \{\phi\} \vdash_{SL} \psi$.

Show each of the following.

26.4 $\vdash_{SL} (\phi \supset \psi) \supset ((\psi \supset \chi) \supset (\phi \supset \chi))$.

26.5 $\vdash_{SL} (\phi \supset \psi) \supset ((\chi \supset \phi) \supset (\chi \supset \psi))$.

26.6 $\vdash_{SL} \phi \supset ((\phi \supset \psi) \supset \psi)$.

26.7* $\vdash_{SL} {\sim}{\sim}\phi \supset \phi$.

26.8 $\vdash_{SL} \phi \supset {\sim}{\sim}\phi$.

26.9 $\vdash_{SL} (\phi \supset {\sim}\psi) \supset (\psi \supset {\sim}\phi)$.

26.10 $\vdash_{SL} ({\sim}\phi \supset \psi) \supset ({\sim}\psi \supset \phi)$.

26.11 $\vdash_{SL} (\phi \supset \psi) \supset ({\sim}\psi \supset {\sim}\phi)$.

26.12 $\vdash_{SL} \phi \supset ({\sim}\phi \supset \psi)$.

26.13 $\vdash_{SL} \phi \supset ({\sim}\psi \supset {\sim}(\phi \supset \psi))$.

26.14 $\vdash_{SL} (\phi \supset \psi) \supset (({\sim}\phi \supset \psi) \supset \psi)$.

26.15 $\vdash_{SL} (\phi \wedge \psi) \supset (\psi \wedge \phi)$.

26.16 $\vdash_{SL} (\phi \vee \psi) \supset (\psi \vee \phi)$.

26.17 $\vdash_{SL} (\phi \wedge \psi) \supset \phi$.

26.18 $\vdash_{SL} \phi \supset (\phi \vee \psi)$.

26.19 $\vdash_{SL}(\phi \equiv \psi) \supset (\sim\phi \equiv \sim\psi)$.

26.20 $\vdash_{SL}(\phi \equiv \psi) \supset ((\chi \supset \phi) \equiv (\chi \supset \psi))$.

26.21 $\vdash_{SL}(\phi \equiv \psi) \supset ((\phi \supset \chi) \equiv (\psi \supset \chi))$.

26.22 $\vdash_{SL}(\sim\phi \supset \psi) \supset ((\chi \supset \psi) \supset ((\phi \supset \chi) \supset \psi))$.

Remember that you may use anything that has already been proved to prove something new. This includes previous exercises and examples. For example, once you have proved Exercise 26.4, you may then use that exercise in the proof of any new result.

26.23* Show that $\vdash_{SL}\phi \equiv \phi' \rightarrow (\sigma)(\tau)((\sigma$ is an SL-expression & τ is an SL-expression & $\psi = \sigma{*}\phi{*}\tau) \rightarrow (\sigma{*}\phi'{*}\tau \in ST_{SL}$ & $\vdash_{SL}\psi \equiv \sigma{*}\phi'{*}\tau))$. This is a very difficult result. You can construct a proof using Theorem 1 and Exercises 20.4 and 20.6. This result shows that SL is closed under substitution of provable equivalents.

§27. Syntactical Consistency. Now we will develop another notion of consistency, a notion which does not involve any interpretation of the language of the sentential logic. Since this new notion can be defined solely in terms of the relationships between SL-sentences themselves, this is a syntactical rather than a semantical notion. Later we will find that in fact these two kinds of consistency are possesed by exactly the same sets of SL-sentences. You should have learned in earlier logic courses that you can derive anything at all from an inconsistent set of premises. On the other hand, if there is at least one thing that you can't derive from some set of premises, then that set of premises must be consistent. This is the idea behind the definition of SL-consistency.

DEFINITION 48. K is SL-consistent $\leftrightarrow (\exists\phi)\sim(K\vdash_{SL}\phi)$.

If K is not SL-consistent, we say that K is SL-inconsistent.

THEOREM 14. K is SL-consistent $\leftrightarrow \sim(\exists\phi)(K\vdash_{SL}\phi$ & $K\vdash_{SL}\sim\phi)$.

Proof. First assume that K is SL-consistent. We will use an indirect proof to show that $\sim(\exists\phi)(K \vdash_{SL} \phi \ \& \ K \vdash_{SL} \sim\phi)$. Suppose $K \vdash_{SL} \phi \ \& \ K \vdash_{SL} \sim\phi$. Since K is SL-consistent by our original assumption, we can let ψ be an SL-sentence such that $\sim K \vdash_{SL} \psi$ by Definition 48. We showed in the last section that $\vdash_{SL} \phi \supset (\sim\phi \supset \psi)$, so by Definition 44 and Theorems 9 and 10, $K \vdash_{SL} \sim\phi \supset \psi \ \& \ K \vdash_{SL} \psi$. This is a contradiction, so $\sim(\exists\phi)(K \vdash_{SL} \phi \ \& \ K \vdash_{SL} \sim\phi)$.

Now assume that $\sim(\exists\phi)(K \vdash_{SL} \phi \ \& \ K \vdash_{SL} \sim\phi)$. Then $\sim(K \vdash_{SL} \langle P_1 \rangle \ \& \ K \vdash_{SL} \sim\langle P_1 \rangle)$, $\sim K \vdash_{SL} \langle P_1 \rangle \vee \sim K \vdash_{SL} \sim\langle P_1 \rangle$, and since both $\langle P_1 \rangle$ and $\sim\langle P_1 \rangle$ are SL-sentences, $(\exists\phi)\sim(K \vdash_{SL} \phi)$. Thus K is SL-consistent by Definition 48.

<u>THEOREM 15.</u> K is SL-consistent $\leftrightarrow \sim(\exists\phi)(K \vdash_{SL} \sim(\phi \supset \phi))$.

<u>THEOREM 16.</u> $K \vdash_{SL} \phi \leftrightarrow K \cup \{\sim\phi\}$ is SL-inconsistent.

Proof. Suppose $K \vdash_{SL} \phi$. Then $K \cup \{\sim\phi\} \vdash_{SL} \phi$ by Theorem 10, $K \cup \{\sim\phi\} \vdash_{SL} \sim\phi$ by Theorem 7, and $K \cup \{\sim\phi\}$ is SL-inconsistent by Theorem 14.

Now suppose that $K \cup \{\sim\phi\}$ is SL-inconsistent. Then by Definition 48, $K \cup \{\sim\phi\} \vdash_{SL} \sim(\langle P_1 \rangle \supset \langle P_1 \rangle)$, and by Theorem 13, $K \vdash_{SL} \sim\phi \supset \sim(\langle P_1 \rangle \supset \langle P_1 \rangle)$. $K \vdash_{SL} (\sim\phi \supset \sim(\langle P_1 \rangle \supset \langle P_1 \rangle)) \supset ((\langle P_1 \rangle \supset \langle P_1 \rangle) \supset \phi)$ by AX3 and Exercise 24.3, and so $K \vdash_{SL} (\langle P_1 \rangle \supset \langle P_1 \rangle) \supset \phi$ by Theorem 9. Since $K \vdash_{SL} \langle P_1 \rangle \supset \langle P_1 \rangle$ by Exercise 23.3, Definition 44, and Theorem 10, $K \vdash_{SL} \phi$ by Theorem 9.

<u>THEOREM 17.</u> (K is SL-consistent & $K \vdash_{SL} \phi) \rightarrow K \cup \{\phi\}$ is SL-consistent.

<u>THEOREM 18.</u> K is SL-consistent $\leftrightarrow (\Gamma)((\Gamma \subseteq K \ \& \ \Gamma$ is finite) $\rightarrow \Gamma$ is SL-consistent).

Proof. Suppose first that K is SL-consistent and $\Gamma \subseteq K$. $\sim K \vdash_{SL} \sim(\phi \supset \phi)$ by Theorem 15, $\sim\Gamma \vdash_{SL} \sim(\phi \supset \phi)$ by Theorem 10, $\sim(\exists\phi)\Gamma \vdash_{SL} \sim(\phi \supset \phi)$, and Γ is SL-consistent by Theorem 15. So $(\Gamma)((\Gamma \subseteq K \ \& \ \Gamma$ is finite) $\rightarrow \Gamma$ is SL-consistent).

Now suppose $(\Gamma)((\Gamma \subseteq K \,\&\, \Gamma$ is finite$) \rightarrow \Gamma$ is SL-consistent). If K is not SL-consistent, then $K \vdash_{SL} \sim(\langle P_1\rangle \supset \langle P_1\rangle)$ by Definition 48 and $(\exists\Gamma)(\Gamma \subseteq K \,\&\, \Gamma$ is finite $\&\, \Gamma \vdash_{SL} \sim(\langle P_1\rangle \supset \langle P_1\rangle))$. But then by Theorem 15 $(\exists\Gamma)(\Gamma \subseteq K \,\&\, \Gamma$ is finite $\&\, \Gamma$ is not SL-consistent), which contradicts our initial assumption. So K is SL-consistent.

THEOREM 19. K is SL-consistent $\leftrightarrow (\Gamma)(\Gamma \subseteq K \rightarrow \Gamma$ is SL-consistent).

Theorem 16 corresponds to the rule of Indirect Proof or *Reductio ad Absurdum* in a natural deduction system. To show that $K \vdash_{SL} \phi$, we accept $\sim\phi$ as an assumed premise to produce a new premise set $K \cup \{\sim\phi\}$. Once we have showed that this new premise set is inconsistent (usually by deriving a contradiction), we conclude that $K \vdash_{SL} \phi$.

EXERCISES

27.1 Prove Theorems 15, 17, and 19.

§28. Maximal SL-consistency.

DEFINITION 49. K is *maximally SL-consistent* $\leftrightarrow$ (K is SL-consistent $\&\, (\phi)(K \cup \{\phi\}$ is SL-consistent $\rightarrow \phi \in K))$.

The idea behind maximal SL-consistency is that a maximally SL-consistent set is as large as a set of SL-sentences can get and still remain SL-consistent. Nothing can be added to a maximally SL-consistent set without producing a set which is SL-*in*consistent. Some of the properties of maximally SL-consistent sets are developed in the following theorems.

THEOREM 20. K is maximally SL-consistent $\rightarrow K = CN_{SL}(K)$.

THEOREM 21. K is maximally SL-consistent $\rightarrow (\phi \in K \leftrightarrow \sim\phi \notin K)$.

THEOREM 22. (K is maximally SL-consistent $\&\, K \vdash_{SL} \phi) \rightarrow$

$\phi \in K$.

THEOREM 23. K is maximally SL-consistent $\rightarrow (\phi \supset \psi \in K \leftrightarrow (\sim\phi \in K \vee \psi \in K))$.

EXERCISES

28.1 Prove Theorems 20, 21, 22, and 23.

§29. Semantical Analogs of Syntactical Theorems. An examination will show that there are many similarities between the results we have established for the two notions of semantical consistency and SL-consistency (syntactical consistency). Eventually we will show that these two notions are very closely related. Another semantic-syntactic pair of concepts which are similar are the concepts of tautological implication and SL-derivability. Here we shall look at some theorems concerning tautological implication which resemble earlier results for SL-derivability. A bit later we shall show just how very closely related these two notions are.

THEOREM 24. $\phi \in K \rightarrow K \models \phi$.

THEOREM 25. $\phi \in AX_{SL} \rightarrow (K \models \phi \;\&\; \models \phi)$.

THEOREM 26. $(K \models \phi \;\&\; K \models \phi \supset \psi) \rightarrow K \models \psi$.

Proof. Assume that $K \models \phi \;\&\; K \models \phi \supset \psi$. We want to show that $K \models \psi$; so by Definition 38 we need to show that $(v)((\chi)(\chi \in K \rightarrow I_v(\chi) = 1) \rightarrow I_v(\psi) = 1)$. Suppose v is a valuation such that $(\chi)(\chi \in K \rightarrow I_v(\chi) = 1)$. Since $K \models \phi \;\&\; K \models \phi \supset \psi$, $(\chi)(\chi \in K \rightarrow I_v(\chi) = 1) \rightarrow I_v(\phi) = 1$ and $(\chi)(\chi \in K \rightarrow I_v(\chi) = 1) \rightarrow I_v(\phi \supset \psi) = 1$ by Definition 38. So $I_v(\phi) = 1 \;\&\; I_v(\phi \supset \psi) = 1$, and by Definition 37.3, $I_v(\phi) = 0 \vee I_v(\psi) = 1$. But $I_v(\phi) \neq 0$, so $I_v(\psi) = 1$. Thus $(\chi)(\chi \in K \rightarrow I_v(\chi) = 1) \rightarrow I_v(\psi) = 1$, and $K \models \psi$ by Definition 38.

THEOREM 27. $(K \models \phi \;\&\; K \subseteq \Gamma) \rightarrow \Gamma \models \phi$.

THEOREM 28. $\models\phi \rightarrow K\models\phi$.

THEOREM 29. $K \cup \{\phi\}\models\psi \leftrightarrow K\models\phi \supset \psi$.

Proof. First assume that $K \cup \{\phi\}\models\psi$. By Definition 38 we want to show that $(v)((\chi)(\chi \varepsilon K \rightarrow I_v(\chi) = 1) \rightarrow I_v(\phi \supset \psi) = 1)$. We begin by supposing that v is a valuation such that $(\chi)(\chi \varepsilon K \rightarrow I_v(\chi) = 1)$. We have two cases to consider: either $I_v(\phi) = 0$ or $I_v(\phi) = 1$. If $I_v(\phi) = 0$, then $I_v(\phi \supset \psi) = 1$ by Definition 37.3. If $I_v(\phi) = 1$, then since $(\chi)(\chi \varepsilon K \rightarrow I_v(\chi) = 1)$ we conclude that $(\chi)(\chi \varepsilon K \cup \{\phi\} \rightarrow I_v(\chi) = 1)$. But $K \cup \{\phi\}\models\psi$, so $(\chi)(\chi \varepsilon K \cup \{\phi\} \rightarrow I_v(\chi) = 1) \rightarrow I_v(\psi) = 1$ by Definition 38 and $I_v(\psi) = 1$. Then $I_v(\phi \supset \psi) = 1$ by Definition 37.3. In either case, then, $I_v(\phi \supset \psi) = 1$. Therefore $(\chi)(\chi \varepsilon K \rightarrow I_v(\chi) = 1) \rightarrow I_v(\phi \supset \psi) = 1$, and $K\models\phi \supset \psi$ by Definition 38.

Now assume that $K\models\phi \supset \psi$. Then $K \cup \{\phi\}\models\phi$ by Theorem 24, $K \cup \{\phi\}\models\phi \supset \psi$ by Theorem 27, and $K \cup \{\phi\}\models\psi$ by Theorem 26.

EXERCISES

29.1 Prove Theorems 24, 25, 27, and 28.

§30. The Lindenbaum Lemma for SL.

THEOREM 30. (The Lindenbaum Lemma for SL.) K is SL-consistent $\rightarrow (\exists\Gamma)(K \subseteq \Gamma$ & Γ is maximally SL-consistent).

Proof. We need to show that we can start with an SL-consistent set K and build it up into a maximally SL-consistent set. The strategy is to look at each SL-sentence in turn, adding it to K if doing so will not make the resulting set SL-inconsistent. Actually after we have added several SL-sentences to K, we can only add another if doing so will not make the set we have already produced by augmenting K inconsistent. We keep up this process until we have either added or rejected every SL-sentence. Then we whould have added everything that can be added to K without resulting in an SL-inconsistent set. Now we need to make this precise.

Assume K is SL-consistent. S_{SL} is countable, so by a result from set theory we know that the set of all finite sequences of members of S_{SL} is also countable, i.e., the set of SL-expressions is countable. But ST_{SL} is an infinite subset of the set of SL-expressions, so ST_{SL} is countable. Therefore we can let $f\colon N \xrightarrow{\text{onto}} ST_{SL}$. What f allows us to do is to look at the SL-sentences one at a time.

Suppose we can add f(1) to K without producing an SL-inconsistent set. Suppose, that is, that $K \cup \{f(1)\}$ is SL-consistent. Then we want to add f(1) to K. On the other hand, if $K \cup \{f(1)\}$ is not SL-consistent, we want to reject f(1). Whether or not we add f(1) to K, we will call the set we have after we consider f(1) K_1. Then

$$K_1 = \begin{cases} K \cup \{f(1)\} \text{ if } K \cup \{f(1)\} \text{ is SL-consistent} \\ K \text{ if } K \cup \{f(1)\} \text{ is not SL-consistent} \end{cases}.$$

Next we examine f(2). If we can add f(2) to K_1 without producing an SL-inconsistent set, we do so. Otherwise, we reject f(2). If we let K_2 be the set we have after we have added or rejected f(2), then we have

$$K_2 = \begin{cases} K_1 \cup \{f(2)\} \text{ if } K_1 \cup \{f(2)\} \text{ is SL-consistent} \\ K_1 \text{ if } K_1 \cup \{f(2)\} \text{ is not SL-consistent} \end{cases}.$$

We proceed in this manner for each positive n. In general, then, if we let K_n be the set which results from adding or rejecting f(n), we have for each $n \neq 1$ that

$$K_n = \begin{cases} K_{n-1} \cup \{f(n)\} \text{ if } K_{n-1} \cup \{f(n)\} \text{ is SL-consistent} \\ K_{n-1} \text{ if } K_{n-1} \cup \{f(n)\} \text{ is not SL-consistent} \end{cases}.$$

This gives us infinitely many sets $K_1, K_2, \ldots$ We need to prove certain things about these sets.

First we will use mathematical induction to show that

$(n)(K_n$ is SL-consistent).

Basis step. If $K \cup \{f(1)\}$ is SL-consistent, then $K_1 = K \cup \{f(1)\}$ and thus K_1 is SL-consistent. If $K \cup \{f(1)\}$ is not SL-consistent, then $K_1 = K$. But K is SL-consistent by our original assumption, so K_1 is SL-consistent. So in either case, K_1 is SL-consistent.

Induction step. Assume that $(n)(n < k \rightarrow K_n$ is SL-consistent). If $K_{k-1} \cup \{f(k)\}$ is SL-consistent, then $K_k = K_{k-1} \cup \{f(k)\}$ and thus K_k is SL-consistent. If $K_{k-1} \cup \{f(k)\}$ is not SL-consistent, then $K_k = K_{k-1}$. But $k - 1 < k$, so K_{k-1} is SL-consistent by our inductive hypothesis. So in either case, K_k is SL-consistent.

Therefore by mathematical induction, $(n)(K_n$ is SL-consistent).

Next we will use mathematical induction to show that $(n)(m)(n \leq m \rightarrow K_n \subseteq K_m)$.

Basis step. Of course $K_1 \subseteq K_1$. But $(m)(m \leq 1 \rightarrow m = 1)$. So $(m)(m \leq 1 \rightarrow K_m \subseteq K_1)$.

Induction step. Assume that $(n)(n < k \rightarrow (m)(m \leq n \rightarrow K_m \subseteq K_n))$. Clearly $K_{k-1} \subseteq K_k$ & $K_k \subseteq K_k$. But $(m)(m \leq k \rightarrow (m \leq k - 1 \vee m = k))$. But $k - 1 < k$, so $(m)(m \leq k - 1 \rightarrow K_m \subseteq K_{k-1})$ by our inductive hypothesis. Since containment is a transitive relation, we then know that $(m)(m \leq k - 1 \rightarrow K_m \subseteq K_k)$. And since $K_k \subseteq K_k$, we can strengthen this to $(m)(m \leq k \rightarrow K_m \subseteq K_k)$.

Then by mathematical induction, $(n)(m)(n \leq m \rightarrow K_n \subseteq K_m)$.

We will use the sets $K_1, K_2, \ldots$ to build the desired maximally SL-consistent set Γ. We let $\Gamma = \{\phi: (\exists n)(\phi \in K_n)\}$. Since $K \subseteq K_1$, it is obvious that $K \subseteq \Gamma$ & $(n)(K_n \subseteq \Gamma)$. Now we need to show that Γ is maximally SL-consistent.

First we show that Γ is SL-consistent. We do this by showing that $(\Delta)((\Delta \subseteq \Gamma$ & Δ is finite) $\rightarrow \Delta$ is SL-consistent). Suppose $\Delta \subseteq \Gamma$ & Δ is finite. If $\phi \in \Delta$, then $\phi \in \Gamma$ and

$(\exists n)(\phi \in K_n)$. For each $\phi \in \Delta$, let n_ϕ be the smallest positive integer such that $\phi \in K_n$. Since Δ is finite, $\{n_\phi : \phi \in \Delta\}$ will also be finite, having no more members than does Δ. Let n be the largest member of $\{n_\phi : \phi \in \Delta\}$. (We can do this only because $\{n_\phi : \phi \in \Delta\}$ is finite.) Then $(\phi)(\phi \in \Delta \rightarrow (\phi \in K_{n_\phi}$ & $n_\phi \leq n))$. But since $(n)(m)(m \leq n \rightarrow K_m \subseteq K_n)$, we can conclude that $(\phi)(\phi \in \Delta \rightarrow \phi \in K_n)$. So $\Delta \subseteq K_n$. But $(n)(K_n$ is SL-consistent), so Δ is SL-consistent by Theorem 19. Hence $(\Delta)((\Delta \subseteq \Gamma$ & Δ is finite) $\rightarrow \Delta$ is SL-consistent), and Γ is SL-consistent by Theorem 18.

The last thing we need to show is that Γ is <u>maximally</u> SL-consistent i.e., that $\Gamma \cup \{\phi\}$ is SL-consistent $\rightarrow \phi \in \Gamma$. Suppose that $\Gamma \cup \{\phi\}$ is SL-consistent. Since the function f is <u>onto</u> ST_{SL}, $(\exists n)(f(n) = \phi)$. If n = 1, then $K \cup \{f(1)\} \subseteq \Gamma \cup \{\phi\}$ and $K \cup \{f(1)\}$ is SL-consistent by Theorem 19. But then $K_1 = K \cup \{f(1)\}$, $\phi \in K_1$, and $\phi \in \Gamma$. If $n \neq 1$, then $K_{n-1} \cup \{f(n)\} \subseteq \Gamma \cup \{\phi\}$ and $K_{n-1} \cup \{f(n)\}$ is SL-consistent by Theorem 19. But then $K_n = K_{n-1} \cup \{f(n)\}$, $\phi \in K_n$, and $\phi \in \Gamma$. So in either case, $\phi \in \Gamma$. Hence $\Gamma \cup \{\phi\}$ is SL-consistent $\rightarrow \phi \in \Gamma$.

Therefore $K \subseteq \Gamma$ & Γ is maximally SL-consistent, completing our proof.

We should notice that unless K is already maximally SL-consistent, in which case $\Gamma = K$, the set Γ which we construct will depend upon the function f. A single SL-consistent set K might be contained in infinitely many maximally SL-consistent sets. For example, suppose $\phi \notin K$, $\sim\phi \notin K$, $K \cup \{\phi\}$ is SL-consistent, and $K \cup \{\sim\phi\}$ is SL-consistent. (This would be the case, e.g., if $K = \emptyset$ and $\phi = \langle P_1 \rangle$.) If $f(1) = \phi$, then $\phi \in \Gamma$; but if $f(1) = \sim\phi$, then $\sim\phi \in \Gamma$.

What are the implications of the Lindenbaum Lemma? Suppose we have some theory, say a physical theory. If our physics is consistent, then Theorem 30 tells us that we can incorporate our physics into a consistent and <u>complete</u> description of the world. Maximal SL-consistency can be thought of, then, as a kind of completeness. Biology, physics, astrology, or whatever, is only a partial description of the world. Although each may be consistent, yet each leaves certain matters undetermined. A complete account of the world, which would correspond to a maximally SL-consistent set of sentences, would leave nothing undetermined. It would provide a determinate answer to every question. Of course a complete theory of the world need not be a true theory, even though it is consistent. We can have a consistent description of the world, one which answers every question which can be asked about the world, and yet that theory may give false answers to many of our questions. But the question of truth or falsity can not be dealt with so long as we restrict ourselves to syntax. The notions of being true or false involve interpreting our symbols, and interpretation is the domain of semantics.

EXERCISES

30.1* In which maximally SL-consistent sets is AX_{SL} contained?

30.2 In which maximally SL-consistent sets is ST_{SL} contained?

30.3 In which maximally SL-consistent sets is AT_{SL} contained?

§31. Soundness and Completeness. We have already seen remarkable similarities between the syntactical theorems and the semantical theorems of this chapter. Just how similar are our syntactical and our semantical results? How should our syntax and our semantics fit together? This can not be determined within the system itself but must be determined on extra-systemic grounds. Let's think for a moment about what it is we want a formal system to do. We want a set of rules and axioms which allow us to derive conclusions from sets of premises. But not just any set of rules and axioms will do. We only want to be able to derive a conclusion from a set of premises if it is impossible for the premises to be all true and the conclusion to be false. In other words, we only want to be able to provide derivations for intuitively valid arguments. We would reject as unsuitable any formal system which allowed us to show that the conclusion of an invalid argument followed from its premises. When a formal system only lets us provide derivations for valid arguments, we say that the formal system is <u>sound</u>. Of course validity as we are thinking of it here is a semantical notion, so whether or not a formal system is sound will depend upon how we are interpreting the language of the system. The usual way of interpreting the sentential logic is in terms of truth functions as we have done here. So we want to be able to show that $K \vdash_{SL} \phi$ only if it is impossible for every member of K to be true and ϕ to be false, i.e., only if $K \models \phi$. If we could show this, then we would say that the formal system SL was <u>sound</u> with respect to the standard truth-functional interpretation of the formal language of SL. Fortunately it is very easy to prove this given the results we already have.

<u>THEOREM 31.</u> (Soundness of SL.) $K \vdash_{SL} \phi \rightarrow K \models \phi$.

Proof. We can restate this theorem as $CN_{SL}(K) \subseteq \{\phi: K \models \phi\}$. So an easy way to prove the theorem is to do an induction on $CN_{SL}(K)$.

Basis step. $K \subseteq \{\phi: K \models \phi\}$ by Theorem 24 and $AX_{SL} \subseteq \{\phi: K \models \phi\}$ by Theorem 25.

Induction step. $\{\phi: K \models \phi\}$ is closed under <u>modus ponens</u> by Thorem 26.

Therefore $CN_{SL}(K) \subseteq \{\phi: K \models \phi\}$ by Theorem 12.

This theorem relates the notion of SL-derivability to that of tautological implication in a certain way. As a corollary, we establish an interesting relationship between our two notions of consistency.

COROLLARY 31.1. K is semantically consistent → K is SL-consistent.

But soundness is not the only extrasystemic requirement we place upon our formal system. Certainly we don't want our formal system to allow derivations for arguments which are not valid, but at the same time we ask that a formal system allow a derivation for every argument that is valid. We don't want our formal system to be so strong that it condones invalid arguments, but we want it to be strong enough to endorse every valid argument. In other words, we demand a formal system which is exactly strong enough to enable us to provide derivations for all and only valid arguments. We say that a formal system which satisfies the requirement that it provides derivations for all valid arguments is complete (or as some authors say, adequate) with respect to the notion of validity we have in mind. Once again, since our notion of validity is a semantical notion, the completeness requirement will be different if we interpret the language of the formal system differently. What we want for SL is that it be complete with respect to the standard truth-functional interpretation. In order to show completeness, we first show the converse of Corollary 31.1. In fact the relation between this result and the more obvious completeness results is so close that the converse of Corollary 31.1 is usually thought of as a version of completeness.

THEOREM 32. (Completeness, first version.) K is SL-consistent → K is semantically consistent.

Proof. Suppose K is SL-consistent. Then by the Lindenbaum Lemma we can let Γ be a maximally SL-consistent set such that $K \subseteq \Gamma$. We define a valuation v as follows: for each atomic SL-sentence ϕ, let $v(\phi) = 1$ if $\phi \in \Gamma$ and let $v(\phi) = 0$ if

$\phi \notin \Gamma$. We will do an induction on ST_{SL} to show that $ST_{SL} \subseteq \{\phi: I_v(\phi) = 1 \leftrightarrow \phi \in \Gamma\}$. For convenience, we will let $\Delta = \{\phi: I_v(\phi) = 1 \leftrightarrow \phi \in \Gamma\}$.

Basis step. Let $\phi \in AT_{SL}$. It is clear from the definition of v and Definition 37.1 that $I_v(\phi) = 1 \leftrightarrow \phi \in \Gamma$. So $AT_{SL} \subseteq \Delta$.

Induction step. Suppose $\phi \in \Delta$ & $\psi \in \Delta$. Then $I_v(\sim\phi) = 1$ if and only if $I_v(\phi) = 0$ (by Definition 37.2) if and only if $\phi \notin \Gamma$ (by our inductive hypothesis and the definition of Δ) if and only if $\sim\phi \in \Gamma$ (by Theorem 21 since Γ is maximally SL-consistent). So by the definition of Δ, $\sim\phi \in \Delta$. Furthermore, $I_v(\phi \supset \psi) = 1$ if and only if $I_v(\phi) = 0 \vee I_v(\psi) = 1$ (by Definition 37.3) if and only if $\phi \notin \Gamma \vee \psi \in \Gamma$ (by our inductive hypothesis and the definition of Δ) if and only if $\phi \supset \psi \in \Gamma$ (by Theorem 23 since Γ is maximally SL-consistent). So by the definition of Δ, $\phi \supset \psi \in \Delta$.

Therefore $ST_{SL} \subseteq \Delta$, i.e., $(\phi)(I_v(\phi) = 1 \leftrightarrow \phi \in \Gamma)$, by Theorem 1.

Since $K \subseteq \Gamma$, it follows that $(\phi)(\phi \in K \rightarrow I_v(\phi) = 1)$. So K is semantically consistent by Definition 40.

<u>THEOREM 33.</u> (Completeness, second version.) $K \models \phi \rightarrow K \vdash_{SL} \phi$.

It is this theorem which best captures the intuitive account of completeness which we offered above. This theorem says that if an argument is valid (according to the truth-functional interpretation of our language for sentential logic), then we can provide a derivation for the argument in our formal system. This version of completeness is actually equivalent to the first version.

<u>THEOREM 34.</u> (Completeness, weak version.) $\models \phi \rightarrow \vdash_{SL} \phi$.

It is possible to have a formal system which is complete with respect to a certain interpretation in the weak sense but not in the strong sense. The system may allow us to derive (without any premises) any sentence of the formal language which is "necessarily true" according to the interpretation we give to the language of the system, and yet the formal system may not provide the means for deriving the conclusion from the premises of some argument which is valid according to the interpretation we adopt. So weak completeness really is a weaker result than either of our first two completeness results.

EXERCISES

31.1 Prove Corollary 31.1 and Theorems 33 and 34.

31.2 Prove Theorem 32 using Theorem 33 but without using Theorem 1.

31.3 Show that K is semantically consistent $\leftrightarrow$ $(\Gamma)((\Gamma \subseteq K$ & Γ is finite$) \rightarrow \Gamma$ is semantically consistent$)$.

§32. The Consistency of SL. We know what it is for a set of SL-sentences to be SL-consistent, but do we know that there are any sets of SL-sentences which are SL-consistent? And what might it mean to say that SL itself is consistent? Consistency must always be defined in terms of the derivability relation of a formal system (syntactical consistency) or in terms of the interpretation we give to the language of the system (semantical consistency). Typically the consistency of the system itself is defined in terms of the set of theorems of the system, in this case $\{\phi\colon \vdash_{SL} \phi\}$ or $CN_{SL}(\emptyset)$. We say that the system is itself consistent just in case the set of theorems of the system has the kind of consistency we have defined within the system. So we say that SL is consistent just in case $CN_{SL}(\emptyset)$ is SL-consistent. If we could show this, then we would also have showed that there is at least one subset of ST_{SL}, namely $CN_{SL}(\emptyset)$, which is SL-consistent.

THEOREM 35. (Consistency of SL.) $CN_{SL}(\emptyset)$ is SL-consistent.

Proof. By Theorems 31 and 33, $CN_{SL}(\emptyset) = \{\phi\colon \models\phi\}$. Thus the set of theorems of SL and the set of tautologies are one and the same. Now let v be any valuation whatsoever. If $\models\phi$, then since $(\chi)(\chi \in \emptyset \rightarrow I_v(\chi) = 1)$ is vacuously true because $(\chi)(\chi \notin \emptyset)$, $I_v(\phi) = 1$. So $(\phi)(\models\phi \rightarrow I_v(\phi) = 1)$, and $\{\phi\colon \models\phi\}$ is semantically consistent by Definition 40. Then $CN_{SL}(\emptyset)$ is semantically consistent, and $CN_{SL}(\emptyset)$ is SL-consistent by Corollary 31.1.

Notice that we used the notion of semantical consistency to prove that SL was itself consistent. Most consistency proofs, but not all, involve semantics. To prove consistency, you prove that every theorem of the system has some property which some sentences lack. In the case of SL, we showed that every valuation made every theorem come out true. It is easy enough to see that every valuation will make every contradiction come out false. So no contradiction could be a theorem and our set of theorems must be consistent. In general we may prove that a system is consistent by showing that every theorem has some semantical property which not every sentence of the system has.

EXERCISES

32.1 Show that AX_{SL} is SL-consistent. (Hint: Show that AX_{SL} is semantically consistent.)

32.2 Show that $\emptyset$ is SL-consistent.

32.3 Show that AT_{SL} is SL-consistent.

CHAPTER 3

Predicate Logic

§33. Predicate Logic Symbols. To discuss the predicate logic we must have ways of referring to quantifiers, variables, constants, and predicates. For this purpose we introduce some additional primitive constants and predicates into our metalanguage. Besides the two logical constants '$\underline{n}$' and '$\underline{i}$', we will require another logical constant '$\underline{u}$' which we will read as 'the universal quantifier symbol'. We will assume that we have available countably many variables in any predicate logic object language we discuss, and for each positive integer n we introduce the constant '$\underline{v}_n$' which we will read as 'the nth variable symbol'. In addition we will need some new primitive predicates in our metalanguage. One of these will be '---- is a constant'. Also for each positive integer n we will need the predicate '---- is an n-place predicate'.

Instead of adding primitive predicates to our metalanguage it seems that we might have added a new constant, say '$\underline{c}_n$', for each positive integer n, a constant which would be read 'the nth constant symbol'. We could have done something similar for predicates. But this would only be acceptable if there were only countably many constants and predicates. We are assuming, though, that there are uncountably many constants and predicates. Indeed, we are making a very strong assumption about the richness of our supply of constants and predicates.

Recall that in Chapter 1 we showed that there is no set which has as its members exactly those things for which the open sentence 'x $\notin$ x' is true. We assume that something similar is true where constants and predicates are concerned. We assume that $\sim(\exists A)(x)(x \varepsilon A \leftrightarrow$ x is a constant) and we assume that $(n)\sim(\exists A)(x)(x \varepsilon A \leftrightarrow$ x is an n-place predicate). No matter how large a set of constants and predicates we may have, then, there are always more constants and predicates available which do not belong to our set than there are in our set. We call these our <u>richness assumptions</u> concerning predicate logic symbols.

Besides our richness assumptions, we also make several <u>distinctness assumptions</u>. We have already assumed that $\underline{n} \neq \underline{i}$, but now we assume that $\underline{n} \neq \underline{u}$, that $\underline{i} \neq \underline{u}$, and that none of $\underline{n}$, $\underline{i}$, or $\underline{u}$ is a variable symbol, a constant, or a predicate of any number of places. We assume that $(m)(n)(m \neq n \rightarrow \underline{v}_m \neq \underline{v}_n)$ and that no variable symbol is either a constant or a predicate. We also assume that no predicate is a constant and that (m)(n)(x)((m $\neq$ n & x is an m-place predicate) $\rightarrow$ x is not an n-place predicate).

<u>DEFINITION 50.</u> $VR = \{x: (\exists n)(x = \langle \underline{v}_n \rangle)\}$.

We call the members of VR <u>variable expressions</u> and we will use the Greek letter 'α', 'β', and 'γ' as special variables which range over variable expressions.

<u>DEFINITION 51.</u> x is a <u>PL-symbol</u> $\leftrightarrow$ (x ε $\{\underline{n},\underline{i},\underline{u}\}$ $\vee$ $(\exists n)(x = \underline{v}_n)$ $\vee$ x is a constant $\vee$ $(\exists n)$(x is an n-place predicate)).

We make one last distinctness assumption that no PL-symbol is a sequence of PL-symbols.

Because of our richness assumptions for PL-symbols, we know that $\sim(\exists A)(x)(x \varepsilon A \leftrightarrow$ x is a PL-symbol). Since a formal language is a 3-place sequence the first member of which is the set of symbols of the language, there is nothing which is the language of predicate logic. Instead we shall find that predicate logic is the study of a family of languages all of whose symbols are PL-symbols.

DEFINITION 52. σ is a PL-expression $\leftrightarrow$ σ is a finite sequence of PL-symbols.

DEFINITION 53. x is a constant expression $\leftrightarrow$ $(\exists y)$(y is a constant & x = <y>).

We will use 'c', 'c_1', 'c_2', etc., as special variables which range over constant expressions.

DEFINITION 54. x is an n-place predicate expression $\leftrightarrow$ $(\exists y)$(y is an n-place predicate & x = <y>).

We will sometimes simply say 'predicate expression' when we are not concerned with the number of places of a predicate expression. We will use 'F', 'G', 'H', etc., as special variables which range over predicate expressions. Where σ and τ are PL-expressions, we have the following definition.

DEFINITION 55.

$$\sim\sigma = \langle \underline{n} \rangle * \sigma.$$
$$\sigma \supset \tau = \langle \underline{i} \rangle * \sigma * \tau.$$
$$\sigma \wedge \tau = \sim(\sigma \supset \sim\tau).$$
$$\sigma \vee \tau = \sim\sigma \supset \tau.$$
$$\sigma \equiv \tau = (\sigma \supset \tau) \wedge (\tau \supset \sigma).$$
$$\bigwedge \alpha\sigma = \langle \underline{u} \rangle * \alpha * \sigma.$$
$$\bigvee \alpha\sigma = \sim \bigwedge \alpha \sim\sigma.$$

§34. Predicate Logic Languages.

As we mentioned in the last section, there is no such thing as the language of predicate logic. Instead we will examine a family of languages which we will call predicate logic languages or PL-languages. Each of these languages will have as its basis a set of constants and predicates. Each of these languages will in turn determine a formal system.

For sentential logic the smallest expression considered was an atomic SL-sentence. We had no referring expressions or predicate expressions out of which our SL-sentences were built. We have already defined predicate expressions and we are now ready to define the notion of a predicate logic term.

DEFINITION 56. x is a PL-term $\leftrightarrow$ (x ε VR $\vee$ x is a constant expression).

While atomic SL-sentences are simple in that they are 1-place sequences, the atomic formulas of predicate logic are complex in that each must involve at least one predicate expression and at least one PL-term.

DEFINITION 57. σ is an atomic PL-formula $\leftrightarrow$ $(\exists n)(\exists F)(\exists x_1)\ldots(\exists x_n)$(F is an n-place predicate expression & x_1 is a PL-term & ... & x_n is a PL-term & $\sigma = F{*}x_1{*}\ldots{*}x_n$).

Just as in the case of SL-sentences, predicate logic formulas are constructed, beginning with the atomic PL-formulas. There is an important difference in the construction procedure, however, since later lines of a predicate logic construction may be generalizations of earlier lines.

DEFINITION 58. σ is a PL-construction $\leftrightarrow$ $(n)(n \leq \ell(\sigma) \rightarrow (\sigma_n$ is an atomic PL-formula $\vee (\exists i)(i < n \;\&\; \sigma_n = {\sim}\sigma_i) \vee (\exists i)(\exists j)(i < n \;\&\; j < n \;\&\; \sigma_n = \sigma_i \supset \sigma_j) \vee (\exists i)(\exists \alpha)(i < n \;\&\; \sigma_n = \bigwedge \alpha \sigma_i)))$.

DEFINITION 59. x is a PL-formula $\leftrightarrow$ $(\exists\sigma)(\sigma$ is a PL-construction & $\sigma_{\ell(\sigma)} = x)$.

In this chapter we will use 't', 't_1', 't_2'. etc., as special variables which range over PL-terms and we will use 'ϕ', 'ψ', 'χ', and 'θ' as special variables which range over PL-formulas.

We are now ready to define the notion of a PL-language.

DEFINITION 60. x is a PL-language $\leftrightarrow$ $(\exists A)(\exists B)(\exists C)(\exists D)$

(A is at most countable & A is recursive & $(y)(y \in A \to$ (y is a constant $\vee$ $(\exists n)$(y is an n-place predicate))) & $x = \langle B;C;D \rangle$ & $B = A \cup \{\underline{n},\underline{i},\underline{u}\} \cup \{\underline{v}_n : n \in N\}$ & $C = VR \cup \{\langle y \rangle : y \in A$ & y is a constant$\}$ & $D = \{\phi : \phi$ is a PL-formula & $(n)(n \leq \ell(\phi) \to \phi_n \in B)\})$.

Let's unpack this definition. First we have a set of constants and predicates A which is recursive and which is either finite or countably infinite. This set will be unique for each PL-language, and for each PL-language we will call the corresponding set A the base of the language. Next we have three sets B, C, and D, all defined in terms of A. Since A is recursive, so are B, C, and D. The set B contains all of the constants and predicates in A, all of the variable symbols, and our three logical constants $\underline{n}$, $\underline{i}$, and $\underline{u}$. So B is a recursive set of PL-symbols. The set C contains all variable expressions and all constant expressions which can be formed from members of B. So C is a recursive set of finite sequences of members of B, all of which are PL-terms. Finally, since every member of D is a PL-formula every member of which is a member of B, D is also a recursive set of finite sequences of members of B. Then by Definition 27, every PL-language is a formal language. We will use 'L', 'L_1', 'L_2', etc., as special variables which range over PL-languages. Where L is a PL-language, we will let 'L_B' denote the base of L. Thus $L_B = S_L - (\{\underline{n},\underline{i},\underline{u}\} \cup VR)$.

We could omit the stipulation in Definition 60 that the base of a PL-language may be at most countable. By including this stipulation we insure that for every PL-language L, both TM_L and FM_L are either empty or countable. We will need this assumption when we prove the predicate logic version of the Lindenbaum Lemma. If we delete this stipulation we can still prove a Lindenbaum Lemma for PL-languages but we must then use transfinite induction instead of mathematical induction. This would require the development of additional set-theoretic notions and techniques.

Where L is a PL-language, $x \in L_B$, and x is a predicate, we will say that $\langle x \rangle$ is a predicate expression *of* L. If $c \in TM_L$, we will say that c is a constant expression *of* L. And of course we will call members of S_L *L-symbols*, members of TM_L *L-terms*, and members of FM_L *L-formulas*. We can also define the notion of an atomic L-formula.

DEFINITION 61. $AT_L = \{\phi: \phi \text{ is an atomic PL-formula } \& \ (n)(n \leq \ell(\phi) \rightarrow \phi_n \in S_L)\}$.

Before looking at a concrete example of a PL-language, we will introduce a more convenient and familiar notation for writing atomic PL-formulas.

DEFINITION 62. (F is an n-place predicate expression & t_1 is a PL-term & ... & t_n is a PL-term) $\rightarrow$ $(Ft_1 \ldots t_n = F{*}t_1{*} \ldots {*}t_n)$.

Definition 62 allows us to eliminate the unfamiliar concatenation sign from our names for atomic PL-formulas.

Now let's look at a very simple PL-language. Whenever we wish to discuss a particular PL-language we will specify the intended language by identifying its base. As we will see in Exercise 34.4, the base determines the entire language. Let $A = \{x,y,z\}$ such that x is a constant, y is a 1-place predicate, and z is a 2-place predicate. Let $c = \langle x \rangle$, let $F = \langle y \rangle$, and let $G = \langle z \rangle$. Let L be the PL-language such that $L_B = A$. Then $S_L = \{x,y,z,\underline{n},\underline{i},\underline{u}\} \cup \{v_n: n \in N\}$, $TM_L = \{c\} \cup VR$, and $AT_L = \{Fc, Gcc\} \cup \{F\alpha: \alpha \in VR\} \cup \{Gc\alpha: \alpha \in VR\} \cup \{G\alpha c: \alpha \in VR\} \cup \{G\alpha\beta: \alpha \in VR \ \& \ \beta \in VR\}$. Now let's show that $\phi \in FM_L$ where $\phi = \mathbf{V}\langle \underline{v}_{13}\rangle(Fc \vee G\langle \underline{v}_{67}\rangle\langle \underline{v}_{101}\rangle)$. Clearly every member of ϕ is an L-symbol. All we need to show, then, is that ϕ is a PL-formula. To do this we need to show that there is a PL-construction whose last member is ϕ. Let σ be the 7-place sequence such that:

σ_1 = Fc	(atomic PL-formula);
σ_2 = G<$\underline{v}_{67}$><$\underline{v}_{101}$>	(atomic PL-formula);
σ_3 = ~Fc	(= ~σ_1);
σ_4 = Fc v G<$\underline{v}_{67}$><$\underline{v}_{101}$>	(= $\sigma_3 \supset \sigma_2$ by Definition 55, line 4);
σ_5 = ~(Fc v G<$\underline{v}_{67}$><$\underline{v}_{101}$>)	(= ~σ_4);
σ_6 = $\bigwedge$<$\underline{v}_{13}$>~(Fc v G<$\underline{v}_{67}$><$\underline{v}_{101}$>)	(= $\bigwedge\alpha\sigma_5$); and
σ_7 = $\bigvee$<$\underline{v}_{13}$>(Fc v G<$\underline{v}_{67}$><$\underline{v}_{101}$>)	(= ~σ_6 by Definition 55, line 7).

Then σ is a PL-construction and $\sigma_{\ell(\sigma)} = \phi$. So $\phi \in FM_L$.

EXERCISES

Let c_1 and c_2 be constant expressions and let F and G be 2-place predicate expressions.

34.1 Which of the following are atomic PL-formulas: Fc_1, $G\alpha c_2$, $F\alpha\beta\gamma$, $G\beta\alpha$, $G\beta$, $F\alpha\alpha \supset G\alpha\alpha$? Explain your answers.

34.2 Show that $Fc_1c_2 \vee \sim\bigvee\alpha G\beta\gamma$ is a PL-formula.

34.3 Show that $\bigwedge c_1Fc_1c_1$ is not a PL-formula where $\bigwedge c_1\phi$ = <$\underline{u}$>*c_1*ϕ.

34.4 Show that (A is recursive & A is at most countable & (x)(x ε A → (x is a constant ∨ (∃n)(x is an n-place predicate))) → (∃L)(L is a PL-language & L_B = A & (L')((L' is a PL-language & L'_B = A) → L = L')).

34.5* Show that (t)(∃L)(t ε TM_L).

34.6 Show that (ϕ)(∃L)(ϕ ε FM_L).

§35. An Induction Principle for PL-formulas.

THEOREM 36. (Induction Principle for FM_L.) $(AT_L \subseteq A$ & $(\phi)(\phi \in A \rightarrow \sim\phi \in A)$ & $(\phi)(\psi)((\phi \in A$ & $\psi \in A) \rightarrow \phi \supset \psi \in A)$ & $(\phi)(\phi \in A \rightarrow (\alpha)(\bigwedge\alpha\phi \in A))) \rightarrow FM_L \subseteq A$.

Both the proof and the application of Theorem 36 parallel those of Theorem 1. In the basis step of an induction on FM_L we show that AT_L is contained in some set or that every atomic L-formula has some property. In the induction step we show that whenever ϕ and ψ belong to the set or have the property in question, then so do all of $\sim\phi$, $\phi \supset \psi$, and $\Lambda\alpha\phi$. Of course this last claim must be established for each variable expression α.

EXERCISES

35.1 Prove Theorem 36.

35.2* Show that $\phi \in FM_L \rightarrow \langle\phi_{\ell(\phi)}\rangle \in TM_L$.

35.3 Show that $\phi \in FM_L \rightarrow (\exists n)(\exists m)(\phi_n$ is an m-place predicate).

§36. Free and Bound Variable Expressions. The usual introductory symbolic logic textbook provides a set of rules which allow us to eliminate and introduce quantifiers. At least one of these rules will have restrictions which concern the free or bound occurrence of certain variable expressions in the previous lines of the derivation and/or in the line we are about to write down. If we violate these restrictions we will be able to provide derivations for arguments which we intuitively judge to be invalid. Let's consider a simple example.

1.	(∃x)(Cx)	premise
2.	(∃x)(Dx)	premise
3.	Cx	1, Existential Instantiation
4.	Dx	2, Existential Instantiation
5.	Cx & Dx	3,4, Conjunction
6.	(y)(Cy & Dy)	5, Universal Generalization

Suppose our first premise says that something is a cat and our second premise says that something is a dog. Then our conclusion says that everything is a "feline canine". Our premises are both true but our conclusion is false. Anyone who has studied a natural deduction system for predicate logic knows that we have violated the usual restrictions placed upon Existential Instantiation and Universal Generalization in constructing this derivation. Line 4 is improper because 'x' appears free in a previous line and line 6 is improper because 'x' appears free in a previous line obtained by Existential Instantiation. There is nothing wrong with line 3, though, even though 'x' occurs in earlier lines because 'x' does not occur free in any earlier lines. This example shows that we can not apply our quantifier rules properly unless we can distinguish between free and bound occurrences of variable expressions. The easiest way to do this is to define what it is for a variable expression to occur bound and then to define a free occurrence as any occurrence which is not bound.

DEFINITION 63. $OB(\alpha,n,\phi) \leftrightarrow (\langle\phi_n\rangle = \alpha \mathbin{\&} (\exists\psi)(\psi_1 = \underline{u} \mathbin{\&} \langle\psi_2\rangle = \alpha \mathbin{\&} (\exists x)((x = 0 \vee x \varepsilon N) \mathbin{\&} x < n \mathbin{\&} n \leq x + \ell(\psi) \mathbin{\&} (k)(k \leq \ell(\psi) \rightarrow \psi_k = \phi_{k + x}))))$.

We read '$OB(\alpha,n,\phi)$' as 'α occurs bound at the nth place in ϕ'. Let us see exactly what this involves. First, in order for $OB(\alpha,n,\phi)$, α must occur at the nth place in ϕ, i.e., the nth member of ϕ must be the same variable symbol as is the first and only member of α. Second, the occurrence of α at the nth place in ϕ must be an occurrence which "falls within the scope of a universal quantifier which binds occurrences of α". And this is what the rest of the definition spells out. For the relevant occurrence of α to fall within the scope of a quantifier binding α, there must be a formula of the form $\bigwedge\alpha\psi$ such that this formula occurs as part of ϕ and the relevant occurrence of α occurs within this formula as it occurs in ϕ.

Let's look at an example. Let $\phi = Fc \supset \bigwedge\alpha F\alpha$ and let $\psi = \bigwedge\alpha F\alpha$. Then by Definition 55, $\phi = \langle\underline{i}\rangle{*}Fc{*}\langle\underline{u}\rangle{*}\alpha{*}F\alpha$ and $\psi = \langle\underline{u}\rangle{*}\alpha{*}F\alpha$. We see that α occurs at the fifth and seventh places in ϕ. Furthermore we see by examination that $\langle\phi_5\rangle = \alpha \mathbin{\&} \psi_1 = \underline{u} \mathbin{\&} \langle\psi_2\rangle = \alpha \mathbin{\&} 3 < 5 \mathbin{\&} 5 \leq 3 + \ell(\psi) \mathbin{\&} (k)(k \leq \ell(\psi) \rightarrow \psi_k = \phi_{3 + k})$. So by Definition 63, $OB(\alpha,5,\phi)$. We can also see that $OB(\alpha,7,\phi)$. So every occurrence of α in ϕ is a bound occurrence.

Let's consider another example. Now let $\phi = \bigwedge\alpha Fc \supset F\alpha$. By Definition 55, $\phi = \langle\underline{i}\rangle*\langle\underline{u}\rangle*\alpha*Fc*F\alpha$. The only formula which occurs within ϕ whose first member is $\underline{u}$ is ψ where $\psi = \bigwedge\alpha Fc = \langle\underline{u}\rangle*\alpha*Fc$. Now α occurs at the seventh place in ϕ, but the only non-negative integer m such that $(k)(k \leq \ell(\psi) \rightarrow \psi_k = \phi_{k+m})$ is 1 and it is <u>not</u> the case that $7 \leq 1 + \ell(\psi)$. So $\sim OB(\alpha,7,\phi)$. We do note, though, that $OB(\alpha,3,\phi)$.

Although you probably were not provided with such a precise definition of the notion of a bound occurrence of a variable expression in any introductory logic textbook you may have studied, you nevertheless probably developed the ability to determine whether a particular occurrence of a variable expression was bound. All that Definition 63 does is make the condition which you use in exercising that ability precise. (It is not unusual that people are able to do something without being able to explain exactly how it is that they do it.) You should find that the defining condition for a variable expression occurring bound in a formula which is incorporated into Definition 63 is true for a variable expression in a formula in exactly the same cases in which the ability you developed in your introductory logic course tells you that that occurrence of that variable expression is bound. In other words, our precise definition should exactly agree with the imprecise account contained in most introductory symbolic logic textbooks.

<u>DEFINITION 64.</u> $OF(\alpha,n,\phi) \leftrightarrow (\langle\phi_n\rangle = \alpha \;\&\; \sim OB(\alpha,n,\phi))$.

Once you understand Definition 63 the meaning of Definition 64 should be clear. As an example, $OF(\alpha,7,\bigwedge\alpha Fc \supset F\alpha)$.

<u>DEFINITION 65.</u> $BV(\phi) = \{\alpha\colon (\exists n)(OB(\alpha,n,\phi))\}$.

<u>DEFINITION 66.</u> $FV(\phi) = \{\alpha\colon (\exists n)(OF(\alpha,n,\phi))\}$.

$BV(\phi)$ and $FV(\phi)$ are, respectively, the set of variable expressions which occur bound in ϕ and the set of variable expressions which occur free in ϕ. Of course a single variable expression may have both free and bound occurrences in the same PL-formula. For example, $BV(\bigwedge \alpha Fc \supset F\alpha) = FV(\bigwedge \alpha Fc \supset F\alpha) = \{\alpha\}$.

In sentential logic we make no distinction between an SL-formula and an SL-sentence. We do make such a distinction in the case of predicate logic. Only certain PL-formulas are PL-sentences.

DEFINITION 67. ϕ is a PL-sentence $\leftrightarrow FV(\phi) = \emptyset$.

DEFINITION 68. $ST_L = \{\phi: \phi \in FM_L \;\&\; \phi$ is a PL-sentence$\}$.

Examples of arguments found in introductory symbolic logic texts normally include only the sort of thing we mean by a PL-sentence as premises and conclusions. Formulas which are not PL-sentences usually only show up as intermediate steps in derivations in such texts. The reason for this is that there do not seem to be any sentences in natural languages which correspond to PL-formulas which are not also PL-sentences.

EXERCISES

36.1 Determine the following: $BV(\bigwedge \alpha F\beta)$, $FV(\bigvee \alpha F\beta)$, $BV(\bigwedge \alpha F\beta \supset F\alpha)$, and $FV(\bigwedge \alpha(F\beta \supset F\alpha))$.

36.2 Show that ϕ is an atomic PL-formula $\rightarrow FV(\phi) = \{\alpha: (\exists n)(<\phi_n> = \alpha)\}$.

36.3 Show that $FV(\phi) = FV({\sim}\phi) \;\&\; BV(\phi) = BV({\sim}\phi)$.

36.4 Show that $FV(\phi \supset \psi) = FV(\phi) \cup FV(\psi) \;\&\; BV(\phi \supset \psi) = BV(\phi) \cup BV(\psi)$.

36.5 Show that ${\sim}OB(\alpha,1,\phi) \;\&\; {\sim}OF(\alpha,1,\phi)$.

36.6* Show that $<(\bigwedge \alpha\phi)_n> = \beta \rightarrow (OB(\beta,n,\bigwedge \alpha\phi) \leftrightarrow (\alpha = \beta \vee (n > 2 \;\&\; OB(\beta,n-2,\phi))))$.

36.7 Show that $(\alpha \neq \beta \rightarrow {\sim}OB(\beta,2,\bigwedge \alpha\phi)) \;\&\; {\sim}OF(\beta,2,\bigwedge \alpha\phi)$.

36.8 Show that $FV(\bigwedge \alpha\phi) = FV(\phi) - \{\alpha\} \;\&\; BV(\bigwedge \alpha\phi) = BV(\phi) \cup \{\alpha\}$.

§37. Substitution of Terms. The rules of a natural deduction system for predicate logic frequently allow or require the substitution of one term for another in a formula. The most common substitutions are substitutions of a constant expression or a variable expression for a freely occurring variable expression and substitutions of a variable expression for a constant expression. We will define functions which accomplish such substitutions in this section.

We begin by looking at the problem of substituting a constant expression or a variable expression for a free variable expression. We must take particular care when we substitute a variable expression for a free variable expression. Suppose, for example, we wish to replace all free occurrences of α in $\bigwedge\beta F\alpha$ with some variable expression. Assuming that $\alpha \neq \beta$, the single occurrence of α in $\bigwedge\beta F\alpha$ is free so we can replace it with some other variable expression. But if we replace α by β in $\bigwedge\beta F\alpha$ to produce $\bigwedge\beta F\beta$, we end up with no free occurrence of any variable expression. While we have $OF(\alpha,4,\bigwedge\beta F\alpha)$, we have $OB(\beta,4,\bigwedge\beta F\beta)$. We could express what has happened by saying that we have replaced a free occurrence of a variable expression by a bound occurrence of a variable expression, and this we do not want to do. We want a function which replaces only free occurrences of variable expressions and which replaces them with constant expressions or with occurrences of variable expressions which are themselves free.

DEFINITION 69. We define for each PL-language L, each $t \in TM_L$, and each $\alpha \in VR$ a function $|\alpha/t|: TM_L \cup FM_L \longrightarrow TM_L \cup FM_L$ recursively as follows:

1. $|\alpha/t|t' = \begin{cases} t' \text{ if } \alpha \neq t' \\ t \text{ if } \alpha = t' \end{cases}$;
2. $|\alpha/t|Ft_1\ldots t_n = F*|\alpha/t|t_1* \ldots *|\alpha/t|t_n$;
3. $|\alpha/t|{\sim}\phi = {\sim}|\alpha/t|\phi$;

4. $|\alpha/t|(\phi \supset \psi) = |\alpha/t|\phi \supset |\alpha/t|\psi$; and

5. $$|\alpha/t|\bigwedge\beta\phi = \begin{cases} \bigwedge\beta|\alpha/t|\phi \text{ if } \alpha \neq \beta \;\&\; t \neq \beta \\ \bigwedge\beta\phi \text{ if } \alpha = \beta \vee t = \beta \end{cases}.$$

Where $x \in TM_L \cup FM_L$ we call $|\alpha/t|x$ <u>the result of replacing free occurrences of</u> α <u>in</u> x <u>by free occurrences of</u> t. Of course we can think of any occurrence of a constant expression as being a free occurrence since a quantifier can never bind an occurrence of a constant expression. Strictly speaking, though, only occurrences of variable expressions may be bound or free.

Let's look at a few examples to see how Definition 69 works and to make sure the functions we have defined do what they are supposed to do. Let α, β, and γ be three different variable expressions and let c be a constant expression. What would we have if we replaced all free occurrences of α with free occurrences of β in the PL-formula $(\bigwedge\alpha F\alpha \vee \bigvee\beta F\alpha) \supset \bigwedge\gamma Gc\alpha$? First we need to locate the free occurrences of α in this formula. We see that α occurs free in $\bigvee\beta F\alpha$ and in $\bigwedge\gamma Gc\alpha$. But if we replace the occurrence of α in $\bigvee\beta F\alpha$ with β, we produce a bound occurrence of β where we previously had a free occurrence of α. So the only occurrence of α which we can replace is the occurrence in $\bigwedge\gamma Gc\alpha$. Applying the skill developed in learning to use a natural deduction system, we find that the result of replacing all free occurrences of α with free occurrences of β in $(\bigwedge\alpha F\alpha \vee \bigvee\beta F\alpha) \supset \bigwedge\gamma Gc\alpha$ is $(\bigwedge\alpha F\alpha \vee \bigvee\beta F\alpha) \supset \bigwedge\gamma Gc\beta$. Let's see if this is what we get when we use the function defined in Definition 69 for the variable expressions α and β and for the language generated by the set of PL-symbols {x,y,z} such that F = <x>, G = <y>, and c = <z>.

$|\alpha/\beta|((\bigwedge\alpha F\alpha \vee \bigvee\beta F\alpha) \supset \bigwedge\gamma Gc\alpha) =$

$|\alpha/\beta|((\sim\bigwedge\alpha F\alpha \supset \sim\bigwedge\beta{\sim}F\alpha) \supset \bigwedge\gamma Gc\alpha) =$

$|\alpha/\beta|(\sim\bigwedge\alpha F\alpha \supset \sim\bigwedge\beta{\sim}F\alpha) \supset |\alpha/\beta|\bigwedge\gamma Gc\alpha =$

$(|\alpha/\beta|\sim\bigwedge\alpha F\alpha \supset |\alpha/\beta|\sim\bigwedge\beta{\sim}F\alpha) \supset \bigwedge\gamma|\alpha/\beta|Gc\alpha =$

$(\sim|\alpha/\beta|\bigwedge\alpha F\alpha \supset \sim|\alpha/\beta|\bigwedge\beta{\sim}F\alpha) \supset \bigwedge\gamma G|\alpha/\beta|c|\alpha/\beta|\alpha =$

$(\sim\bigwedge\alpha F\alpha \supset \sim\bigwedge\beta{\sim}F\alpha) \supset \bigwedge\gamma Gc\beta =$

$(\bigwedge\alpha F\alpha \vee \bigvee\beta F\alpha) \supset \bigwedge\gamma Gc\beta$

In this case at least our function replaces every free occurrence of α with a free occurrence of β except for the one free occurrence of α which can not be replaced by a free occurrence of β. Later, when we formulate our axioms for predicate logic, we will be interested only in proper substitutions of one variable expression for another. A substitution is proper only if every free occurrence of a variable being replaced is in fact replaceable by a free occurrence of the replacing variable. In other words, $|\alpha/\beta|$ produces a proper substitution of free occurrences of β for free occurrences of α in ϕ if and only if $\alpha = \beta \vee \alpha \notin FV(|\alpha/\beta|\phi)$. This condition of propriety will be a condition for one of our predicate logic axiom schemas.

Suppose that instead of replacing α with another variable expression β, we want to replace all free occurrences of α with c. Then the question of propriety does not arise since we are not restricted from replacing the occurrence of α in $\bigvee\beta F\alpha$ with c since the resulting occurrence of c can not be a bound occurrence. So our result should be $(\bigwedge\alpha F\alpha \vee \bigvee\beta Fc) \supset \bigwedge\gamma Gcc$. Let's see if we get the same result using our replacement function $|\alpha/c|$.

$|\alpha/c|((\bigwedge\alpha F\alpha \vee \bigvee\beta F\alpha) \supset \bigwedge\gamma Gc\alpha) =$

$|\alpha/c|((\sim\bigwedge\alpha F\alpha \supset \sim\bigwedge\beta{\sim}F\alpha) \supset \bigwedge\gamma Gc\alpha) =$

$|\alpha/c|(\sim\bigwedge\alpha F\alpha \supset \sim\bigwedge\beta{\sim}F\alpha) \supset |\alpha/c|\bigwedge\gamma Gc\alpha =$

$(|\alpha/c|\sim\bigwedge\alpha F\alpha \supset |\alpha/c|\sim\bigwedge\beta{\sim}F\alpha) \supset \bigwedge\gamma|\alpha/c|Gc\alpha =$

$(\sim|\alpha/c|\bigwedge\alpha F\alpha \supset \sim|\alpha/c|\bigwedge\beta{\sim}F\alpha) \supset \bigwedge\gamma G|\alpha/c|c|\alpha/c|\alpha =$

$(\sim\bigwedge\alpha F\alpha \supset \sim\bigwedge\beta|\alpha/c|{\sim}F\alpha) \supset \bigwedge\gamma Gcc =$

$(\sim\bigwedge\alpha F\alpha \supset \sim\bigwedge\beta{\sim}|\alpha/c|F\alpha) \supset \bigwedge\gamma Gcc =$

$(\sim\bigwedge\alpha F\alpha \supset \sim\bigwedge\beta{\sim}F|\alpha/c|\alpha) \supset \bigwedge\gamma Gcc =$

$(\sim\bigwedge\alpha F\alpha \supset \sim\bigwedge\beta{\sim}Fc) \supset \bigwedge\gamma Gcc =$

$(\bigwedge\alpha F\alpha \vee \bigvee\beta Fc) \supset \bigwedge\gamma Gcc$

Here our replacement function performs exactly as we wish.

DEFINITION 70. We define for each PL-language L, each constant expression c of L, and each $\alpha \in$ VR a function $|c/\alpha|: TM_L \cup FM_L \longrightarrow TM_L \cup FM_L$ recursively as follows:

1. $|c/\alpha|t = \begin{cases} t \text{ if } c \neq t \\ \alpha \text{ if } c = t \end{cases}$;
2. $|c/\alpha|Ft_1 \ldots t_n = F|c/\alpha|t_1 \ldots |c/\alpha|t_n$;
3. $|c/\alpha|{\sim}\phi = {\sim}|c/\alpha|\phi$;
4. $|c/\alpha|(\phi \supset \psi) = |c/\alpha|\phi \supset |c/\alpha|\psi$; and
5. $|c/\alpha|\bigwedge\beta\phi = \begin{cases} \bigwedge\beta|c/\alpha|\phi \text{ if } \alpha \neq \beta \\ \bigwedge\beta\phi \text{ if } \alpha = \beta \end{cases}$.

We have defined what it means for a variable expression to occur free or bound in a PL-formula, but we have not yet defined the general notion of what it is for any PL-expression to occur in another. We will find this to be a very useful notion.

DEFINITION 71. $OC(\sigma) = \{\tau: (\exists\rho)(\exists\pi)(\sigma = \rho{*}\tau{*}\pi)\}$.

If $\tau \in OC(\sigma)$, we say that τ occurs in σ. Recall that we introduced the notion of an empty sequence in Chapter 1. Using this notion we can show that for any PL-expression σ, $\sigma \in OC(\sigma)$. We simply note that $\sigma = \emptyset{*}\sigma{*}\emptyset$.

EXERCISES

37.1 Assume that α, β, and γ are three distinct variable expressions and determine each of the following:

a. $|\alpha/\beta|F\alpha c$;
b. $|\alpha/\beta|\bigwedge\gamma(F\alpha \wedge \bigvee\beta G\alpha\beta)$;
c. $|\alpha/\beta|(\bigwedge\beta F\beta \supset \bigvee\beta G\alpha c)$; and
d. $|\alpha/\beta|(\bigwedge\alpha Fc \supset \bigwedge\beta G\alpha c)$.

37.2 What are the members of $OC(\bigwedge\alpha{\sim}Fc)$?

37.3* Show that $\alpha \notin FV(|\alpha/c|\phi)$. Hint: Use Theorem 36. Give an example of a PL-formula ϕ such that $\alpha \in FV(|\alpha/\beta|\phi)$.

37.4 Show that $(c \in TM_L \ \& \ t \in TM_L) \to (|\alpha/\beta|t \in TM_L \ \& \ |\alpha/c|t \in TM_L \ \& \ |c/\alpha|t \in TM_L)$.

37.5 Show that $(c \in TM_L \ \& \ \phi \in FM_L) \to (|\alpha/\beta|\phi \in FM_L \ \& \ |\alpha/c|\phi \in FM_L \ \& \ |c/\alpha|\phi \in FM_L)$.

37.6 Show that $(\sigma \in OC(\tau) \ \& \ \tau \in OC(\rho)) \to \sigma \in OC(\rho)$.

37.7 Show that $(n)(|c/\alpha| \Lambda\alpha_1 \ldots \Lambda\alpha_n\phi = \Lambda\alpha_1 \ldots \Lambda\alpha_n\phi \vee |c/\alpha| \Lambda\alpha_1 \ldots \Lambda\alpha_n\phi = \Lambda\alpha_1 \ldots \Lambda\alpha_n|c/\alpha|\phi)$. Hint: Use mathematical induction.

37.8 Show that $c \notin OC(\phi) \to |c/\alpha|\phi = \phi$. Hint: First show that $c \neq t \to |c/\alpha|t = t$. Provide a PL-formula ϕ such that $|c/\alpha|\phi \neq \phi$.

37.9 Show that $t \notin OC(\phi) \to |t/\alpha||\alpha/t|\phi = \phi$. Provide a PL-formula ϕ such that $|c/\alpha||\alpha/c|\phi \neq \phi$.

37.10 Show that $|c/\alpha||\beta/\alpha|\phi = |\beta/\alpha||c/\alpha|\phi$.

37.11 Show that $(c \in OC(|\alpha/t|\phi) \ \& \ c \neq t) \to c \in OC(\phi)$.

37.12* Show that $c \notin OC(|c/\alpha||\beta/c|\phi) \to |c/\alpha||\beta/c|\phi = |c/\alpha||\beta/\alpha|\phi$. Provide a PL-formula ϕ such that $|c/\alpha||\beta/c|\phi \neq |c/\alpha||\beta/\alpha|\phi$.

37.13 Show that $(\alpha \neq \beta \ \& \ c \neq t) \to |c/\alpha||\beta/t|\phi = |\beta/t||c/\alpha|\phi$.

37.14 Show that $(\beta \in FV(|c/\alpha|\phi) \ \& \ \beta \neq \alpha) \to \beta \in FV(\phi)$.

37.15 Show that $c \in OC(|c/\alpha|\phi) \to \alpha \in BV(\phi)$. Provide a PL-formula ϕ such that $c \in OC(|c/\alpha|\phi)$.

37.16 Show that $(c \notin OC(|c/\alpha|\phi) \ \& \ \beta \notin OC(\phi)) \to |\beta/\alpha||c/\beta|\phi = |c/\alpha|\phi$.

§38. Predicate Logic Axioms.

DEFINITION 72. ϕ is a generalization of $\psi \leftrightarrow (\exists n)(\exists\alpha_1) \ldots (\exists\alpha_n)(\phi = \psi \vee \phi = \Lambda\alpha_1 \ldots \Lambda\alpha_n\psi)$.

DEFINITION 73. $AX_L = \{\phi: (\exists\psi)(\exists\chi)(\exists\theta)(\exists t)(\psi \in FM_L \ \& \ \chi \in FM_L \ \& \ \theta \in FM_L \ \& \ t \in TM_L \ \& \ \phi$ is a generalization of one of the following:

AX1. $\psi \supset (\chi \supset \psi)$;

AX2. $(\psi \supset (\chi \supset \theta)) \supset ((\psi \supset \chi) \supset (\psi \supset \theta))$;

AX3. $(\sim\psi \supset \sim\chi) \supset (\chi \supset \psi)$;

AX4. $\bigwedge\alpha(\psi \supset \chi) \supset (\bigwedge\alpha\psi \supset \bigwedge\alpha\chi)$;

AX5. $\bigwedge\alpha\psi \supset |\alpha/t|\psi$ if $(\alpha = t \vee \alpha \notin FV(|\alpha/t|\psi)$;

AX6. $\psi \supset \bigwedge\alpha\psi$ if $\alpha \notin FV(\psi))\}$.

We see that $AX_L \subseteq FM_L$. AX_L is recursive since FM_L is and since Definition 73 tells us how to determine whether a member of FM_L is also an L-axiom. We complicate our definition of L-axioms by including all generalizations of L-formulas of one of the forms AX1-AX6 because this makes it possible for us to omit quantifier rules from our list of basic inference rules for predicate logic. By defining our axioms in this way we will be able to show that we can use a rule of universal generalization, etc., but the only rule we will build into the system at the foundation will once again be *modus ponens*. Notice also the restriction on the form AX5. This is the propriety restriction mentioned in the last section. An L-formula of the form indicated in AX5 will only be an L-axiom if we can *properly* substitute t for α in ψ.

Having defined the symbols, terms, formulas, and axioms of a system of predicate logic, it only remains for us to define the derivability relation for such a system. Once we do this we will be able to specify a unique formal system corresponding to each predicate logic language.

§39. Predicate Logic Derivations.

DEFINITION 74. σ is an *L-derivation of* ϕ *from* K $\leftrightarrow$ $(K \cup \{\phi\} \subseteq FM_L \;\&\; \sigma_{\ell(\sigma)} = \phi \;\&\; (n)(n \leq \ell(\sigma) \rightarrow (\sigma_n \in K \vee \sigma_n \in AX_L \vee (\exists i)(\exists j)(i < n \;\&\; j < n \;\&\; \sigma_i = \sigma_j \supset \sigma_n))))$.

DEFINITION 75. $K \vdash_L \phi \leftrightarrow (\exists\sigma)(\sigma$ is an L-derivation of ϕ from K).

We read '$K \vdash_L \phi$' as 'ϕ *is derivable from* K *in* L'.

DEFINITION 76. $\vdash_L \phi \leftrightarrow \emptyset \vdash_L \phi$.

We read '$\vdash_L \phi$' as 'ϕ is an L-theorem' or 'ϕ is derivable in L'.

DEFINITION 77. $CN_L(K) = \{\phi: K \vdash_L \phi\}$.

We read '$CN_L(K)$' as 'the set of consequences of K in L'. We frequently want to prove that all members of $CN_L(K)$ have some common property. To facilitate such proofs we first establish an induction principle for $CN_L(K)$.

THEOREM 37. (Induction Principle for $CN_L(K)$.) $(K \subseteq A$ & $AX_L \subseteq A$ & A is closed under modus ponens$) \rightarrow CN_L(K) \subseteq A$.

THEOREM 38. $(K \subseteq FM_L$ & $\phi \varepsilon K) \rightarrow K \vdash_L \phi$.

THEOREM 39. $(K \subseteq FM_L$ & $\phi \varepsilon AX_L) \rightarrow (K \vdash_L \phi$ & $\vdash_L \phi)$.

THEOREM 40. $(K \vdash_L \phi$ & $K \vdash_L \phi \supset \psi) \rightarrow K \vdash_L \psi$.

THEOREM 41. $(K \subseteq \Gamma$ & $\Gamma \subseteq FM_L$ & $K \vdash_L \phi) \rightarrow \Gamma \vdash_L \phi$.

THEOREM 42. $(L_B \subseteq L'_B$ & $K \vdash_L \phi) \rightarrow K \vdash_{L'} \phi$.

As we have defined it, '$\vdash_L$' does not strictly speaking denote a relation between sets of L-formulas and individual L-formulas. But we can introduce a new use of '$\vdash_L$' which serves this function. We let $\vdash_L = \{<K,\phi>: K \vdash_L \phi\}$. Then we see that $\Sigma_L = <S_L;TM_L;FM_L;AX_L;\vdash_L>$ is a formal system whenever L is a PL-language. We call such a formal system a predicate logic.

THEOREM 43. (Deduction Theorem for Σ_L.) $K \cup \{\phi\} \vdash_L \psi \leftrightarrow K \vdash_L \phi \supset \psi$.

THEOREM 44. $K \vdash_L \phi \leftrightarrow (\exists\Gamma)(\Gamma \subseteq K$ & Γ is finite & $\Gamma \vdash_L \phi)$.

THEOREM 45. (c is a constant expression of L & $(\psi)(\psi \varepsilon K \rightarrow c \notin OC(\psi))$ & $c \notin OC(|c/\alpha|\phi)$ & $\alpha \notin FV(\phi)$ & $K \vdash_L \phi) \rightarrow K \vdash_L \Lambda\alpha|c/\alpha|\phi$.

Theorem 45 is one version of the rule of Universal Generalization. This particular version allows us to generalize with respect to a constant expression c so long as c does not occur in any of our premises. In the next theorem we will show that we may also generalize with respect to a variable expression in certain circumstances. We will use many of the results listed as exercises at the end of Section 37 in our proof of Theorem 45.

Proof. Assume $K \subseteq FM_L$ & c is a constant expression of L & $(\phi)(\phi \in K \rightarrow c \notin OC(\phi))$. We will use Theorem 37 to show that $CN_L(K) \subseteq \Gamma$ where $\Gamma = \{\phi: K \vdash_L \phi$ & $(\alpha)((c \notin OC(|c/\alpha|\phi)$ & $\alpha \notin FV(\phi)) \rightarrow K \vdash_L \Lambda\alpha|c/\alpha|\phi)\}$.

Basis step. Suppose $\phi \in K$ & $c \notin OC(|c/\alpha|\phi)$ & $\alpha \notin FV(\phi)$. Then $K \vdash_L \phi$ by Theorem 38. Since $(\psi)(\psi \in K \rightarrow c \notin OC(\psi))$ by our initial assumption, $c \notin OC(\phi)$. So $|c/\alpha|\phi = \phi$ by Exercise 37.8 and $\Lambda\alpha|c/\alpha|\phi = \Lambda\alpha\phi$. But $\phi \supset \Lambda\alpha\phi \in AX_L$ by AX6, so $K \vdash_L \phi \supset \Lambda\alpha\phi$ by Theorem 39, and $K \vdash_L \Lambda\alpha\phi$ by Theorem 40. So $K \subseteq \Gamma$. Now suppose $\phi \in AX_L$ & $c \notin OC(|c/\alpha|\phi)$ & $\alpha \notin FV(\phi)$. Then $K \vdash_L \phi$ by Theorem 39, and we must show that $K \vdash_L \Lambda\alpha|c/\alpha|\phi$ in order to show that $\phi \in \Gamma$. ϕ must be a generalization of some L-formula ψ where ψ is of one of the forms AX1-AX6. Let $\alpha_1,\ldots,\alpha_n$ be variable expressions such that $\phi = \Lambda\alpha_1\ldots\Lambda\alpha_n\psi$. Then $|c/\alpha|\phi = \phi \vee |c/\alpha|\phi = \Lambda\alpha_1\ldots\Lambda\alpha_n|c/\alpha|\psi$ by Exercise 37.7. If $|c/\alpha|\phi = \phi$, then $\Lambda\alpha|c/\alpha|\phi \in AX_L$ and $K \vdash_L \Lambda\alpha|c/\alpha|\phi$ by Theorem 39. Suppose, though, that $|c/\alpha|\phi \neq \phi$. Then we must consider each of the six forms ψ may take as separate cases.

Case 1. $\psi = \chi \supset (\theta \supset \chi)$. Then $|c/\alpha|\phi = \Lambda\alpha_1\ldots\Lambda\alpha_n|c/\alpha|\psi = \Lambda\alpha_1\ldots\Lambda\alpha_n(|c/\alpha|\chi \supset (|c/\alpha|\theta \supset |c/\alpha|\chi))$, and $\Lambda\alpha|c/\alpha|\phi \in AX_L$ by AX1. But then $K \vdash_L \Lambda\alpha|c/\alpha|\phi$ by Theorem 39.

Cases 2 and 3 are similar to case 1.

Case 4. $\psi = \Lambda\beta(\chi \supset \theta) \supset (\Lambda\beta\chi \supset \Lambda\beta\theta)$. Then $|c/\alpha|\phi = \Lambda\alpha_1\ldots\Lambda\alpha_n(|c/\alpha|\Lambda\beta(\chi \supset \theta) \supset (|c/\alpha|\Lambda\beta\chi \supset |c/\alpha|\Lambda\beta\theta))$. If $\alpha = \beta$, then $|c/\alpha|\phi = \phi$. If $\alpha \neq \beta$, then $|c/\alpha|\phi = \Lambda\alpha_1\ldots\Lambda\alpha_n(\Lambda\beta(|c/\alpha|\chi \supset |c/\alpha|\theta) \supset (\Lambda\beta|c/\alpha|\chi \supset \Lambda\beta|c/\alpha|\theta))$. In either case $\Lambda\alpha|c/\alpha|\phi \in AX_L$ by AX4, and $K \vdash_L \Lambda\alpha|c/\alpha|\phi$ by Theorem 39.

Case 5. $\psi = \Lambda\beta\chi \supset |\beta/t|\chi$. Then $|c/\alpha|\phi = \Lambda\alpha_1 \ldots \Lambda\alpha_n (|c/\alpha| \Lambda\beta\chi \supset |c/\alpha||\beta/t|\chi)$. We must divide this case into four subcases.

Case 5a. $\alpha = \beta$ & $c = t$. Then $|c/\alpha|\phi = \Lambda\alpha_1 \ldots \Lambda\alpha_n(|c/\alpha| \Lambda\alpha\chi \supset |c/\alpha||\alpha/c|\chi) = \Lambda\alpha_1 \ldots \Lambda\alpha_n(\Lambda\alpha\chi \supset |c/\alpha||\alpha/c|\chi)$. We have assumed that $c \notin OC(|c/\alpha|\phi)$; since $\chi \varepsilon OC(|c/\alpha|\phi)$, $c \notin OC(\chi)$ by Exercise 37.6. Then $|c/\alpha||\alpha/c|\chi = \chi$ (= $|\alpha/\alpha|\chi$) by Exercise 37.9. So $\Lambda\alpha|c/\alpha|\phi = \Lambda\alpha\Lambda\alpha_1 \ldots \Lambda\alpha_n(\Lambda\alpha\chi \supset |\alpha/\alpha|\chi)$. But then $\Lambda\alpha|c/\alpha|\phi \varepsilon AX_L$ by AX5, and $K \vdash_L \Lambda\alpha|c/\alpha|\phi$.

Case 5b. $\alpha = \beta$ & $c \neq t$. Then $|c/\alpha|\phi = \Lambda\alpha_1 \ldots \Lambda\alpha_n(|c/\alpha| \Lambda\alpha\chi \supset |c/\alpha||\alpha/t|\chi) = \Lambda\alpha_1 \ldots \Lambda\alpha_n(\Lambda\alpha\chi \supset |c/\alpha||\alpha/t|\chi)$. As in Case 5a, $c \notin OC(\chi)$; so since $c \neq t$, $c \notin OC(|\alpha/t|\chi)$ by Exercise 37.11. But then $|c/\alpha||\alpha/t|\chi = |\alpha/t|\chi$ by Exercise 37.8, and $|c/\alpha|\phi = \phi$. Then $\Lambda\alpha|c/\alpha|\phi \varepsilon AX_L$ by AX5 and $K \vdash_L \Lambda\alpha|c/\alpha|\phi$.

Case 5c. $\alpha \neq \beta$ & $c = t$. Then $|c/\alpha|\phi = \Lambda\alpha_1 \ldots \Lambda\alpha_n (\Lambda\beta|c/\alpha|\chi \supset |c/\alpha||\beta/c|\chi)$. Since $c \notin OC(|c/\alpha|\phi)$ and $|c/\alpha||\beta/c|\chi \varepsilon OC(|c/\alpha|\phi)$, $c \notin OC(|c/\alpha||\beta/c|\chi)$ by Exercise 37.6. But then $|c/\alpha||\beta/c|\chi = |c/\alpha||\beta/\alpha|\chi$ by Exercise 37.12, and $|c/\alpha||\beta/\alpha|\chi = |\beta/\alpha||c/\alpha|\chi$ by Exercise 37.10. Therefore $\Lambda\alpha|c/\alpha|\phi = \Lambda\alpha\Lambda\alpha_1 \ldots \Lambda\alpha_n(\Lambda\beta|c/\alpha|\chi \supset |\beta/\alpha||c/\alpha|\chi)$, $\Lambda\alpha|c/\alpha|\phi \varepsilon AX_L$ by AX5, and $K \vdash_L \Lambda\alpha|c/\alpha|\phi$.

Case 5d. $\alpha \neq \beta$ & $c \neq t$. Then $|c/\alpha|\phi = \Lambda\alpha_1 \ldots \Lambda\alpha_n (\Lambda\beta|c/\alpha|\chi \supset |c/\alpha||\beta/t|\chi)$. But $|c/\alpha||\beta/t|\chi = |\beta/t||c/\alpha|\chi$ by Exercise 37.13, so $\Lambda\alpha|c/\alpha|\phi = \Lambda\alpha\Lambda\alpha_1 \ldots \Lambda\alpha_n(\Lambda\beta|c/\alpha|\chi \supset |\beta/t||c/\alpha|\chi)$, $\Lambda\alpha|c/\alpha|\phi \varepsilon AX_L$ by AX5, and $K \vdash_L \Lambda\alpha|c/\alpha|\phi$.

So in any of the cases 5a-5d, $K \vdash_L \Lambda\alpha|c/\alpha|\phi$.

Case 6. $\psi = \chi \supset \Lambda\beta\chi$ & $\beta \notin FV(\chi)$. Then $|c/\alpha|\phi = \Lambda\alpha_1 \ldots \Lambda\alpha_n(|c/\alpha|\chi \supset |c/\alpha| \Lambda\beta\chi)$. If $\alpha \neq \beta$, then $|c/\alpha|\phi = \Lambda\alpha_1 \ldots \Lambda\alpha_n(|c/\alpha|\chi \supset \Lambda\beta|c/\alpha|\chi)$. But since $\alpha \neq \beta$ and $\beta \notin FV(\chi)$, $\beta \notin FV(|c/\alpha|\chi)$ by Exercise 37.14. So $\Lambda\alpha|c/\alpha|\phi \varepsilon AX_L$ by AX6. Suppose, though, that $\alpha = \beta$. Then $|c/\alpha|\phi = \Lambda\alpha_1 \ldots \Lambda\alpha_n(|c/\alpha|\chi \supset \Lambda\beta\chi)$. Since we have assumed that $c \notin OC(|c/\alpha|\phi)$, it follows by Exercise 37.6 that $c \notin OC(\chi)$. So $|c/\alpha|\chi = \chi$ by

Exercise 37.8, $\Lambda\alpha|c/\alpha|\phi = \Lambda\alpha\phi$, and $\Lambda\alpha|c/\alpha|\phi \in AX_L$ by AX6. In either case, then, $\Lambda\alpha|c/\alpha|\phi \in AX_L$ and $K \vdash_L \Lambda\alpha|c/\alpha|\phi$.

This exhausts all the forms that ψ may take. Therefore $AX_L \subseteq \Gamma$ and our basis step is complete.

Induction step. Suppose $\psi \in \Gamma$ & $\psi \supset \phi \in \Gamma$ & $c \notin OC(|c/\alpha|\phi)$ & $\alpha \notin FV(\phi)$. By the definition of Γ, $K \vdash_L \psi$ & $K \vdash_L \psi \supset \phi$; so $K \vdash_L \phi$ by Theorem 40. Pick a variable expression β such that $\alpha \neq \beta$ and $\beta \notin OC(\psi \supset \phi)$. Then $c \notin OC(|c/\alpha|(\psi \supset \phi))$ by Exercise 37.15, and $c \notin OC(|c/\alpha|\phi)$. Since $\beta \notin OC(\psi \supset \phi)$, $\beta \notin FV(\psi)$ & $\beta \notin FV(\psi \supset \phi)$. Then since $\psi \in \Gamma$ & $\psi \supset \phi \in \Gamma$, $K \vdash_L \Lambda\beta|c/\beta|\psi$ & $K \vdash_L \Lambda\beta|c/\beta|(\psi \supset \phi)$. Since $\Lambda\beta|c/\beta|(\psi \supset \phi) = \Lambda\beta(|c/\beta|\psi \supset |c/\beta|\phi)$, $K \vdash_L \Lambda\beta(|c/\beta|\psi \supset |c/\beta|\phi)$. $K \vdash_L \Lambda\beta(|c/\beta|\psi \supset |c/\beta|\phi) \supset (\Lambda\beta|c/\beta|\psi \supset \Lambda\beta|c/\beta|\phi)$ by AX4 and Theorem 39. Therefore $K \vdash_L \Lambda\beta|c/\beta|\psi \supset \Lambda\beta|c/\beta|\phi$ & $K \vdash_L \Lambda\beta|c/\beta|\phi$ by Theorem 40. $K \vdash_L \Lambda\alpha(\Lambda\beta|c/\beta|\phi \supset |\beta/\alpha||c/\beta|\phi)$ by AX5 and Theorem 39, $K \vdash_L \Lambda\alpha(\Lambda\beta|c/\beta|\phi \supset |\beta/\alpha||c/\beta|\phi) \supset (\Lambda\alpha\Lambda\beta|c/\beta|\phi \supset \Lambda\alpha|\beta/\alpha||c/\beta|\phi)$ by AX4 and Theorem 39, and $K \vdash_L \Lambda\alpha\Lambda\beta|c/\beta|\phi \supset \Lambda\alpha|\beta/\alpha||c/\beta|\phi$ by Theorem 40. Since $\alpha \notin FV(\phi)$ and $\alpha \neq \beta$, $\alpha \notin FV(|c/\beta|\phi)$ and $K \vdash_L \Lambda\beta|c/\beta|\phi \supset \Lambda\alpha\Lambda\beta|c/\beta|\phi$ by AX6 and Theorem 39. But then $K \vdash_L \Lambda\alpha\Lambda\beta|c/\beta|\phi$ and $K \vdash_L \Lambda\alpha|\beta/\alpha||c/\beta|\phi$ by Theorem 40. Then since $\beta \notin OC(\phi)$ and $c \notin OC(|c/\alpha|\phi)$, $|\beta/\alpha||c/\beta|\phi = |c/\alpha|\phi$ by Exercise 37.16, and hence $K \vdash_L \Lambda\alpha|c/\alpha|\phi$. So Γ is closed under <u>modus ponens</u>.

Therefore $CN_L(K) \subseteq \Gamma$ by Theorem 37, and we have our result immediately by the definition of Γ.

<u>THEOREM 46.</u> $(K \vdash_L \phi \;\&\; (\psi)(\psi \in K \rightarrow \alpha \notin FV(\psi))) \rightarrow K \vdash_L \Lambda\alpha\phi$.

Proof. Suppose $(\psi)(\psi \in K \rightarrow \alpha \notin FV(\psi))$. We shall do an induction on $CN_L(K)$ to show that $CN_L(K) \subseteq \Gamma$ where $\Gamma = \{\phi: K \vdash_L \Lambda\alpha\phi\}$.

Basis step. Suppose $\phi \in K$. Then $K \vdash_L \phi$ by Theorem 38, $\alpha \notin FV(\phi)$ by our original hypothesis, $K \vdash_L \phi \supset \Lambda\alpha\phi$ by AX6 and Theorem 39, and $K \vdash_L \Lambda\alpha\phi$ by Theorem 40. So $K \subseteq \Gamma$. Now suppose $\phi \in AX_L$. Then $\Lambda\alpha\phi \in AX_L$ and $K \vdash_L \Lambda\alpha\phi$ by Theorem 39. So $AX_L \subseteq \Gamma$.

Induction step. Suppose $\psi \in \Gamma$ & $\psi \supset \phi \in \Gamma$. Then by the definition of Γ, $K \vdash_L \bigwedge\alpha\psi$ & $K \vdash_L \bigwedge\alpha(\psi \supset \phi)$. But $K \vdash_L \bigwedge\alpha(\psi \supset \phi) \supset (\bigwedge\alpha\psi \supset \bigwedge\alpha\phi)$ by AX4 and Theorem 39, $K \vdash_L \bigwedge\alpha\psi \supset \bigwedge\alpha\phi$ by Theorem 40, $K \vdash_L \bigwedge\alpha\phi$ by Theorem 40, and $\phi \in \Gamma$. So Γ is closed under modus ponens.

Then $CN_L(K) \subseteq \Gamma$ by Theorem 37.

THEOREM 47. $(\psi)(\psi \in K \rightarrow \alpha \notin FV(\psi)) \rightarrow K \vdash_L \phi \leftrightarrow K \vdash_L \bigwedge\alpha\phi)$.

THEOREM 48. $(\alpha \notin FV(\phi)$ & $\beta \notin FV(|\beta/\alpha|\phi)) \rightarrow (K \vdash_L \bigwedge\beta\phi \leftrightarrow K \vdash_L \bigwedge\alpha|\beta/\alpha|\phi)$.

THEOREM 49. $(L_B \subseteq L'_B$ & $L'_B - L_B$ is a set of constants & $K \cup \{\phi\} \subseteq FM_L$ & $K \vdash_{L'} \phi) \rightarrow K \vdash_L \phi$.

EXERCISES

39.1* Prove Theorems 37-44 and 47-49. Hint: For Theorem 48, show that $\alpha \notin FV(\phi) \rightarrow |\alpha/\beta||\beta/\alpha|\phi = \phi$.

39.2* Assume that F is a 1-place predicate expression of L, G is a 2-place predicate expression of L, and c and c' are constant expressions of L. Show each of the following.

a. $\vdash_L Gcc \supset \bigvee\alpha\bigvee\beta G\alpha\beta$.

b. $\vdash_L \bigvee\alpha\bigwedge\beta G\alpha\beta \supset \bigwedge\beta\bigvee\alpha G\alpha\beta$.

c. $\vdash_L \bigwedge\alpha(F\alpha \supset \bigwedge\beta\bigwedge\gamma G\gamma\beta) \supset (\bigvee\alpha F\alpha \supset \bigwedge\beta G\beta\beta)$.

39.3* Show that $(\phi \in FM_L$ & $\alpha \notin OC(\phi)) \rightarrow \vdash_L \bigvee\alpha(\bigvee\beta\phi$ $|\beta/\alpha|\phi)$.

§40. Interpreting PL-languages. As we might expect, providing an interpretation for a language involving predicates, constants, and quantifiers is a good deal more complicated than providing an interpretation for the language of the sentential logic. We must provide an interpretation for each constant or predicate expression of a PL-language. We must also specify a universe of discourse which we can use to interpret our variable expressions. Once we do this, we can build up to an interpretation of the formulas of L. Of course we will want our formulas to have truth values just as SL-sentences do. We will also want our interpretation of the logical constants '$\underline{n}$' and '$\underline{i}$' to correspond closely with the interpretation these symbols are given in the sentential logic.

We begin by defining the notion of a model indexed by a PL-language L. Such a model specifies the domain of discourse and provides interpretations for all of the members of $\{\langle x\rangle : x \in L_B\}$.

> <u>DEFINITION 78.</u> $\mathcal{A}$ is an <u>L-model</u> $\leftrightarrow (\exists A)(\exists R)(\mathcal{A} = \langle A;R\rangle$ & $A \neq \emptyset$ & $R:\{x: x$ is a constant expression of L $\vee$ x is a predicate expression of L$\} \longrightarrow A \cup \text{Power}(\{y: y$ is a finite sequence of members of A$\})$ & (c)(c is a constant expression in L $\rightarrow R(c) \in A$) & (F)(n)(F is an n-place predicate expression in L $\rightarrow$ R(F) is a set of n-place sequences of members of A)).

Definition 78 is rather complicated and requires some explanation. Suppose $\mathcal{A} = \langle A;R\rangle$ is an L-model. We will often refer to L as '$L_{\mathcal{A}}$' and to A as '$U_{\mathcal{A}}$'. $U_{\mathcal{A}}$ is the universe of discourse which our model specifies for L. If we interpret L in terms of the model $\mathcal{A}$, then we can only use the language of L to say things about the members of $U_{\mathcal{A}}$. Of course we could change our universe of discourse, but this would mean that we were interpreting L differently and with respect to a different L-model. Constant expressions in L are interpreted as referring to some member of the universe of discourse. Thus for any constant expression c of L, our interpretation function R picks out a member R(c) of $U_{\mathcal{A}}$. Where c is a constant expression of L, we will often refer to R(c) as '$c_{\mathcal{A}}$'. Finally, we must interpret the predicate expressions of L. Intuitively a 1-place predicate expression stands for some property which things in our universe of discourse may or may not possess, a 2-place predicate expression stands for a relation which may or may not hold between two members of our universe of discourse, and so on. Let F be an n-place predicate expression in L. If n = 1, F stands for a property; if n ≠ 1, F stands for a relation which may hold between n-many things in our universe of discourse. In either case, the interpretation of F will be a set of n-place sequences. Each sequence in this set will be a group of objects in our universe of discourse which stand in the relation for which F stands, to each other. Of course if n = 1, then R(F) will be a set of 1-place sequences and each sequence in R(F) will have as its first and only member some object in our universe of discourse which we take to possess the property for which F stands. We will often refer to R(F) as '$F_{\mathcal{A}}$'.

<u>DEFINITION 79.</u> $\mathcal{A}$ is a <u>model</u> ↔ (∃L)($\mathcal{A}$ is an L-model).

We will use the capital script letters '$\mathcal{A}$', '$\mathcal{B}$', '$\mathcal{C}$', etc., as special variables ranging over models.

Besides the constant expressions and predicate expressions of L, we also need a way of interpreting the variable expressions. Because variable expressions <u>are</u> variable, however, they will not be given a determinate and unchanging interpretation in a model in the way constant and predicate expressions are. Instead each variable may stand for any member of the universe of discourse specified in the model.

<u>DEFINITION 80.</u> a is an <u>assignment</u> <u>in</u> $\mathcal{A}$ ↔ a:VR ⟶ $U_{\mathcal{A}}$.

Each assignment interprets each variable expression as standing for some specific member of the universe of discourse, but of course there will be infinitely many assignments in a model so long as the universe of discourse for that model has at least two members. The value (or extension) which a term takes in a model will depend, then, upon the assignment we have in mind.

<u>DEFINITION 81.</u> a is an assignment in $\mathcal{A}$ → ((c)(c is a constant expression of L → Val(c,$\mathcal{A}$,a) = $c_{\mathcal{A}}$) &

$(\alpha)(\mathrm{Val}(\alpha,A,a) = a(\alpha))$.

We see that the value or extension of a constant expression does not change with a change in the assignment while the extension of a variable expression does. This keeps the interpretation of constant expressions constant while allowing the interpretation of a variable expression to range over the entire universe of discourse.

Intuitively certain objects satisfy "open sentences" or "sentence functions" while others do not. For example, $\emptyset$ satisfies the open sentence 'x is a set', but the Statue of Liberty does not satisfy this open sentence. In a similar fashion, the members of the universe of discourse of a model may or may not satisfy an open sentence of the language of the model. Suppose A is a model and F is a 1-place predicate expression of L_A. Under what conditions does a member $x \in U_A$ satisfy the open sentence $F\alpha$? Since F_A is the set of 1-place sequences such that each member of a member of F_A has the property for which F stands, our intuitive answer is that x satisfies $F\alpha$ just in case $\langle x\rangle \in F_A$. Put another way, $F\alpha$ is in some sense true when we think of α as standing for a member of a member of F_A, and we think of α as doing this when we consider an assignment a for A such that $\langle a(\alpha)\rangle \in F_A$. This allows us to think of the assignment a itself as satisfying $F\alpha$. Where c is a constant expression in L, we can also think of an assignment a as satisfying or not satisfying the "closed sentence" Fc. Of course it really doesn't matter what a is in this case because Fc will be true or false regardless of what a assigns to anything. To talk about satisfying sentences like Fc is to stretch the notion of satisfaction a bit, but by doing this we can say what it means for an assignment to satisfy an atomic formula in general without having to worry about whether that atomic formula actually contains any free variables. Putting all of this together, we arrive at the following definition.

DEFINITION 82. a is an assignment in $A \rightarrow$

1. ((F is an n-place predicate expression of L_A & $t_1 \varepsilon TM_{L_A}$ & ... & $t_n \varepsilon TM_{L_A}$) $\rightarrow$ (a satisfies (sat) $Ft_1...t_n$ in $A \leftrightarrow$ $<Val(t_1,A,a);...;Val(t_n,A,a)> \varepsilon F_A$) &
2. $\phi \varepsilon FM_{L_A} \rightarrow$ (a sat $\sim\phi$ in $A \leftrightarrow$ a non-sat ϕ in A) &
3. ($\phi \varepsilon FM_{L_A}$ & $\psi \varepsilon FM_{L_A}$) $\rightarrow$ (a sat $\phi \supset \psi$ in $A \leftrightarrow$ (a non-sat ϕ in A $\vee$ a sat ψ in A)) &
4. $\phi \varepsilon FM_{L_A} \rightarrow$ (a sat $\Lambda\alpha\phi$ in $A \leftrightarrow (x)(x \varepsilon U_A \rightarrow a(\alpha|x)$ sat ϕ in A))).

Definition 82 gives us the conditions under which any assignment a for A satisfies any formula in L_A. Perhaps we should say a few additional words about clause 4 of this definition. It is not enough for a to satisfy $\Lambda\alpha\phi$ that the single object $a(\alpha)$ satisfy ϕ. Instead we want every object in our universe of discourse to satisfy ϕ. The way we say this is to say that ϕ would still be satisfied no matter what a assigned to α. And this is exactly what clause 4 of Definition 82 says.

We are finally ready to say what it means for a formula to be true in a model. Definition 82 tells us what it means for an assignment for a model to satisfy a formula, but an assignment interprets each variable as referring to a single object. Our variables should be allowed to range over the entire universe of discourse. In other words, for a formula to be true in a model it should be satisfied in that model regardless of the particular assignment we choose.

DEFINITION 83. $\phi \varepsilon FM_{L_A} \rightarrow$ (ϕ is true in $A \leftrightarrow$ (a)(a is an assignment for $A \rightarrow$ a sat ϕ in A)).

Let's combine all the definitions in this section in one simple example. Suppose L has only one constant expression c, one 1-place predicate expression F, and one 2-place predicate expression G. Then $A = <\{0,1\};\{<c;0>,<F;\{<0>,<1>\}>;<G;\{<0;0>\}>\}>$ is an L-model such that $U_A = \{0,1\}$, $c_A = 0$, $F_A =$

$\{\langle 0\rangle;\langle 1\rangle\}$, and $G_A = \{\langle 0;0\rangle\}$. If we use the L-model A to interpret our language L, we will only be able to use L to talk about 0 and 1. For every variable expression α, let $a(\alpha) = 1$. Then a is an assignment in A.

Does a sat Fc in A? It does just in case $\langle Val(c,A,a)\rangle \in F_A$, i.e., just in case $\langle c_A\rangle \in F_A$, i.e., just in case $\langle 0\rangle \in \{\langle 0\rangle,\langle 1\rangle\}$, which of course it is.

Does a sat Fα in A? It does just in case $\langle Val(\alpha,A,a)\rangle \in F_A$, i.e., just in case $\langle a(\alpha)\rangle \in F_A$, i.e., just in case $\langle 1\rangle \in \{\langle 0\rangle,\langle 1\rangle\}$, which of course it is.

Does a sat Gcα in A? It does just in case $\langle Val(c,A,a); Val(\alpha,A,a)\rangle \in G_A$, i.e., just in case $\langle c_A;a(\alpha)\rangle \in G_A$, i.e., just in case $\langle 0;1\rangle \in \{\langle 0;0\rangle\}$, which of course it is not.

Is Fα true in A? Yes it is. To see this, let a' be any assignment for A. Then $a'(\alpha) = 0 \vee a'(\alpha) = 1$ by Definition 80. If $a'(\alpha) = 0$, then $Val(\alpha,A,a') = a'(\alpha)$ by Definition 81, $\langle Val(\alpha,A,a')\rangle \in F_A$, and a' sat F$\alpha$ in A by Definition 82. If $a'(\alpha) = 1$, then by a similar argument, a' sat Fα in A. Therefore every assignment satisfies Fα in A and Fα is true in A by Definition 83.

EXERCISES

Let L and A be as in the example above and let a be an assignment for A such that $a(\alpha) = 0$ and $a(\beta) = 1$. Justify your answers for the following.

40.1 Does a sat $G\alpha\alpha$ in A?

40.2 Does a sat $G\alpha\beta$ in A?

40.3 Does a sat $G\alpha c$ in A?

40.4 Does a sat $\sim Gc\beta$ in A?

40.5 Does a sat $Gc\beta \supset Gcc$ in A?

40.6 Does a sat $\bigwedge\beta(Gc\beta \supset G\beta c)$ in A?

40.7 Does a sat $\bigwedge\beta Gc\beta$ in A?

40.8 Is $\bigvee\gamma G\gamma\gamma$ true in A?

40.9 Is $\bigvee\gamma{\sim}F\gamma$ true in A?

§41. Some Semantical Theorems. In this section we will look at five theorems which give us additional information about the relationship between a formula and an assignment which satisfies it in some model for a language of the formula.

THEOREM 50. (a is an assignment for A & a' is an assignment for A & $\phi \in FM_{L_A}$ & $FV(\phi) \subseteq \{\alpha_1,\ldots,\alpha_n\}$ & $x_1 \in U_A$ & ... & $x_n \in U_A$) $\rightarrow$ ($a(\alpha_1|x_1)\ldots(\alpha_n|x_n)$ sat ϕ in $A \leftrightarrow a'(\alpha_1|x_1)\ldots(\alpha_n|x_n)$ sat ϕ in A).

Proof. Let a and a' be assignments for A. We proceed by induction on FM_{L_A}. Let $K = \{\phi;\ \phi \in FM_{L_A}$ & $(n)((FV(\phi) \subseteq \{\alpha_1,\ldots\alpha_n\}$ & $x_1 \in U_A$ & ... & $x_n \in U_A) \rightarrow (a(\alpha_1|x_1)\ldots(\alpha_n|x_n)$ sat ϕ in $A \leftrightarrow a'(\alpha_1|x_1)\ldots(\alpha_n|x_n)$ sat ϕ in $A))\}$.

Basis step. Let $Ft_1\ldots t_m \in AT_{L_A}$ such that $FV(Ft_1\ldots t_m) \subseteq \{\alpha_1,\ldots,\alpha_n\}$. Then $a(\alpha_1|x_1)\ldots(\alpha_n|x_n)$ sat $Ft_1\ldots t_m$ in $A \leftrightarrow \langle Val(t_1,A,a(\alpha_1|x_1)\ldots(\alpha_n|x_n));\ \ldots\ ;Val(t_m,A,a(\alpha_1|x_1)\ldots(\alpha_n|x_n))\rangle \in F_A$ and $a'(\alpha_1|x_1)\ldots(\alpha_n|x_n)$ sat $Ft_1\ldots t_m$ in $A \leftrightarrow \langle Val(t_1,A,a'(\alpha_1|x_1)\ldots(\alpha_n|x_n));\ldots;Val(t_m,A,a'(\alpha_1|x_1)\ldots(\alpha_n|x_n))\rangle \in F_A$. Let $i \leq m$. Then since $FV(Ft_1\ldots t_m) \subseteq \{\alpha_1,\ldots,\alpha_n\}$, either t_i is a constant expression or there is a largest $j \leq n$ such that $t_i = \alpha_j$. In the first case, $Val(t_i,A,a(\alpha_1|x_1)\ldots(\alpha_n|x_n)) = t_{iA} = Val(t_i,A,a'(\alpha_1|x_1)\ldots(\alpha_n|x_n))$, and in the second case, $Val(t_i,A,a(\alpha_1|x_1)\ldots(\alpha_n|x_n)) = a(\alpha_1|x_1)\ldots(\alpha_n|x_n)(\alpha_j) = x_j = a'(\alpha_1|x_1)\ldots(\alpha_n|x_n)(\alpha_j) = Val(t_i,A,a'(\alpha_1|x_1)\ldots(\alpha_n|x_n))$. So $\langle Val(t_1,A,a(\alpha_1|x_1)\ldots(\alpha_n|x_n));\ \ldots\ ;Val(t_m,A,a'(\alpha_1|x_1)\ldots(\alpha_n|x_n))\rangle = \langle Val(t_1,A,a(\alpha_1|x_1)\ldots(\alpha_n|x_n));\ \ldots\ ;Val(t_m,A,a'(\alpha_1|x_1)\ldots(\alpha_n|x_n))\rangle$. So $Ft_1\ldots t_m \in K$ and $AT_{L_A} \subseteq K$.

Induction step. Suppose $\phi \in K$ & $\psi \in K$.

If $FV(\phi) \subseteq \{\alpha_1,\ldots,\alpha_n\}$, then since $\phi \in K$, $a(\alpha_1|x_1)\ldots(\alpha_n|x_n)$ sat ${\sim}\phi$ in A if and only if $a(\alpha_1|x_1)\ldots(\alpha_n|x_n)$ non-sat ϕ in A if and only if $a'(\alpha_1|x_1)\ldots(\alpha_n|x_n)$ non-sat ϕ in A if and only if $a'(\alpha_1|x_1)\ldots(\alpha_n|x_n)$ sat ${\sim}\phi$ in A. So ${\sim}\phi \in K$.

Similarly, we show that $\phi \supset \psi \in K$.

If $FV(\Lambda\alpha\phi) \subseteq \{\alpha_1,\ldots,\alpha_n\}$, then $FV(\phi) \subseteq \{\alpha,\alpha_1,\ldots,\alpha_n\}$, and since $\phi \in K$, $a(\alpha_1|x_1)\ldots(\alpha_n|x_n)$ sat $\Lambda\alpha\phi$ in A if and only if $(x)(x \in U_A \rightarrow a(\alpha_1|x_1)\ldots(\alpha_n|x_n)(\alpha|x)$ sat ϕ in $A)$ if and only if $(x)(x \in U_A \rightarrow a'(\alpha_1|x_1)\ldots(\alpha_n|x_n)(\alpha|x)$ sat ϕ in $A)$ if and only if $a'(\alpha_1|x_1)\ldots(\alpha_n|x_n)$ sat $\Lambda\alpha\phi$ in A. So $\Lambda\alpha\phi \in K$.

Then by Theorem 36, $FM_{L_A} \subseteq K$.

<u>THEOREM 51.</u> $\phi \in FM_{L_A} \rightarrow (\phi$ is true in $A \leftrightarrow \Lambda\alpha\phi$ is true in $A)$.

<u>THEOREM 52.</u> $\phi \in ST_{L_A} \rightarrow ((\exists a)(a$ is an assignment for A & a sat ϕ in $A) \leftrightarrow (a)(a$ is an assignment for $A \rightarrow a$ sat ϕ in $A))$.

<u>THEOREM 53.</u> $(\phi \in FM_{L_A}$ & $\alpha \notin FV(\phi)$ & $x \in U_A$ & a is an assignment for $A) \rightarrow (a$ sat ϕ in $A \leftrightarrow a(\alpha|x)$ sat ϕ in $A)$.

<u>THEOREM 54.</u> $(\phi \in FM_{L_A}$ & $t \in TM_{L_A}$ & $(\alpha = t \vee \alpha \notin FV(|\alpha/t|\phi))$ & a is an assignment for $A) \rightarrow (a$ sat $|\alpha/t|\phi$ in $A \leftrightarrow a(\alpha|Val(t,A,a))$ sat ϕ in $A)$.

Theorem 50 tells us that once we know what values an assignment takes for the free variable expressions in a formula, we can determine whether or not the assignment satisfies the formula. Although an assignment takes on some member of the universe of discourse for each variable expression, only the values which the assignment takes for the variable expressions actually occurring in a given formula affect the satisfaction or non-satisfaction of that formula. Theorem 51 tells us that a formula is true in a model just in case its "universal closure" is true in that model. Theorem 52 tells us that if a formula contains no free variable expressions, then either every assignment satisfies it or none does.

EXERCISES

41.1 Prove Theorems 51, 52, 53, and 54.

41.2 Show that (a is an assignment for $\mathcal{A}$ & $x \in U_{\mathcal{A}}$ & c is a constant expression of $L_{\mathcal{A}}$) → Val(c,$\mathcal{A}$,a) = Val(c,$\mathcal{A}$,a($\alpha|x$)).

41.3 Show that (a is an assignment for $\mathcal{A}$ & $x \in U_{\mathcal{A}}$ & $\alpha \neq \beta$) → Val(β,$\mathcal{A}$,a) = Val(β,$\mathcal{A}$,a($\alpha|x$)).

41.4 Show that (a is an assignment for $\mathcal{A}$ & a' is an assignment for $\mathcal{A}$ & $\phi \in FM_{L_{\mathcal{A}}}$ & (α)($\alpha \in FV(\phi)$ → a(α) = a'(α)) → (a sat ϕ in $\mathcal{A}$ ↔ a' sat ϕ in $\mathcal{A}$). Hint: Use Theorem 36.

§42. Semantical Consistency. Intuitively a sentence is consistent if there is some way of interpreting it which would make it come out true. The way we interpret PL-sentences and PL-formulas is in terms of models. We would expect, then, to define consistency for a PL-formula as consisting in being true in at least one model. And this is exactly what we can do for PL-sentences, but we need a broader notion of consistency for PL-formulas which are not PL-sentences, i.e., for PL-formulas which contain free occurrences of variable expressions. The interpretation of such PL-formulas depends upon our choice of an assignment in a way that the interpretation of PL-sentences does not. (Recall that Theorem 52 says that a PL-sentence is satisfied by all or by none of the assignments for a model.) In order to accommodate PL-formulas which are not PL-sentences, we define semantical consistency in terms of satisfaction rather than in terms of truth-in-a-model.

DEFINITION 84. (a is an assignment for $\mathcal{A}$ & $K \subseteq FM_{L_{\mathcal{A}}}$) → (a simultaneously satisfies (sim-sat) K in $\mathcal{A}$ ↔ (ϕ)($\phi \in K$ → a sat ϕ in $\mathcal{A}$)).

DEFINITION 85. $K \subseteq FM_{L_{\mathcal{A}}}$ → (K is sim-sat in $\mathcal{A}$ ↔ ($\exists$a)(a is an assignment for $\mathcal{A}$ & a sim-sat K in $\mathcal{A}$).

DEFINITION 86. K is semantically consistent ↔

$(\exists A)(K \subseteq FM_{L_A}$ & K is sim-sat in A).

DEFINITION 87. A is a model for K $\leftrightarrow$ ($K \subseteq FM_{L_A}$ & $(\phi)(\phi \in K \rightarrow \phi$ is true in A)).

DEFINITION 88. K has a model $\leftrightarrow$ $(\exists A)$(A is a model for K).

DEFINITION 89. $K \models_L \phi \leftrightarrow (K \cup \{\phi\} \subseteq FM_L$ & (A)(a)((A is an L-model & a is an assignment for A & a sim-sat K in A) $\rightarrow$ a sat ϕ in A)).

DEFINITION 90. $K \models \phi \leftrightarrow (\exists L)(K \models_L \phi)$.

Definitions 89 and 90 define a notion which we might informally call semantic entailment. Essentially they say that K semantically entails ϕ just in case it is impossible to satisfy K without also satisfying ϕ.

DEFINITION 91. $\models \phi \leftrightarrow \emptyset \models \phi$.

DEFINITION 92. ϕ is logically true $\leftrightarrow \models \phi$.

EXERCISES

42.1 Show that ϕ is logically true $\leftrightarrow (\exists L)(\phi \in FM_L$ & (A)(A is an L-model $\rightarrow \phi$ is true in A)).

Let c be a constant expression, let F be a 1-place predicate expression, and let G be a 2-place predicate expression.

42.2 Show that {Fc} is semantically consistent.

42.3 Show that {~Fc} is semantically consistent.

42.4* Show that {Gcα,Fc,Fα} is semantically consistent.

42.5 Show that {Fα} has a model.

42.6 Show that $K \subseteq ST_L \rightarrow$ (K is semantically consistent $\leftrightarrow$ K has a model).

§43. Semantical Analogs of Syntactical Theorems. The following results are semantical analogs of theorems found in Section 39.

THEOREM 55. $\phi \in K \rightarrow K \models \phi$.

THEOREM 56. $(\Gamma \subseteq K \subseteq FM_L \;\&\; \Gamma \models_L \phi) \rightarrow K \models_L \phi$.

THEOREM 57. $(K \models \phi \;\&\; K \models \phi \supset \psi) \rightarrow K \models \psi$.

THEOREM 58. $\phi \in AX_L \rightarrow (K \models \phi \;\&\; \models \phi)$.

THEOREM 59. $\models \phi \rightarrow K \models \phi$.

THEOREM 60. $K \cup \{\phi\} \models \psi \leftrightarrow K \models \phi \supset \psi$.

The proofs for most of these theorems resemble the proofs of the corresponding theorems for sentential logic found in Section 29. As an example we will look at a partial proof for Theorem 58. Let ϕ be a generalization of AX6, i.e., let $\phi = \bigwedge\alpha_1 \ldots \bigwedge\alpha_n(\psi \supset \bigwedge\alpha\psi)$ for some ψ and some $\alpha, \alpha_1, \ldots, \alpha_n$ such that $\alpha \notin FV(\psi)$. Now let L be a language such that $K \cup \{\phi\} \subseteq FM_L$, let $\mathcal{A}$ be an L-model, and let a be an assignment for $\mathcal{A}$. By Definition 82, a sat ϕ in $\mathcal{A}$ if and only if for all $x_1, \ldots, x_n$ such that $\{x_1, \ldots, x_n\} \subseteq U_{\mathcal{A}}$, $a(\alpha_1|x_1)\ldots(\alpha_n|x_n)$ sat $\psi \supset \bigwedge\alpha\psi$ in $\mathcal{A}$ if and only if $(a(\alpha_1|x_1)\ldots(\alpha_n|x_n)$ non-sat ψ in $\mathcal{A}$ or $(x)(x \in U_{\mathcal{A}} \rightarrow a(\alpha_1|x_1)\ldots(\alpha_n|x_n)(\alpha|x)$ sat ψ in $\mathcal{A}))$. If $a(\alpha_1|x_1)\ldots(\alpha_n|x_n)$ non-sat ψ in $\mathcal{A}$ we are done, so suppose $a(\alpha_1|x_1)\ldots(\alpha_n|x_n)$ sat ψ in $\mathcal{A}$ and let $x \in U_{\mathcal{A}}$. Then since $\alpha \notin FV(\psi)$, $a(\alpha_1|x_1)\ldots(\alpha_n|x_n)(\alpha|x)$ sat ψ in $\mathcal{A}$ by Theorem 53. Therefore, for any L-model $\mathcal{A}$ and any assignment a for $\mathcal{A}$, a sat ϕ in $\mathcal{A}$. So $K \models_L \phi$ and $\emptyset \models_L \phi$ by Definition 89, $\emptyset \models_L \phi$ by Definition 91, and $K \models \phi$ and $\models \phi$ by Definition 90.

EXERCISES

43.1 Show that $(K \cup \{\phi\} \;\&\; L_B \subseteq L'_B) \rightarrow (K \models_L \phi \leftrightarrow K \models_{L'} \phi)$.

43.2 Prove Theorems 55-58.

43.3 Show the importance of the restriction on AX5 by constructing a model $\mathcal{A}$ for a language L with a single (1-place) predicate expression F and no constant expressions, and an assignment a for $\mathcal{A}$ such that a non-sat $\bigwedge\alpha(F\alpha \supset \bigwedge\beta F\alpha) \supset (F\beta \supset$

$\wedge$ βFα).

43.4 Prove Theorems 59 and 60.

§44. Syntactical Consistency and Maximal Consistency. Corresponding to our notion of semantical consistency we have a syntactical notion of consistency, i.e., a notion of consistency which is defined in terms of relations between expressions in the language at which we are looking, without regard for the way in which we interpret that language. As in the case of sentential logic, we will count a set of formulas of a PL-language as being consistent just in case we can not derive a contradiction from that set of formulas. Once we get a contradiction, of course, we can then derive anything whatsoever. It is this last fact which we actually incorporate into our definition of syntactical consistency and maximal consistency.

DEFINITION 93. K is L-consistent $\leftrightarrow$ (K $\subseteq$ FM_L & $(\exists\phi)(\phi \in FM_L$ & $\sim K \vdash_L \phi$)).

DEFINITION 94. K is maximally L-consistent $\leftrightarrow$ (K is L-consistent & (ϕ)(K $\cup$ $\{\phi\}$ is L-consistent $\rightarrow \phi \in$ K)).

Now we turn to a number of theorems involving L-consistency and maximal L-consistency. These theorems should be familiar as predicate logic counterparts of theorems for sentential logic which we saw in the last chapter.

THEOREM 61. K is L-consistent $\leftrightarrow$ (K $\subseteq$ FM_L & $\sim(\exists\phi)(\phi \in FM_L$ & $K \vdash_L \phi$ & $K \vdash_L {\sim}\phi$)).

THEOREM 62. K is L-consistent $\leftrightarrow$ (K $\subseteq$ FM_L & $\sim(\exists\phi)(\phi \in FM_L$ & $K \vdash_L {\sim}(\phi \supset \phi)$)).

THEOREM 63. $K \vdash_L \phi \leftrightarrow$ (K $\cup$ $\{\phi\} \subseteq FM_L$ & K $\cup$ $\{{\sim}\phi\}$ is not L-consistent).

THEOREM 64. ($K \vdash_L \phi$ & K is L-consistent) $\rightarrow$ K $\cup$ $\{\phi\}$ is

L-consistent.

THEOREM 65. K is L-consistent $\leftrightarrow$ $(\Gamma)((\Gamma \subseteq K \,\&\, \Gamma$ is finite$) \rightarrow \Gamma$ is L-consistent$)$.

THEOREM 66. (K is maximally L-consistent & $\phi \in FM_L) \rightarrow (\phi \in K \leftrightarrow {\sim}\phi \notin K)$.

THEOREM 67. (K is maximally L-consistent & $\phi \in FM_L) \rightarrow (\phi \in K \leftrightarrow K \vdash_L \phi)$.

THEOREM 68. (K is maximally L-consistent & $\phi \in FM_L$ & $\psi \in FM_L) \rightarrow (\phi \supset \psi \in K \leftrightarrow ({\sim}\phi \in K \vee \psi \in K))$.

THEOREM 69. (Lindenbaum Lemma.) K is L-consistent $\rightarrow$ $(\exists\Gamma)(\Gamma$ is maximally L-consistent & $K \subseteq \Gamma)$.

The proof of the Lindenbaum Lemma for L is exactly parallel to the proof of the Lindenbaum Lemma for SL offered in the previous chapter. If we allowed for PL-languages with uncountably infinite sets of symbols, we would have to use transfinite induction in our proof of the Lindenbaum Lemma for L.

EXERCISES

44.1 Prove Theorems 61-68.

§45. ω-completeness. In the last chapter, we proved that SL is complete with respect to the standard truth-functional interpretation by taking a syntactically consistent set of SL sentences and using it to construct a valuation which made every member of that set true. To do this, it was first necessary to show that the SL-consistent set of SL-sentences with which we began was contained in some maximally SL-consistent set. We will use a similar technique to prove completeness for a PL-logic with language L, with respect to the class of L-models. We will use a consistent set of L-sentences to construct a model for that set. It turns out, though, that we have to construct a set containing the maximally L-consistent set K of L-sentences with which we start which contains K, which is maximally L'-consistent for some language L' such that K is contained in $ST_{L'}$, and which satisfies an even stronger condition. It is this set which we actually use to construct our model of K. The added condition which this superset of K must satisfy is given in our next definition.

DEFINITION 95. K is maximally L-consistent and ω-complete ↔ (K is maximally L-consistent & $(\phi)(\alpha)(\bigvee\alpha\phi \in K \rightarrow (\exists t)(t \in TM_L \ \& \ (t = \alpha \vee \alpha \notin FV(|\alpha/t|\phi)) \ \& \ |\alpha/t|\phi \in K)))$.

What Definition 95 requires in addition to maximal L-consistency is that whenever an L-formula of the form '$\bigvee\alpha\phi$' is a member of K, then there is some L-term t which can properly be substituted for α in ϕ such that $|\alpha/t|\phi \in K$. We have a result for such sets which will be essential for our completeness theorems.

THEOREM 70. K is maximally L-consistent and ω-complete $\rightarrow (\phi)(\alpha)(\bigwedge\alpha\phi \in K \leftrightarrow (t)((t \in TM_L \ \& \ (t = \alpha \vee \alpha \notin FV(|\alpha/t|\phi))) \rightarrow |\alpha/t|\phi \in K))$.

EXERCISES

45.1 Prove Theorem 70.

§46. Soundness and Completeness.

THEOREM 71. (Soundness.) $K \vdash_L \phi \rightarrow K \models_L \phi$.

COROLLARY 71.1. K is semantically consistent → (∃L) (K is L-consistent).

THEOREM 72. (K is L-consistent & $K \subseteq ST_L$) → K has a model.

Proof. Suppose K is L-consistent & $K \subseteq ST_L$. By our richness assumption for constants, let C be a countably infinite set of constant expressions such that no member of C is a constant expression of L. Let $S_{L'} = S_L \cup \{\langle x\rangle : \langle x\rangle \in C\}$ and let L' be the corresponding PL-language. $\Theta = \{ \bigvee\alpha\phi : \phi \in FM_{L'}\}$ is countable, so we can let $f{:}N \xrightarrow{\text{onto}} \Theta$. For each n, we will represent f(n) as $\bigvee\alpha_n\phi_n$ and we will let c_n be a member of C such that $(k)(k \leq n \rightarrow c_n \notin OC(\bigvee\alpha_k\phi_k))$. We can pick such a c_n for each n since C is countably infinite and there are only finitely many $\bigvee\alpha_k\phi_k$ such that $k \leq n$. For each n, let $\psi_n = \bigvee\alpha_n\phi_n \supset |\alpha_n/c_n|\phi_n$, and let $\Gamma = K \cup \{\psi_n : n \in N\}$.

<u>Lemma 1.</u> $(n)(K \cup \{\psi_1,\ldots,\psi_n\}$ is L'-consistent). We will provide the basis step for a proof of this lemma which uses mathematical induction and leave the induction step to the reader. Suppose $K \cup \{\psi_1\}$ is not L'-consistent. Then $K \cup \{\psi_1\} \vdash_{L'} {\sim}(\psi_1 \supset \psi_1)$, $K \vdash_{L'} \psi_1 \supset {\sim}(\psi_1 \supset \psi_1)$, and $K \vdash_{L'} (\psi_1 \supset \psi_1) \supset {\sim}\psi_1$. But $K \vdash_{L'} (\psi_1 \supset \psi_1)$, so $K \vdash_{L'} {\sim}\psi_1$, i.e., $K \vdash_{L'} {\sim}(\bigvee\alpha_1\phi_1 \supset |\alpha_1/c_1|\phi_1)$. Let β be a variable expression such that $\beta \notin OC(\phi_1)$. Then since c_1 does not occur in any member of K, $K \vdash_{L'} \bigwedge\beta|c_1/\beta|{\sim}(\bigvee\alpha_1\phi_1 \supset |\alpha_1/c_1|\phi_1)$. But then since $c_1 \notin OC(\bigvee\alpha_1\phi_1)$ and hence $c_1 \notin OC(\phi_1)$, $\bigwedge\beta|c_1/\beta|{\sim}(\bigvee\alpha_1\phi_1 \supset |\alpha_1/c_1|\phi_1) = \bigwedge\beta{\sim}(\bigvee\alpha_1\phi_1 \supset |\alpha_1/\beta|\phi_1)$. (Proof of this is left to the reader.) So $K \vdash_{L'} \bigwedge\beta{\sim}(\bigvee\alpha_1\phi_1 \supset |\alpha_1/\beta|\phi_1)$. But $K \vdash_{L'} {\sim}\bigwedge\beta{\sim}(\bigvee\alpha_1\phi_1 \supset |\alpha_1/\beta|\phi_1)$ by Exercise 39.1, so K is not L'-consistent. Since this contradicts our initial assumption, we conclude that after all $K \cup \{\psi_1\}$ must be L'-consistent.

Now let $\Gamma' \subseteq \Gamma$ such that Γ' is finite. Then for sufficiently large n, $\Gamma' \subseteq K \cup \{\psi_1,\ldots,\psi_n\}$ and Γ' is L'-consistent. So every finite subset of Γ is L'-consistent and Γ is L'-consistent by Theorem 65. By the Lindenbaum Lemma, we can let Δ be a maximally L'-consistent set such that $\Gamma \subseteq \Delta$. Then $K \subseteq \Delta$. Let $\bigvee\alpha\phi \in \Delta$. Then $\bigvee\alpha\phi \supset |\alpha/c_n|\phi \in \Gamma$ for some n, $\bigvee\alpha\phi \supset |\alpha/c_n|\phi \in \Delta$ since $\Gamma \subseteq \Delta$, and $|\alpha/c_n|\phi \in \Delta$ since Δ is maximally L'-consistent. Thus Δ is maximally L'-consistent and ω-complete.

We will use Δ to build an L'-model for K. Let U = {c: c is a constant expression of L'}. For each c ε U, let R(c) = c, and for each n ε N and each n-place predicate expression F of L', let $R(F) = \{<c_1,\ldots,c_n>: \{c_1,\ldots,c_n\} \subseteq U \,\&\, Fc_1\ldots c_n \,\varepsilon\, \Delta\}$. Then $A = <U,R>$ is an L'-model. Let a be any assignment for A and let $\Omega = \{\phi: (n)(\alpha_1)\ldots(\alpha_n)(c_1)\ldots(c_n)((\{c_1,\ldots,c_n\} \subseteq U \,\&\, |\alpha_1/c_1|\ldots|\alpha_n/c_n|\phi \,\varepsilon\, ST_{L'}) \rightarrow (a \text{ sat } |\alpha_1/c_1|\ldots|\alpha_n/c_n|\phi \text{ in } A \leftrightarrow |\alpha_1/c_1|\ldots|\alpha_n/c_n|\phi \,\varepsilon\, \Delta))\}$. We will do an induction on $FM_{L'}$ to show that $FM_{L'} \subseteq \Omega$.

Basis step. Let $Ft_1\ldots t_n \,\varepsilon\, AT_{L'}$ and let $\{\alpha_1,\ldots,\alpha_m\} \subseteq VR$ and $\{c_1,\ldots,c_m\} \subseteq U$ such that $|\alpha_1/c_1|\ldots|\alpha_m/c_m|Ft_1\ldots t_n \,\varepsilon\, ST_{L'}$. Then a sat $|\alpha_1/c_1|\ldots|\alpha_m/c_m|Ft_1\ldots t_n$ in $A \leftrightarrow$ a sat $F|\alpha_1/c_1|\ldots|\alpha_m/c_m|t_1 \;.\;.\;.\; |\alpha_1/c_1|\ldots|\alpha_m/c_m|t_n$ in $A \leftrightarrow$ $<Val(|\alpha_1/c_1|\ldots|\alpha_m/c_m|t_1,A,a), \;.\;.\;.\; ,Val(|\alpha_1/c_1|\ldots|\alpha_m/c_m|t_n,A,a)> \,\varepsilon\, R(F) \leftrightarrow F|\alpha_1/c_1|\ldots|\alpha_m/c_m|t_1 \;.\;.\;.\; |\alpha_1/c_1|\ldots|\alpha_m/c_m|t_n \,\varepsilon\, \Delta \leftrightarrow |\alpha_1/c_1|\ldots|\alpha_m/c_m|Ft_1\ldots t_n \,\varepsilon\, \Delta$. So $Ft_1\ldots t_n \,\varepsilon\, \Omega$.

Induction step. Suppose $\phi \,\varepsilon\, \Omega \,\&\, \{\alpha_1,\ldots,\alpha_n\} \subseteq VR \,\&\, \{c_1,\ldots,c_n\} \subseteq U \,\&\, |\alpha_1/c_1|\ldots|\alpha_n/c_n|{\sim}\phi \,\varepsilon\, ST_{L'}$. Then $|\alpha_1/c_1|\ldots|\alpha_n/c_n|\phi \,\varepsilon\, ST_{L'}$ by Exercise 36.3 and Definition 68. So a sat $|\alpha_1/c_1|\ldots|\alpha_n/c_n|{\sim}\phi$ in $A \leftrightarrow$ a sat ${\sim}|\alpha_1/c_1|\ldots|\alpha_n/c_n|\phi$ in $A \leftrightarrow$ a non-sat $|\alpha_1/c_1|\ldots|\alpha_n/c_n|\phi$ in $A \leftrightarrow |\alpha_1/c_1|\ldots|\alpha_n/c_n|\phi \notin \Delta$ (since $|\alpha_1/c_1|\ldots|\alpha_n/c_n|\phi \,\varepsilon\, ST_{L'} \,\&\, \phi \,\varepsilon\, \Omega) \leftrightarrow {\sim}|\alpha_1/c_1|\ldots|\alpha_n/c_n|\phi \,\varepsilon\, \Delta$ (since Δ is maximally L'-consistent) $\leftrightarrow |\alpha_1/c_1|\ldots|\alpha_n/c_n|{\sim}\phi \,\varepsilon\, \Delta$. So ${\sim}\phi \,\varepsilon\, \Omega$.

Similarly, we can show that $\phi \supset \psi \,\varepsilon\, \Omega$.

Next suppose $\phi \,\varepsilon\, \Omega \,\&\, \{\alpha_1,\ldots,\alpha_n\} \subseteq VR \,\&\, \{c_1,\ldots,c_n\} \subseteq U \,\&\, |\alpha_1/c_1|\ldots|\alpha_n/c_n| \Lambda\alpha\phi \,\varepsilon\, ST_{L'}$. Note that each $|\alpha_i/c_i|$ will either disappear or move from the left of '$\Lambda\alpha$' to the right, depending on whether $\alpha_i = \alpha$. So there is a subset $\{\beta_1,\ldots,\beta_m\} \subseteq \{\alpha_1,\ldots,\alpha_n\}$ and a subset $\{d_1,\ldots,d_m\} \subseteq \{c_1,\ldots,c_n\}$ such that $|\alpha_1/c_1|\ldots|\alpha_n/c_n| \Lambda\alpha\phi = \Lambda\alpha|\beta_1/d_1|\ldots|\beta_m/d_m|\phi$. Then a sat $|\alpha_1/c_1|\ldots|\alpha_n/c_n|\Lambda\alpha\phi$ in $A \leftrightarrow$ a sat $\Lambda\alpha|\beta_1/d_1|\ldots|\beta_m/d_m|\phi$ in A $\leftrightarrow (c)(c \,\varepsilon\, U \rightarrow a(\alpha|c)$ sat $|\beta_1/d_1|\ldots|\beta_m/d_m|\phi$ in $A) \leftrightarrow$

(c)(c ε U → a(α|Val(c,A,a)) sat $|\beta_1/d_1|\ldots|\beta_m/d_m|\phi$ in A) (since (c)(c ε U → Val(c,A,a) = c)) ↔ (c)(c ε U → a sat $|\alpha/c||\beta_1/d_1|\ldots|\beta_m/d_m|\phi$ in A) (by Theorem 54) ↔ (c)(c ε U → $|\alpha/c||\beta_1/d_1|\ldots|\beta_m/d_m|\phi \in \Delta$) (since $|\alpha/c||\beta_1/d_1|\ldots|\beta_m/d_m|\phi \in ST_{L'}$, & $\phi \in \Omega$). We leave it to the reader to show that $|\alpha/c||\beta_1/d_1|\ldots|\beta_m/d_m|\phi \in ST_{L'}$. Now we need to show that (c)(c ε U → $|\alpha/c||\beta_1/d_m|\ldots|\beta_m/d_m|\phi \in \Delta$) ↔ (t)((t ε $TM_{L'}$ & (t = α ∨ α ∉ FV($|\alpha/c||\beta_1/d_1|\ldots|\beta_m/d_m|\phi$))) → $|\alpha/t||\beta_1/d_1|\ldots|\beta_m/d_m|\phi \in \Delta$). The inference from right to left is obvious, so suppose (c)(c ε U → $|\alpha/c||\beta_1/d_1|\ldots|\beta_m/d_m|\phi \in \Delta$) & t ε $TM_{L'}$ & (t = α ∨ α ∉ FV($|\alpha/t||\beta_1/d_1|\ldots|\beta_m/d_m|\phi$)). We need to show that $|\alpha/t||\beta_1/d_1|\ldots|\beta_m/d_m|\phi \in \Delta$. If t ε U, then $|\alpha/t||\beta_1/d_1|\ldots|\beta_m/d_m| \in \Delta$, so suppose t ε VR. If $|\alpha/t||\beta_1/d_1|\ldots|\beta_m/d_m|\phi \notin \Delta$, then $\sim|\alpha/t||\beta_1/d_1|\ldots|\beta_m/d_m|\phi \in \Delta$ since Δ is maximally L'-consistent, $\sim|\alpha/t||\beta_1/d_1|\ldots|\beta_m/d_m|\phi \supset \bigvee\alpha\sim|\beta_1/d_1|\ldots|\beta_m/d_m|\phi \in \Delta$ (proof is left to the reader), $\bigvee\alpha\sim|\beta_1/d_1|\ldots|\beta_m/d_m|\phi \in \Delta$ since Δ is maximally L'-consistent, (∃c)(c ε U & $\bigvee\alpha\sim|\beta_1/d_1|\ldots|\beta_m/d_m|\phi \supset |\alpha/c||\beta_1/d_1|\ldots|\beta_m/d_m|\sim\phi \in \Delta$) by the definition of Δ, (∃c)(c ε U & $|\alpha/c||\beta_1/d_1|\ldots|\beta_m/d_m|\sim\phi \in \Delta$) since Δ is maximally L'-consistent, (∃c)(c ε U & $|\alpha/c||\beta_1/d_1|\ldots|\beta_m/d_m|\phi \in \Delta$ & $\sim|\alpha/c||\beta_1/d_1|\ldots|\beta_m/d_m|\phi \in \Delta$) since (c)(c ε U → $|\alpha/c||\beta_1/d_1|\ldots|\beta_m/d_m|\phi \in \Delta$), and Δ is not L'-consistent by Theorem 62. This contradicts a result we showed earlier, so $|\alpha/t||\beta_1/d_1|\ldots|\beta_m/d_m|\phi \in \Delta$. Continuing with our argument, then, (c)(c ε U → $|\alpha/c||\beta_1/d_1|\ldots|\beta_m/d_m|\phi \in \Delta$) ↔ (t)((t ε $TM_{L'}$ & (t = α ∨ α ∉ FV($|\alpha/t||\beta_1/d_1|\ldots|\beta_m/d_m|\phi$))) → $|\alpha/t||\beta_1/d_1|\ldots|\beta_m/d_m|\phi \in \Delta$) ↔ $\bigwedge\alpha|\beta_1/d_1|\ldots|\beta_m/d_m|\phi \in \Delta$ (by Theorem 70). So $\bigwedge\alpha\phi \in \Omega$.

Thus, $FM_{L'} \subseteq \Omega$. But $K \subseteq \Delta \cap ST_{L'}$, so a sim-sat K in A. Since we chose a arbitrarily, this means every assignment for A sim-sat K in A and A is a model for K.

<u>THEOREM 73.</u> (Completeness.) (∃L)(K is L-consistent) → (∃A)(K is sim-sat in A).

Proof. Suppose K is L-consistent. Let C = $\{c_1, c_2, \ldots\}$

be a countably infinite set of constant expressions such that $(n)(c_n$ is not a constant expression of L). We know that such a set C exists by our richness assumption for constants. Let $S_{L'} = S_L \cup \{x: (\exists n)(c_n = <x>)\}$. For each $\phi \in K$, let $f(\phi) = |<v_{i_1}>/c_{i_1}|\ldots|<v_{i_k}>/c_{i_k}|\phi$ if $FV(\phi) = \{<v_{i_1}>,\ldots,<v_{i_k}>\}$, and let $\Gamma = \{f(\phi): \phi \in K\}$.

Lemma 2. $\Gamma \subseteq ST_{L'}$.

Next we will show that Γ is L'-consistent. Suppose Γ is not L'-consistent. Then by Theorem 65 we will let Γ' be a finite subset of Γ such that Γ' is not L'-consistent. Let $K' = K \cap \Gamma'$ and let $\Gamma' - K = \{\phi_1,\ldots,\phi_n\}$. Then $\Gamma' = K' \cup \{\phi_1,\ldots,\phi_n\}$. Let ϕ be an L'-sentence such that $VR \cap OC(\phi) = \emptyset$. Since Γ' is not SL-consistent, $K' \cup \{\phi_1,\ldots,\phi_n\} \vdash_{L'} \sim(\phi \supset \phi)$ by Definition 93, $K' \vdash_{L'} (\phi_1 \wedge \ldots \wedge \phi_n) \supset \sim(\phi \supset \phi)$ by the Deduction Theorem and other results. Let $\{c_{i_1},\ldots,c_{i_k}\} = \{c: c \in C \;\&\; (\exists j)(j \leq n \;\&\; c \in OC(\phi_j))\}$.

Lemma 3. $K' \vdash_{L'} \bigwedge\alpha_{i_1}\ldots\bigwedge\alpha_{i_k}|c_{i_1}/\alpha_{i_1}|\ldots|c_{i_k}/\alpha_{i_k}|((\phi_1 \wedge \ldots \wedge \phi_n) \supset \sim(\phi \supset \phi))$.

Lemma 4. $K' \vdash_{L'} |c_{i_1}/\alpha_{i_1}|\ldots|c_{i_k}/\alpha_{i_k}|((\phi_1 \wedge \ldots \wedge \phi_n) \supset \sim(\phi \supset \phi))$.

Lemma 5. $(j)(j \leq n \rightarrow |c_{i_1}/\alpha_{i_1}|\ldots|c_{i_k}/\alpha_{i_k}|\phi_j \in K)$.

By the Deduction Theorem and other results, $K' \cup \{|c_{i_1}/\alpha_{i_1}|\ldots|c_{i_k}/\alpha_{i_k}|\phi_j: j \leq n\} \vdash_{L'} \sim(|c_{i_1}/\alpha_{i_1}|\ldots|c_{i_k}/\alpha_{i_k}|\phi \supset |c_{i_1}/\alpha_{i_1}|\ldots|c_{i_k}/\alpha_{i_k}|\phi)$. But $K' \cup \{|c_{i_1}/\alpha_{i_1}|\ldots|c_{i_k}/\alpha_{i_k}|\phi_j: j \leq n\} \subseteq K$ by Lemma 5, so K is not L'-consistent by Theorem 65. But then we can use Theorem 49 to conclude that K is not L-consistent, contrary to our initial assumption. So Γ is L'-consistent after all.

By Theorem 72, we let $\mathcal{A} = <U,R>$ be a model for Γ. For each $<v_n> \in VR$, let $a(<v_n>) = R(c_n)$. Then a is an assignment for $\mathcal{A}$.

Lemma 6. a sim-sat K in $\mathcal{A}$.

This completes our proof.

There are a couple of other completeness results, all of which are either equivalent to or weaker than Theorem 73. We list these as corollaries.

COROLLARY 73.1. $K \vdash \phi \leftrightarrow K \models \phi$.

COROLLARY 73.2. $\vdash \phi \leftrightarrow \models \phi$.

EXERCISES

46.1 Prove Theorem 71.

46.2 Prove Lemma 1, Theorem 72.

46.3 Prove Lemmas 2-6, Theorem 73. Hint: Use Theorem 45 to prove Lemma 3.

46.4 Prove the corollaries to Theorem 73.

46.5 Let L be a language which has countably many 1-place predicate expressions $F_1, F_2, \ldots$, and no constant expressions. For each positive integer n, let $\phi_n = \bigvee\alpha({\sim}F_1\alpha \wedge \ldots \wedge {\sim}F_n\alpha)$. Let $K = \{F_n\alpha\colon \alpha \in VR \mathbin{\&} n \in N\} \cup \{\phi_n\colon n \in N\}$. Show that K is L-consistent & $(\Gamma)(K \subseteq \Gamma \rightarrow \Gamma$ is not maximally L-consistent and ω-complete).

CHAPTER 4

Modal Logic

§47. Possibility and Necessity. Most readers will have already studied natural deduction systems for sentential and predicate logic, but many will not be familiar with any version of modal logic. Just as the sentential and the predicate logic are motivated by the desire to clarify certain logical features of ordinary discourse and thought, so too is modal logic, but modal logic is intended to take into account features of ordinary language which we can not adequately represent using sentential and predicate logic. In particular modal logic is intended to clarify the way in which we employ the notions of possibility and necessity in our thought and speech in somewhat the same way sentential logic shows the role truth functions play in our thinking and talking.

You may live another ten years or you may not, but what you can not do is both live another ten years and not live another ten years. To both live another ten years and not live another ten years is impossible, to do one or the other is necessary, and living another ten years is possible as is also, I am afraid, not living another ten years. The kind of possibility and necessity we are talking about is logical possibility and necessity. Something which is neither logically impossible nor logically necessary, something such that both it and its negation are possible, is called contingent.

Logical possibility and necessity are not the only kinds of possibility and necessity which we commonly use in our thought and speech. We also frequently employ the notions of physical possibility and necessity. It is physically possible for a man to run a mile in less than four minutes, but it is physically impossible for a man to run faster than light travels. (At least, modern physics tells us that this is impossible.) It is logically possible that you may live another thousand years, but it may be physically impossible for you to do so. The fictional character Superman is a logical possibility, yet it is a physical necessity that no such character exists.

Although logical and physical possibility and necessity are different notions, they have certain common features, and there may be other notions of possibility and necessity which differ from either of these. There are also other concepts which are not concepts of possibility and necessity in any straightforward sense but which seem to have a logical structure similar to that of logical possibility and necessity. We want to develop formal systems and semantics for all of these related concepts which will allow us to represent the logical properties of notions of these kinds.

It may turn out that not all of the logical properties of logical possiblity and necessity and physical possibility and necessity are the same. And when we try to use similar methods to analyze notions from ethics and epistemology and to explore the logical structure of tenses, we almost surely will run into important differences. We will almost certainly need to develop several formal systems for such a variety of purposes. In this chapter we will develop four of the best-known modal logics: Kr, T, S4 and S5. There are many different modal logics, in fact there are infinitely many, but only a few have received the attention which has been given to these four. All modal logics share the same language but no two have exactly the same theorems. Most of these modal logics are interesting only from a formal point of view since they appear to have no interesting applications to or counterparts in ordinary thought and speech. In other words, most of these logics do not represent the structure of notions, whether of possibility and necessity or of something else, which we actually use. The four formal systems Kr, T, S4, and S5, however, are more interesting in this respect since they may very well turn out to represent the logical structures of common notions.

EXERCISES

Indicate for each of the following sentences whether that sentence asserts something which is logically possible, logically impossible, logically necessary, physically possible, physically impossible, or physically necessary. Remember that a single sentence may fall into more than one of these categories. The reader should be warned that some of these examples are controversial.

47.1 No bachelor is married.

47.2 Some bachelors are bald.

47.3 Iron rusts.

47.4 Everyone knows that two plus two is four.

47.5 Pure gold is yellow.

47.6 Gold is a metal.

47.7 Water freezes at 0^0 centigrade.

47.8 The oldest spy in the world is a spy.

§48. The Language of Modal (Sentential) Logic. It is possible to develop a system of modal logic which includes constants, predicates, and quantifiers, but we will not introduce such a system of quantified modal logic here. Instead we will look at systems of modal logic which require us to add only one additional symbol to the symbols of SL. We are, then, referring to such modal sentential logics whenever we say 'modal logics' in this chapter.

We begin by introducing the logical constant '$\underline{l}$' which we read as 'the necessity symbol', and which we assume to refer to an object which is distinct from any SL-symbol.

DEFINITION 96. $S_{\Box} = S_{SL} \cup \{\underline{l}\}$.

We call the members of $S_{\Box}$ modal symbols. We assume that no modal symbol is a sequence of modal symbols.

DEFINITION 97. σ is a modal expression $\leftrightarrow$ σ is a finite sequence of modal symbols.

Where σ and τ are modal expressions, we have the following definition:

DEFINITION 98. $\sim\sigma = \langle\underline{n}\rangle * \sigma$.

$\sigma \supset \tau = \langle\underline{i}\rangle * \sigma * \tau$.

$\sigma \vee \tau = \sim\sigma \supset \tau$.

$\sigma \wedge \tau = \sim(\sigma \supset \sim\tau)$.

$\sigma \equiv \tau = (\sigma \supset \tau) \wedge (\tau \supset \sigma)$.

$\Box\sigma = \langle\underline{l}\rangle * \sigma$.

$\Diamond\sigma = \sim\Box\sim\sigma$.

DEFINITION 99. σ is a modal construction $\leftrightarrow$ $(n)(n \leq \ell(\sigma) \rightarrow (\sigma_n \in AT_{SL} \vee (\exists i)(i < n \,\&\, \sigma_n = \sim\sigma_i) \vee (\exists i)(\exists j)(i < n \,\&\, j < n \,\&\, \sigma_n = \sigma_i \supset \sigma_j) \vee (\exists i)(i < n \,\&\, \sigma_n = \Box\sigma_i)))$.

DEFINITION 100. $ST_{\Box} = \{\phi: (\exists\sigma)(\sigma$ is a modal construction and $\sigma_{\ell(\sigma)} = \phi)\}$.

We will use ϕ, ψ, χ, and θ in this chapter as special variables which range over modal sentences, i.e., over members of $ST_{\Box}$. We will use K, Γ, and Δ as special variables which range over subsets of $ST_{\Box}$.

THEOREM 74. (Induction Principle for $ST_{\Box}$.) $(AT_{SL} \subseteq A$

$\& (\phi)(\phi \in A \rightarrow {\sim}\phi \in A) \& (\phi)(\psi)((\phi \in A \& \psi \in A) \rightarrow \phi \supset \psi \in A) \& (\phi)(\phi \in A \rightarrow \Box\phi \in A)) \rightarrow ST_\Box \subseteq A.$

DEFINITION 101. $L_\Box = \langle S_\Box;\emptyset;ST_\Box\rangle$.

$L_\Box$ is a formal language which we will call the modal language.

DEFINITION 102. ϕ is a modal generalization of $\psi \leftrightarrow (\phi = \psi \vee (\exists\sigma)((n)(n \leq \ell(\sigma) \rightarrow \sigma_n = \underline{1}) \& \phi = \sigma{*}\psi))$.

EXERCISES

48.1 Prove Theorem 74.

48.2 Show that $ST_{SL} \subseteq ST_\Box$.

48.3 Which of the following are modal generalizations of ϕ: $\Diamond\phi$, $\Box\Diamond\phi$, $\Box\phi$? Explain your answer.

§49. The Relational World System Interpretation of the Modal Language. Most people will agree that the world might have been different from the way it is. For example, George Washington might not have been the first President of the United States, Napoleon might not have lost at Waterloo, or even physical laws might have been different. The gravitational constant might have been just a bit greater or the speed of light might have been just a bit slower. When we say that something which didn't happen nevertheless could have happened, we are essentially saying that if things had worked out differently, then that thing would have happened. Our talk of possibility and necessity, of what could have been the case and of what must be the way it is, implicitly involves us in talking about different ways things might have been, or what some people have called counterfactual situations. Another very common term for these various ways things might have been (or might be) is possible worlds. Intuitively something is possible if it happens in some possible world and it is necessary if it happens in all possible worlds.

For present purposes all we need to know about a possible world is which sentences are true in it and which sentences are false. So we will think of possible worlds as functions which tell us which modal sentences are true and which are false. Of course a sentence and its negation can't both be true at the same world, and if an implication is true at a world, then either its antecedent is false or its consequent is true at that world.

DEFINITION 103. w is a world $\leftrightarrow$ $(w:ST_{\Box} \longrightarrow \{0,1\}$ & $(\phi)(\psi)((w(\sim\phi) = 1 \leftrightarrow w(\phi) = 0)$ & $(w(\phi \supset \psi) = 1 \leftrightarrow (w(\phi) = 0 \vee w(\psi) = 1))))$.

Intuitively $\Box\phi$ is true if ϕ would be true no matter what the world was like, i.e., if ϕ is true in every world. But this isn't quite right. If the notion of necessity we have in mind is logical necessity, then we might want to say that $\Box\phi$ is true just in case ϕ is true in every world. But what if the notion of necessity we have in mind is physical necessity or even some other kind of necessity we haven't considered? In some worlds water might boil at 50^0C or acid might turn blue litmus paper yellow. When we are trying to decide whether something is physically possible or physically necessary, we don't want to consider what would happen if physical laws were different. The worlds we look at in a case like this will be less than all of the worlds. For physical necessity we will look only at worlds in which all and only those physical laws hold which actually hold. Only certain worlds will be physical alternatives to the way things actually are. Given some other notion of necessity, say X-necessity, only certain worlds will be X-alternatives to the way things actually are. Whatever kind of necessity X we have in mind, and whatever kind of alternative X to the way things actually are goes along with that notion, we will say that a world which is that kind of an alternative to the way things actually are is X-accessible from the way things actually are or from the actual world. Thus we have the notion of an accessibility relation between worlds where a different accessibility relation may be involved for each different kind of necessity. So $\Box\phi$ is true just in case ϕ is true at every accessible world.

DEFINITION 104. $\mathcal{A}$ is a relational world system (RWS) $\leftrightarrow (\exists U)(\exists R)(\mathcal{A} = \langle U;R\rangle \ \&\ U \neq \emptyset \ \&\ (w)(w \in U \rightarrow w$ is a world$) \ \&\ R \subseteq \{\langle w;w'\rangle : w \in U \ \&\ w' \in U\} \ \&\ (w)(\phi)(w \in U \rightarrow (w(\Box\phi) = 1 \leftrightarrow (w')(\langle w;w'\rangle \in R \rightarrow w'(\phi) = 1))))$.

Where $\mathcal{A} = \langle U;R\rangle$ is an RWS we will sometimes denote U as $U_{\mathcal{A}}$ and R as $R_{\mathcal{A}}$. An RWS, then, consists of a set of worlds and an accessibility relation for that set of worlds. If $w \in U_{\mathcal{A}}$, then $w(\Box\phi) = 1$ if and only if $w'(\phi) = 1$ for every world w' in $U_{\mathcal{A}}$ which is accessible from w by the relation $R_{\mathcal{A}}$. We will use capital script letters '$\mathcal{A}$', '$\mathcal{B}$', etc., as special variables ranging over RWS's in the rest of this chapter, and we will use 'w', 'w_1', etc., as special variables ranging over worlds.

DEFINITION 105. ϕ is true in $\mathcal{A} \leftrightarrow (w)(w \in U_{\mathcal{A}} \rightarrow w(\phi) = 1)$.

A modal sentence is true in an RWS just in case that sentence is true at every world in that RWS.

I referred above to the actual world. By this I mean the way things actually are. Formally the actual world is a function $w: ST_{\Box} \longrightarrow \{0,1\}$ such that $w(\phi) = 1$ just in case ϕ is in fact true. We must distinguish between what we mean by the actual world and the world. The actual world is the way the world actually is as opposed to a merely possible world which is a way the world might have been but isn't. We occupy the world; we are inhabitants of it. We don't occupy any possible world, including the actual world, in the way we occupy the world. We might, though, be some kind of constituents of a counterfactual situation or way things might have been. When we formalize the notion of a world and think of worlds as functions from sentences to either 0 or 1, we are of course unlikely to confuse <u>the</u> world with <u>a</u> world, actual or otherwise.

EXERCISES

49.1 Show that $(A)(w)(w \varepsilon U_A \rightarrow (w(\Diamond\phi) = 1 \leftrightarrow (\exists w')(\langle w;w'\rangle \varepsilon R_A \,\&\, w'(\phi) = 1)))$.

49.2 Show that $(w)(w(\phi \supset (\psi \supset \phi)) = 1)$.

49.3 Show that $(w)(w((\phi \supset (\psi \supset \chi)) \supset ((\phi \supset \psi) \supset (\phi \supset \chi))) = 1)$.

49.4 Show that $(w)(w((\sim\phi \supset \sim\psi) \supset (\psi \supset \phi)) = 1)$.

49.5 Show that $(w)((w(\phi) = 1 \,\&\, w(\phi \supset \psi) = 1) \rightarrow w(\psi) = 1)$.

49.6 Show that $(A)(\Box(\phi \supset \psi) \supset (\Box\phi \supset \Box\psi)$ is true in $A)$.

<u>§50. Logistic Systems.</u> There is a family of languages which share some interesting properties with SL. We will call these <u>IN-languages</u> since they all contain the implication and negation symbols among their symbols and since these two symbols play a similar role in the syntax of each of these languages.

<u>DEFINITION 106.</u> L is an <u>IN-language</u> $\leftrightarrow$ (L is a formal language & $\underline{n} \varepsilon S_L$ & $\underline{i} \varepsilon S_L$ & $(\phi)(\psi)((\phi \varepsilon FM_L \,\&\, \psi \varepsilon FM_L) \rightarrow (\langle\underline{n}\rangle{*}\phi \varepsilon FM_L \,\&\, \langle\underline{i}\rangle{*}\phi{*}\psi \varepsilon FM_L)))$.

The language of sentential logic is an IN-language as are all PL-languages. Since all of the modal logics to be developed in this chapter and all of the conditional logics to be developed in the next chapter are based on IN-languages, and since all of the formal systems we are examining in this book also share other important features, we will save some time if we will pause at this time to establish what it is these systems all have in common. Many of the definitions and theorems of this section will resemble others we have seen.

DEFINITION 107. L is an IN-language $\rightarrow$ ($BAX_L = \{\phi$: $(\exists\psi)(\exists\chi)(\exists\theta)(\{\psi,\chi,\theta\} \subseteq FM_L$ & ϕ is one of the following:

AX1. $\psi \supset (\chi \supset \phi)$;

AX2. $(\psi \supset (\chi \supset \theta)) \supset ((\psi \supset \chi) \supset (\psi \supset \theta))$;

AX3. $(\sim\psi \supset \sim\chi) \supset (\chi \supset \psi))\})$.

DEFINITION 108. (L is an IN-language & $K \cup \{\phi\} \subseteq FM_L$) $\rightarrow$ (σ is a <u>modus ponens derivation</u> (<u>MP-derivation</u>) <u>of</u> ϕ <u>from</u> K <u>in</u> L $\leftrightarrow (n)(n \leq \ell(\sigma) \rightarrow (\sigma_n \in K \vee (\exists i)(\exists j)(i < n \;\&\; j < n \;\&\; \sigma_i = \sigma_j \supset \sigma_n))))$.

Where ϕ and ψ are formulas of an IN-language L, we let $\sim\phi = \langle \underline{n} \rangle * \phi$, $\phi \supset \psi = \langle \underline{i} \rangle * \phi * \psi$, etc., just as we did for the language of the sentential logic, all PL-languages, and the modal language.

DEFINITION 109. Σ is a <u>logistic system</u> $\leftrightarrow (\exists S)(\exists T)(\exists F)(\exists A)(\exists D)(\Sigma = \langle S;T;F;A;D \rangle$ & $\langle S;T;F \rangle$ is an IN-language & $BAX_{\langle S;T;F \rangle} \subseteq A \subseteq F$ & $D = \{\langle K;\phi \rangle$: $K \cup \{\phi\} \subseteq F$ & $(\exists\sigma)(\sigma$ is an MP-derivation of ϕ from $K \cup A$ in $\langle S;T;F \rangle)\})$.

THEOREM 75. Σ is a logistic system $\rightarrow$ Σ is a formal system.

In the rest of <u>this section only</u>, we will use 'Σ', etc., as special variables which range over logistic systems, we will use 'K', etc., as special variables which range over sets of formulas of any logistic system we may be discussing, and we will use 'ϕ', 'ψ', and 'χ' as special variables which range over formulas of any logistic system we happen to be discussing. In the <u>next</u> section, we will once again use 'ϕ', etc., and 'K', etc., to range over modal sentences and sets of modal sentences.

DEFINITION 110. $\vdash_{\Sigma} \phi \leftrightarrow \emptyset \vdash_{\Sigma} \phi$.

THEOREM 76. $\phi \in K \rightarrow K \vdash_{\Sigma} \phi$.

THEOREM 77. $\phi \in AX_{\Sigma} \rightarrow (K \vdash_{\Sigma} \phi \;\&\; \vdash_{\Sigma} \phi)$.

THEOREM 78. $(K \vdash_{\Sigma} \phi \ \& \ K \vdash_{\Sigma} \phi \supset \psi) \rightarrow K \vdash_{\Sigma} \psi$.

THEOREM 79. $(K \vdash_{\Sigma} \phi \ \& \ K \subseteq \Gamma) \rightarrow \Gamma \vdash_{\Sigma} \phi$.

THEOREM 80. $K \vdash_{\Sigma} \phi \leftrightarrow (\exists \Gamma)(\Gamma \subseteq K \ \& \ \Gamma$ is finite $\& \ \Gamma \vdash_{\Sigma} \phi)$.

THEOREM 81. $\vdash_{\Sigma} \phi \rightarrow K \vdash_{\Sigma} \phi$.

THEOREM 82. (Induction Principle for $\{\phi: K \vdash_{\Sigma} \phi\}$.)
$(K \subseteq A \ \& \ AX_{\Sigma} \subseteq A \ \&$ A is closed under modus ponens$) \rightarrow$ $\{\phi: K \vdash_{\Sigma} \phi\} \subseteq A$.

THEOREM 83. (Deduction Theorem for Logistic Systems.)
$K \cup \{\phi\} \vdash_{\Sigma} \psi \leftrightarrow K \vdash_{\Sigma} \phi \supset \psi$.

DEFINITION 111. K is Σ-consistent $\leftrightarrow (\exists \phi) \sim K \vdash_{\Sigma} \phi$.

THEOREM 84. K is Σ-consistent $\leftrightarrow \sim(\exists \phi)(K \vdash_{\Sigma} \phi \ \& \ K \vdash_{\Sigma} \sim \phi)$.

THEOREM 85. K is Σ-consistent $\leftrightarrow \sim(\exists \phi)(K \vdash_{\Sigma} \sim(\phi \supset \phi))$.

THEOREM 86. $K \vdash_{\Sigma} \phi \leftrightarrow K \cup \{\sim \phi\}$ is not Σ-consistent.

THEOREM 87. (K is Σ-consistent $\& \ K \vdash_{\Sigma} \phi) \rightarrow K \cup \{\phi\}$ is Σ-consistent.

THEOREM 88. K is Σ-consistent $\leftrightarrow (\Gamma)((\Gamma \subseteq K \ \& \ \Gamma$ is finite$) \rightarrow \Gamma$ is Σ-consistent).

THEOREM 89. K is Σ-consistent $\leftrightarrow (\Gamma)(\Gamma \subseteq K \rightarrow \Gamma$ is Σ-consistent).

DEFINITION 112. Σ is consistent $\leftrightarrow AX_{\Sigma}$ is Σ-consistent.

DEFINITION 113. K is maximally Σ-consistent $\leftrightarrow$ (K is Σ-consistent $\& \ (\phi)(K \cup \{\phi\}$ is Σ-consistent $\rightarrow \phi \in K)$).

THEOREM 90. K is maximally Σ-consistent $\rightarrow (\phi \in K \leftrightarrow K \vdash_{\Sigma} \phi)$.

THEOREM 91. K is maximally Σ-consistent $\rightarrow (\phi \in K \leftrightarrow \sim \phi \notin K)$.

THEOREM 92. (K is maximally Σ-consistent $\& \vdash_{\Sigma} \phi) \rightarrow \phi \in K$.

THEOREM 93. K is maximally Σ-consistent $\rightarrow$ ($\phi \supset \psi \in K \leftrightarrow (\sim\phi \in K \vee \psi \in K)$).

THEOREM 94. (Lindenbaum Lemma for Logistic Systems.) K is Σ-consistent $\rightarrow$ $(\exists\Gamma)(K \subseteq \Gamma$ & Γ is maximally Σ-consistent.)

DEFINITION 114. Σ' is an extension of $\Sigma \leftrightarrow (S_\Sigma \subseteq S_{\Sigma'}$ & $TM_\Sigma \subseteq TM_{\Sigma'}$ & $FM_\Sigma \subseteq FM_{\Sigma'}$ & $\vdash_\Sigma \subseteq \vdash_{\Sigma'})$.

We will say that an extension Σ' of a formal system Σ is a proper extension of Σ just in case $\Sigma \neq \Sigma'$.

EXERCISES

50.1 Prove Theorems 75-94.

§51. Modal Logics. The family of modal logics make up a subfamily of the family of logistic systems.

DEFINITION 115. Σ is a modal logic $\leftrightarrow$ (Σ is a logistic system & $L_\Sigma = L_\Box$).

In the rest of this chapter we will use 'Σ', etc., as special variables which range over modal logics.

DEFINITION 116. Σ is normal $\leftrightarrow (\phi)(\vdash_\Sigma \phi \rightarrow \vdash_\Sigma \Box\phi)$.

All four of the modal logics we shall study are normal. Since all our modal logics are logistic systems, and hence all derivations in these modal logics will be MP-derivations, we can think of each of our modal logics as having only the one inference rule modus ponens. Yet the condition which defines a normal logic also looks something like an inference rule, a rule we can call necessitation. There is a very important difference between a rule like modus ponens and a rule like necessitation. Modus ponens is what we call a truth-preserving rule. In the case of modus ponens, this means that whenever ϕ and $\phi \supset \psi$ are true, then ψ is also true. But necessitation is not truth-preserving since ϕ may be true even though $\Box\phi$ is false. However, necessitation is theoremhood-preserving. If we can prove ϕ without relying upon any premises, then ϕ must be true by the very foundations of our logical system. But then we ought to be able to prove that ϕ must be true, i.e., we ought to be able to prove $\Box\phi$ as a theorem of our modal logic. And we can do this if our modal logic is normal.

But how do we distinguish formally between a truth-preseving rule and a rule which merely preserves theoremhood? Every truth-preserving rule should also be a theoremhood-preserving rule, but not vice versa. We know that modus ponens is truth-preserving for any modal logic Σ because if $K\vdash_{\Sigma}\phi$ & $K\vdash_{\Sigma}\phi \supset \psi$, then $K\vdash_{\Sigma}\psi$. The corresponding result for necessitation, $K\vdash_{\Sigma}\phi \rightarrow K\vdash_{\Sigma}\Box\phi$, can only be relied upon when $K = \emptyset$. We could build necessitation into our definition of a modal derivation, but then it would be much more difficult to show that every modal logic Σ is also a logistic system. Nevertheless, it seems reasonable to expect that the logic of any notions of possibility and necessity, or of any notions much like notions of possibility and necessity in their logical structure, will be normal.

EXERCISES

51.1 Show that ϕ is true in $A \rightarrow \Box\phi$ is true in A.

§52. The Modal Logic Kr. The first and weakest modal logic we shall examine closely is the formal system Kr.

DEFINITION 117. $AX_{Kr} = \{\phi: (\exists\psi)(\psi \in BAX_{L_\Box}$ & ϕ is a modal generalization of $\psi) \vee (\exists\psi)(\exists\chi)(\phi$ is a modal generalization of $\Box(\psi \supset \chi) \supset (\Box\psi \supset \Box\chi))\}$.

DEFINITION 118. $K\vdash_{Kr}\phi \leftrightarrow (\exists\sigma)(\sigma$ is an MP-derivation of ϕ from $K \cup AX_{Kr})$.

DEFINITION 119. $Kr = \langle S_\square; \emptyset; ST_\square; AX_{Kr}; \vdash_{Kr} \rangle$.

THEOREM 95. Kr is a logistic system.

THEOREM 96. Kr is normal.

THEOREM 97. (Σ is a normal extension of Kr & $\vdash_\Sigma \phi \equiv \phi'$ & $(\exists\sigma)(\exists\tau)$($\sigma$ is a modal expression & τ is a modal expression & $\psi = \sigma{*}\phi{*}\tau$ & $\psi' = \sigma{*}\phi'{*}\tau$)) $\rightarrow \vdash_\Sigma \psi \equiv \psi'$.

Theorem 97 tells us that we may substitute provably equivalent modal sentences for each other in normal extensions of Kr, i.e., that if we can prove in a normal extension Σ of Kr that ϕ and ϕ' are equivalent and if ψ' is the result of replacing an occurrence of ϕ by ϕ' in ψ, then we can also prove that ψ and ψ' are equivalent in Σ.

EXERCISES

52.1 Prove Theorems 95 and 96.

52.2 Prove Theorem 97. Hint: See Exercise 26.23.

52.3 Show each of the following.

a. $\vdash_{Kr} \square(\phi \supset \psi) \supset (\Diamond\phi \supset \Diamond\psi)$.

b. $\vdash_{Kr} {\sim}\Diamond\phi \supset \square(\phi \supset \psi)$.

c. $\vdash_{Kr} {\sim}\Diamond\phi \equiv (\square(\phi \supset \psi) \wedge \square(\phi \supset {\sim}\psi))$.

d. $\vdash_{Kr} (\square\phi \vee \square\psi) \supset \square(\phi \vee \psi)$.

e. $\vdash_{Kr} \Diamond(\phi \vee \psi) \equiv (\Diamond\phi \vee \Diamond\psi)$.

f. $\vdash_{Kr} \Diamond(\phi \wedge \psi) \supset (\Diamond\phi \wedge \Diamond\psi)$.

g. $\vdash_{Kr} \square(\phi \equiv \psi) \supset (\square\phi \equiv \square\psi)$.

h. $\vdash_{Kr} \square(\phi \equiv \psi) \supset (\Diamond\phi \equiv \Diamond\psi)$.

i. $\vdash_{Kr} (\Diamond\phi \supset \square\psi) \supset \square(\phi \supset \psi)$.

j. $\vdash_{Kr} (\Diamond\phi \wedge \square\psi) \supset \Diamond(\phi \wedge \psi)$.

k. $\vdash_{Kr} (\square\phi \wedge \square\psi) \equiv \square(\phi \wedge \psi)$.

§53. Canonical Relational World Systems. In this section we will show that for every consistent, normal extension Σ of Kr, there is some RWS A_Σ such that $(\phi)(\vdash_\Sigma \phi \leftrightarrow \phi$ is true in A_Σ).

DEFINITION 120. K is maximally Σ-consistent $\to$ (w_K = f $\leftrightarrow$ ($f:ST_\Box \longrightarrow \{0,1\}$ & $(\phi)(f(\phi) = 1 \leftrightarrow \phi \in K)$)).

THEOREM 98. K is maximally Σ-consistent $\to$ w_K is a world.

DEFINITION 121. $U_\Sigma = \{w_K$: K is maximally Σ-consistent$\}$.

DEFINITION 122. $R_\Sigma = \{\langle w_K;w_\Gamma\rangle: w_K \in U_\Sigma \ \&\ w_\Gamma \in U_\Sigma\ \&\ (\phi)(\Box\phi \in K \to \phi \in \Gamma)\}$.

DEFINITION 123. $A_\Sigma = \langle U_\Sigma;R_\Sigma\rangle$.

THEOREM 99. Σ is a consistent, normal extension of Kr $\to$ A_Σ is an RWS.

Proof. Suppose Σ is a consistent, normal extension of Kr. AX_Σ is Σ-consistent by Definitions 109 and 112, and we can let K be maximally Σ-consistent such that $AX_\Sigma \subseteq K$ by Theorem 94. Then $w_K \in U_\Sigma$ and $U_\Sigma \neq \emptyset$. By Theorem 98, $(w_K)(w_K \in U_\Sigma \to$ w_K is a world). By Definition 122, $R_\Sigma \subseteq \{\langle w_K;w_\Gamma\rangle: w_K \in U_\Sigma \ \&\ w_\Gamma \in U_\Sigma\}$.

Suppose $\langle w_K;w_\Gamma\rangle \in R_\Sigma$ and $w_K(\Box\phi) = 1$. Then $\Box\phi \in K$ by Definition 120, $\phi \in \Gamma$ by Definition 122, and $w_\Gamma(\phi) = 1$ by Definition 120. Next suppose $(w_\Gamma)(\langle w_K;w_\Gamma\rangle \in R_\Sigma \to w_\Gamma(\phi) = 1)$. Then $(w_\Gamma)(\langle w_K;w_\Gamma\rangle \in R_\Sigma \to \phi \in \Gamma)$ by Theorem 120, and $(\Gamma)((\Gamma$ is maximally Σ-consistent & $(\psi)(\Box\psi \in K \to \psi \in \Gamma)) \to \phi \in \Gamma)$ by Definition 122. But then $\sim(\exists\Gamma)(\Gamma$ is maximally Σ-consistent & $\{\psi: \Box\psi \in K) \cup \{\sim\phi\} \subseteq \Gamma)$, and $\{\psi: \Box\psi \in K\} \cup \{\sim\phi\}$ is not Σ-consistent by Theorem 94. So $\{\psi: \Box\psi \in K\} \vdash_\Sigma \phi$ by Theorem 86 and Definition 115. We can pick $\{\psi_1,\ldots,\psi_n\} \subseteq \{\psi: \Box\psi \in K\}$ such that $\{\psi_1,\ldots,\psi_n\} \vdash_\Sigma \phi$ by Theorem 80, and $\vdash_\Sigma (\psi_1 \wedge \ldots \wedge \psi_n) \supset \phi$ by the Deduction Theorem and other obvious results for logistic systems. But Σ is normal, so $\vdash_\Sigma \Box((\psi_1 \wedge \ldots \wedge \psi_n) \supset \phi)$. Since Σ is an extension of Kr, $\vdash_\Sigma \Box((\psi_1 \wedge \ldots \wedge \psi_n) \supset \phi) \supset (\Box(\psi_1 \wedge \ldots \wedge \psi_n) \supset \Box\phi))$ by Definitions 114 and 117 and Theorem 77. So $\vdash_\Sigma \Box(\psi_1$

$\wedge \ldots \wedge \psi_n) \supset \Box\phi$ by Theorem 78, and $K \vdash_{\Sigma} \Box(\psi_1 \wedge \ldots \wedge \psi_n) \supset \Box\phi$ by Theorem 81 and Definition 115. Since $(i)(i \leq n \rightarrow K \vdash_{\Sigma} \Box\psi_i)$, $K \vdash_{\Sigma} \Box(\psi_1 \wedge \ldots \wedge \psi_n)$ by repeated application of Exercise 52.13 and several other results. So $K \vdash_{\Sigma} \Box\phi$, $\Box\phi \in K$, and $w_K(\Box\phi) = 1$. Thus $w_K(\Box\phi) = 1 \leftrightarrow (w_\Gamma)(\langle w_K;w_\Gamma\rangle \in R_\Sigma \rightarrow w_\Gamma(\phi) = 1)$.

A_Σ is an RWS by Definition 104 and our proof is complete. We call A_Σ <u>the canonical relational world system for</u> Σ.

<u>THEOREM 100.</u> Σ is a consistent, normal extension of Kr $\rightarrow$ ($\vdash_{\Sigma}\phi \leftrightarrow \phi$ is true in A_Σ).

The similarity between what we have done here and what we did in the case of SL and PL-logics should be obvious. To establish a proper fit between the syntax and the semantics for SL, we used a maximally SL-consistent set containing some SL-consistent set K to construct a valuation which made every member of K come out true. To establish a proper fit between a PL-logic with language L and the set of L-models, we used a maximally L-consistent ω-complete set Γ containing some L-consistent set K to construct an L-model within which K could be satisfied. Here we are concerned with <u>theorems</u> of our modal logic rather than with sets of consistent sentences. What we have done is to take the maximally Σ-consistent subsets of $ST_\Box$ and used them to construct an RWS in which every theorem of Σ is true. In all three cases, we in effect interpret expressions in a language as <u>standing for themselves</u> by showing certain <u>syntactic</u> structures have the very properties which define the class of entities referred to in the semantics.

EXERCISES

53.1 Prove Theorems 98 and 100. Hint: For Theorem 100, look at the completeness result for SL.

§54. Soundness and Completeness of Kr.

THEOREM 101. (Soundness of Kr.) $\vdash_{Kr}\phi \rightarrow (A)(\phi$ is true in $A)$.

THEOREM 102. (Completeness of Kr.) $(A)(\phi$ is true in $A) \rightarrow \vdash_{Kr}\phi$.

Proof. Suppose $(A)(\phi$ is true in $A)$. Kr is normal by Theorem 96 and Kr is an extension of Kr by Definition 114. Define a function $w: ST_{\Box} \longrightarrow \{0,1\}$ recursively as follows.

1. If $\psi \in AT_{SL}$, let $w(\psi) = 1$.
2. Let $w(\sim\psi) = 1$ if $w(\psi) = 0$ and let $w(\sim\psi) = 0$ otherwise.
3. Let $w(\psi \supset \chi) = 0$ if $w(\psi) = 1$ & $w(\chi) = 0$, and let $w(\psi \supset \chi) = 1$ otherwise.
4. Let $w(\Box\psi) = w(\psi)$.

w is a world. (This can be shown by doing an induction on $ST_{\Box}$.) Let $U = \{w\}$ and let $R = \{<w;w>\}$. $A = <U;R>$ is an RWS. Then by Theorem 101, $\vdash_{Kr}\psi \rightarrow \psi$ is true in A. $w(\sim(<P_1> \supset <P_1>)) = 0$, so $\sim(<P_1> \supset <P_1>)$ is not true in A by Definition 105, $\sim\vdash_{Kr} \sim(<P_1> \supset <P_1>)$, and Kr is consistent. Then A_{Kr} is an RWS by Theorem 99 and ϕ is true in A_{Kr} by our initial assumption. But then $\vdash_{Kr}\phi$ by Theorem 100.

EXERCISES

54.1 Prove Theorem 101.

54.2 Show that the function w defined in the proof of Theorem 102 is a world.

54.3 Show that the structure A defined in the proof of Theorem 102 is an RWS.

54.4* Show that $\sim\vdash_{Kr} \Box<P_1> \supset <P_1>$. You can do this by constructing an RWS $A = <U;R>$ such that $(\exists w)(w \in U$ & $w(\Box<P_1>) = 1$ & $w(<P_1>) = 0)$.

54.5 Show that $\sim\vdash_{Kr} \Box<P_1> \supset \Diamond<P_1>$.

§55. The Modal Logic T.

DEFINITION 124. $AX_T = AX_{Kr} \cup \{\phi: (\exists\psi)(\phi$ is a modal generalization of $\Box\psi \supset \psi)\}$.

DEFINITION 125. $K \vdash_T \phi \leftrightarrow (\exists\sigma)(\sigma$ is an MP-derivation of ϕ from $K \cup AX_T)$.

DEFINITION 126. $T = \langle S_\Box; \emptyset; ST_\Box; AX_T; \vdash_T \rangle$.

THEOREM 103. T is a modal logic.

THEOREM 104. T is a normal extension of Kr.

In fact we know that T is a proper extension of Kr. This follows from Exercise 54.4 and the fact that $\vdash_T \Box\langle P_1\rangle \supset \langle P_1\rangle$.

The new axioms which we add to AX_{Kr} to obtain AX_T seem very plausible, for it is quite reasonable that if ϕ must be the case, then ϕ is the case. One instance where we might not want this, though, is where we interpret $\Box\phi$ as involving some sort of deontic or moral necessity. If we do this we will take $\Box\phi$ to mean that we must see to it that ϕ is true if we are to fulfill all our obligations and we will take $\Diamond\phi$ to mean that we may (or it is possible for us to do this) allow ϕ to become true and still fulfill all of our obligations. We might read '$\Box\phi$' as 'ϕ ought to be the case'. But 'If ϕ ought to be the case, then ϕ is the case' is not logically true; indeed it is all too often not true at all. So an adequate deontic logic or logic of moral concepts will not be an extension of T.

EXERCISES

55.1 Prove Theorems 103 and 104.

55.2 Show each of the following.

a. $\vdash_T \phi \supset \Diamond\phi$.

b. $\vdash_T \Box\phi \supset \Diamond\phi$.

c. $\vdash_T (\Diamond\phi \supset \Diamond\psi) \supset \Diamond(\phi \supset \psi)$.

d. $\vdash_T (\Box\phi \supset \Box\psi) \supset \Diamond(\phi \supset \psi)$.

e. $\vdash_T \Box(\phi \supset \Diamond\phi)$.

§56. Soundness and Completeness of T. We know from Exercise 54.4 that there are RWS's in which some of the axioms of T are not true, so we will obviously not be able to show that a modal sentence is a theorem of T if and only if it is true in every RWS. But we will be able to show that there is a certain class of RWS's such that a modal sentence is a theorem of T if and only if it is true in every RWS in this class. Consider what the extra axioms in T look like. Each of them is a modal generalization of some sentence of the form $\Box\phi \supset \phi$. What restriction could we place on an RWS which would insure that $\Box\phi \supset \phi$ is true in that RWS? Suppose we have an RWS A = $\langle U;R \rangle$ and a world $w \in U$ such that $w(\Box\phi) = 1$. What would insure that $w(\phi) = 1$? We know that since $w(\Box\phi) = 1$, then $w'(\phi)$ = 1 for every $w' \in U$ such that $\langle w;w' \rangle \in R$. So $w(\phi) = 1$ if w is one of those worlds which is accessible from w, i.e., if $\langle w;w \rangle \in R$. This is the very restriction we need.

DEFINITION 127. R_A is reflexive $\leftrightarrow$ $(w)(w \in U_A \rightarrow \langle w;w \rangle \in R_A)$.

THEOREM 105. (Soundness of T.) $\vdash_T \phi \rightarrow (A)(R_A$ is reflexive $\rightarrow \phi$ is true in $A)$.

THEOREM 106. T is consistent.

THEOREM 107. (Completeness of T.) $(A)(R_A$ is reflexive $\rightarrow \phi$ is true in $A) \rightarrow \vdash_T \phi$.

EXERCISES

56.1 Prove Theorems 105-107. Hints: Use Theorem 80 and the proof of Theorem 101 for 105, look at the proof of Theorem 102 for 106, and show that R_T is reflexive for Theorem 107.

56.2 Show that $\sim\vdash_T \Box\langle P_1 \rangle \supset \Box\Box\langle P_1 \rangle$.

§57. The Modal Logic S4.

DEFINITION 128. $AX_{S4} = AX_T \cup \{\phi: (\exists\psi)(\phi$ is a modal generalization of $\Box\psi \supset \Box\Box\psi)\}$.

DEFINITION 129. $K\vdash_{S4}\phi \leftrightarrow (\exists\sigma)(\sigma$ is a MP-derivation of ϕ from $K \cup AX_{S4})$.

DEFINITION 130. $S4 = \langle S_\Box;\emptyset;ST_\Box;AX_{S4};\vdash_{S4}\rangle$.

THEOREM 108. S4 is a modal logic.

THEOREM 109. S4 is a normal extension of both Kr and T.

In fact S4 is a proper extension of both Kr and T.

The intuitive appeal of the new axioms in S4 should be obvious, but once again there may be modal notions for which we do not want $\Box\phi \supset \Box\Box\phi$. Suppose, for example, we have some sort of epistemic necessity in mind. Then we might read '$\Box\phi$' as 'so-and-so knows that ϕ' where so-and-so is some particular person. (Knowledge is admittedly quite a different notion than most notions we would be willing to call necessity, but we could still interpret $L_\Box$ in such a way.) The special axioms of T seem acceptable under this interpretation, for surely it is the case that so-and-so can not know ϕ (although he or she may believe it ever so strongly) unless ϕ is true. But do we want to say that whenever somebody knows something, then he or she knows that he or she knows it? Many philosophers have questioned this and as a result have questioned whether S4 may not be too strong for the logic of knowledge. We might note that we could also have a doxastic interpretation of $L_\Box$ which has us read '$\Box\phi$' as 'so-and-so believes that ϕ'. For doxastic logic we might accept $\Box\phi \supset \Box\Box\phi$ as an axiom, but we would surely reject $\Box\phi \supset \phi$. We begin to see how we might get many variations of the modal logics we are developing when we start interpreting $L_\Box$ in various interesting ways. Besides questioning the characteristic axioms of T and S4, we very likely would not want either an epistemic or a doxastic logic to be normal.

EXERCISES

57.1 Prove Theorems 108 and 109.

57.2* Let $AX_{S4'} = AX_T \cup \{\phi: (\exists\psi)(\exists\chi)(\phi$ is a modal generalization of $\Box(\psi \supset \chi) \supset \Box(\Box\psi \supset \Box\chi))\}$, and define S4' in the usual way. Show that $\vdash_{S4}\phi \leftrightarrow \vdash_{S4'}\phi$. Hint: Use Theorem 82.

57.3 Show each of the following.

a. $\vdash_{S4}\Box\Box\phi \equiv \Box\phi$.

b. $\vdash_{S4}\Diamond\Diamond\phi \equiv \Diamond\phi$.

c. $\vdash_{S4}\Box\phi \supset \Box\Diamond\Box\phi$.

d. $\vdash_{S4}\Diamond\Box\Diamond\phi \supset \Diamond\phi$.

e. $\vdash_{S4}\Box(\phi \supset \psi) \supset \Box(\Box\phi \supset \Box\psi)$.

§58. Soundness and Completeness of S4. To achieve the proper soundness and completeness results for S4, we must restrict the class of RWS's at which we look even further than we did in the case of T.

DEFINITION 131. R_A is transitive $\leftrightarrow$ $(w)(w')(w'')((\langle w;w'\rangle \in R_A \ \& \ \langle w';w''\rangle \in R_A) \rightarrow \langle w;w''\rangle \in R_A)$.

THEOREM 110. (Soundness of S4.) $\vdash_{S4}\phi \rightarrow (A)((R_A$ is reflexive & R_A is transitive) $\rightarrow \phi$ is true in $A)$.

THEOREM 111. S4 is consistent.

THEOREM 112. (Completeness of S4.) $(A)((R_A$ is reflexive & R_A is transitive) $\rightarrow \phi$ is true in $A) \rightarrow \vdash_{S4}\phi$.

EXERCISES

58.1 Prove Theorems 110-112.

58.2 Show that $\sim\vdash_{S4}\Diamond\langle P_1\rangle \supset \Box\Diamond\langle P_1\rangle$.

§59. The Modal Logic S5.

DEFINITION 132. $AX_{S5} = AX_T \cup \{\phi\colon (\exists\psi)(\phi$ is a modal generalization of $\Diamond\psi \supset \Box\Diamond\psi\}$.

DEFINITION 133. $K \vdash_{S5} \phi \leftrightarrow (\exists\sigma)(\sigma$ is an MP-derivation of ϕ from $K \cup AX_{S5})$.

DEFINITION 134. $S5 = \langle S_\Box; \emptyset; ST_\Box; AX_{S5}; \vdash_{S5} \rangle$.

THEOREM 113. S5 is a modal logic.

THEOREM 114. $\vdash_{S5} \Box\phi \supset \Box\Box\phi$.

THEOREM 115. S5 is a normal extension of Kr, T, and S4.

In fact S5 is a proper extension of each of Kr, T, and S4.

One last interpretation of modal logic which we will consider briefly is tense logic. We can think of $\Box$ and $\Diamond$ as being either past tense indicators or future tense indicators. If we think of them as past tense indicators, then we read '$\Box\phi$' as 'It has always been the case that ϕ' and we read '$\Diamond\phi$' as 'It has been the case that ϕ'. Interpreting $L_\Box$ as the language of past tense in this way, we think of worlds as moments of time and the accessibility relation of an RWS becomes the later than relation. For future tense, our accessibility relation is the earlier than relation. So 'It has always been the case that ϕ' is true at moment w just in case ϕ is true at every moment w' such that w is later than w', and 'It has been the case that ϕ' is true at moment w just in case ϕ is true at some moment w' such that w is later than w'. We do not want the special axioms of S5 to hold in a tense logic. For example, ϕ might describe an event which occurred yesterday, so $\Diamond\phi$ is true today. But $\Diamond\phi$ was not true the day before yesterday, so it has not always been the case that $\Diamond\phi$ has been the case, i.e., $\Box\Diamond\phi$ is not true today. The special axioms of S5 do seem attractive, though, for logical and physical necessity. It would seem, for example, that if it is physically possible for

ϕ to be the case, then this possibility must follow from physical law and must therefore be physically necessary.

DEFINITION 135. ϕ is modally closed $\leftrightarrow$ $(n)(\sigma)(\tau)(\phi = \sigma{*}{<}P_n{>}{*}\tau \rightarrow (\exists\sigma')(\exists\sigma'')(\exists\tau')(\exists\tau'')(\exists\psi)(\sigma = \sigma'{*}\sigma'' \;\&\; \tau = \tau'{*}\tau'' \;\&\; \Box\psi = \sigma''{*}{<}P_n{>}{*}\tau'))$.

According to Definition 135, ϕ is modally closed just in case every occurrence of an atomic SL-sentence in ϕ "falls within the scope of" the necessity symbol. We will prove some interesting facts about S5 which involve this notion in the following exercises.

EXERCISES

59.1 Prove Theorems 113-115.

59.2* Show that ϕ is modally closed $\rightarrow \vdash_{S5} \phi \supset \Box\phi$.

59.3 Show that ϕ is modally closed $\rightarrow \vdash_{S5} \Box(\phi \supset \psi) \supset (\phi \supset \Box\psi)$.

59.4 Let $AX_{Br} = AX_T \cup \{\phi\colon (\exists\psi)(\phi$ is a modal generalization of $\psi \supset \Box\Diamond\psi)\}$, and define Br in the usual way. Show that $\vdash_{S5}\phi \leftrightarrow \vdash_{Br}\phi$.

59.5 Show each of the following.

a. $\vdash_{S5} \Diamond\Box\phi \supset \Box\phi$.

b. $\vdash_{S5} {\sim}\Box\phi \supset \Box{\sim}\Box\phi$.

c. $\vdash_{S5} \Box\phi \supset \Box\Box\phi$.

d. $\vdash_{S5} \phi \supset \Box\Diamond\phi$.

e. $\vdash_{S5} (\Diamond\phi \wedge \Diamond\psi) \supset \Diamond((\phi \wedge \Diamond\psi) \vee (\psi \wedge \Diamond\phi))$.

§60. Soundness and Completeness of S5.

DEFINITION 136. R_A is symmetric $\leftrightarrow$ $(w)(w')({<}w;w'{>} \in R_A \rightarrow {<}w';w{>} \in R_A)$.

THEOREM 116. (Soundness of S5.) $\vdash_{S5}\phi \rightarrow (A)((R_A$ is reflexive & R_A is transitive & R_A is symmetric$) \rightarrow \phi$ is true in $A)$.

THEOREM 117. S5 is consistent.

THEOREM 118. (Completeness of S5.) $(\mathcal{A})((R_{\mathcal{A}}$ is reflexive & $R_{\mathcal{A}}$ is transitive & $R_{\mathcal{A}}$ is symmetric$) \rightarrow \phi$ is true in $\mathcal{A}) \rightarrow \vdash_{S5} \phi$.

EXERCISES

60.1 Prove Theorems 116-118.

CHAPTER 5

Conditional Logic

§61. Material and Strict Implication. The goal in developing a conditional logic is to produce a formal system into the language of which we can translate the conditional sentences of ordinary discourse and which adequately captures in its theorems the ways in which we use conditional sentences in our arguments. The goal of a semantics for a formal language of conditionals is to clarify the truth conditions of conditionals and thereby to give at least a partial analysis of the meanings of these kinds of sentences. Of course none of this means anything until we know what conditional sentences are supposed to be. In everyday English conditionals often involve an 'if ...then' construction as in 'If Jones studies hard, then he will not fail' or 'If Jones had not overslept, then he would not have been late for class'. Notice that the verbs in a conditional sentence may be in either the indicative or the subjunctive mood. Notice also that we frequently delete the word 'then' in the 'if...then' construction; we might well shorten our first example to 'If Jones studies hard, he will not fail'. We can also form conditionals by using verbs in the subjunctive mood without using the 'if...then' construction at all, as in 'Had Jones arrived on time, he would have heard the assignment'. It is sentences of these sorts for which we seek a logic and a formal semantics in this chapter.

We have actually seen two different ways in which we may provide a logic for conditionals already. We might translate ordinary conditionals into the language of SL as material implications or we might translate conditionals into the modal language as strict implications. A material implication is an SL-sentence of the form $\phi \supset \psi$ and a strict implication is a modal sentence of the form $\Box(\phi \supset \psi)$. In most introductory symbolic logic texts we are advised to translate conditionals as material implications. We shall see, however, that there are good reasons for rejecting both material and strict implication as adequate formal counterparts for the conditionals of ordinary discourse.

Translating English conditionals as material implications gives rise to the so-called paradoxes of implication. These are represented by the two results $\{\phi\} \vdash_{SL} \psi \supset \phi$ and $\{\sim\phi\} \vdash_{SL} \phi \supset \psi$. If we interpret material implications as ordinary conditionals then these two results tell us that we can infer from the truth of ϕ the truth of 'If ψ, then ϕ', and that we can infer from the falseness of ϕ the truth of 'If ϕ, then ψ'. But both of these results are counterintuitive. Consider the sentence 'The sun rises in the east', which is clearly true. If conditionals could always be interpreted as material implications, then the following sentences would have to be true: 'If the earth revolved in the opposite direction from that in which it actually revolves, then the sun would rise in the east' and 'If the sun didn't rise in the east, then it would rise in the north'. But both of these sentences seem to be false. What this shows is that we can have a false conditional in which the antecedent is false and the consequence is true, and we can have a false conditional in which the antecedent and the consequent are both false. But this doesn't mean that we have simply translated our conditionals into L_{SL} in the wrong way, for we can just as easily find true conditionals with false antecedents. The conditionals of ordinary discourse are not truth-functional. Since SL is sound and complete with respect to a truth-functional interpretation, this means that there is no way we can adequately represent the conditionals of ordinary discourse within the formal language of SL.

In an attempt to resolve the paradoxes of implication, we might insist that there must be some connection between the antecedent and the consequent of a conditional in order for the conditional to be true. It isn't enough that in fact the antecedent of the conditional is false or the consequent of the conditional is true; it must be the case that either the antecedent is false or the consequent is true. This suggests that we should translate ordinary conditionals as strict implications. If we do this, then the only question which remains is that of deciding which modal logic we are to adopt.

This proposal will not work either. In even a weak modal logic like Kr we have such results as $\{\Box(\phi \supset \psi), \Box(\psi \supset \chi)\} \vdash_{Kr} \Box(\phi \supset \chi)$ and $\{\Box(\phi \supset \psi)\} \vdash_{Kr} \Box((\phi \wedge \chi) \supset \psi)$. Where we interpret strict implications as ordinary conditionals these results are unacceptable. Consider the first, for example. Suppose Smith is a person who overworks and as a result is very tense and irritable. Then Smith would be less tense and irritable if she worked less, and Smith would certainly work less if she lost her job. Yet we would surely deny that Smith would be less tense and irritable if she lost her job. Or consider the second result. It is true that a man would be killed if he fell from a plane flying at 10,000 feet, but it is not true that he would be killed if he were wearing a parachute and he fell from a plane flying at 10,000 feet. Because these and other arguments involving conditionals are not acceptable for ordinary conditionals, we can not accept the proposal that such conditionals be interpreted as strict implications.

It sounds as if no conditional should ever be interpreted as either a material or a strict implication, but this is not true. For example, all of the conditionals we have used in proofs in this book should probably be interpreted as either material or strict implications. What we have discovered is that we should not always interpret conditionals in one or the other of these two ways. Most of the conditionals we use in ordinary thought and speech probably should not be interpreted in either of these ways. It is for this reason that we need to develop a new formal system and a new semantics for conditionals.

There is far from total agreement among logicians and philosophers about the exact form that either a conditional logic or a formal semantics for conditionals should take. In fact, it may even turn out that there are several different kinds of conditionals in common use just as there is more than one common notion of necessity. We will develop three different conditional logics in this chapter and provide them all with semantics of one of the more familiar kinds.

EXERCISES

61.1 Find examples of true conditionals which have false antecedents and false consequents, and of true conditionals which have false antecedents and true consequents.

61.2 Can you find examples of false conditionals which have true antecedents and true consequents? Can you find examples of true conditionals which have true antecedents and false consequents?

61.3 Show that $\{\Box(\phi \supset \psi), \Box(\psi \supset \chi)\} \vdash_{Kr} \Box(\phi \supset \chi)$ and that $\{\Box(\phi \supset \psi)\} \vdash_{Kr} \Box((\phi \wedge \chi) \supset \psi)$.

61.4 Find additional counterexamples for the argument forms mentioned in Exercise 61.3, interpreting strict implications as ordinary conditionals.

§62. Conditional (Sentential) Logics and Their Language.

As in the case of modal logic, we will only examine a sentential version of conditional logic. We begin by introducing the constant '$\underline{c}$' into our metalanguage. We read '$\underline{c}$' as 'the conditional symbol' and we assume that the symbol $\underline{c}$ is distinct from any modal symbol and distinct from any sequence of modal symbols.

<u>DEFINITION 137.</u> $S_> = S_{SL} \cup \{\underline{c}\}$.

We call the members of $S_>$ <u>conditional symbols</u>.

<u>DEFINITION 138.</u> σ is a <u>conditional expression</u> $\leftrightarrow$ σ is a finite sequence of conditional symbols.

Where σ and τ are conditional expressions, we have the following definition.

<u>DEFINITION 139.</u> $\sim\sigma = \langle\underline{n}\rangle * \sigma$.

$\sigma \supset \tau = \langle\underline{i}\rangle * \sigma * \tau$.

$\sigma \vee \tau = \sim\sigma \supset \tau$.

$\sigma \wedge \tau = \sim(\sigma \supset \sim\tau)$.

$\sigma \equiv \tau = (\sigma \supset \tau) \wedge (\tau \supset \sigma)$.

$\sigma > \tau = \langle\underline{c}\rangle * \sigma * \tau$.

$\Box\sigma = \sim\sigma > \sigma$.

$\Diamond\sigma = \sim\Box\sim\sigma$.

The definition of '$\Box\phi$' requires some comment. ϕ is necessary just in case ϕ <u>must</u> be the case no matter what else is the case, i.e., if and only if for any ψ we have 'If ψ were the case, then ϕ would be the case'. In particular we have 'If $\sim\phi$ were the case, then ϕ would be the case'. On the other hand, suppose 'If $\sim\phi$ were the case, then ϕ would be the case' were true. Then if $\sim\phi$ were the case, both ϕ and $\sim\phi$ would be the case, which is impossible. Thus $\sim\phi$ could not be the case, i.e., $\sim\phi$ is impossible and hence ϕ is necessary.

<u>DEFINITION 140.</u> σ is a <u>conditional construction</u> $\leftrightarrow$ $(n)(n \leq \ell(\sigma) \rightarrow (\sigma_n \in AT_{SL} \vee (\exists i)(i < n \,\&\, \sigma_n = \sim\sigma_i)$ $(\exists i)(\exists j)(i < n \,\&\, j < n \,\&\, \sigma_n = \sigma_i \supset \sigma_j) \vee (\exists i)(\exists j)(i$

$< n \,\&\, j < n \,\&\, \sigma_n = \sigma_i > \sigma_j)))$.

DEFINITION 141. $ST_> = \{\phi\colon (\exists\sigma)(\sigma$ is a conditional construction $\&\ \sigma_{\ell(\sigma)} = \phi)\}$.

We will use 'ϕ', 'ψ', 'χ', and 'θ' in this chapter as special variables which range over *conditional sentences*, i.e., over the members of $ST_>$. We will use 'K', 'Γ', and 'Δ' as special variables which range over subsets of $ST_>$.

THEOREM 119. (Induction Principle for $ST_>$.) $(AT_{SL} \subseteq A \,\&\, (\phi)(\phi \in A \rightarrow {\sim}\phi \in A) \,\&\, (\phi)(\psi)((\phi \in A \,\&\, \psi \in A) \rightarrow (\phi \supset \psi \in A \,\&\, \phi > \psi \in A))) \rightarrow ST_> \subseteq A$.

DEFINITION 142. $L_> = \langle S_>;\emptyset;ST_>\rangle$.

$L_>$ is an IN-language which we call *the conditional language*.

DEFINITION 143. ϕ is a *conditional generalization* of $\psi \leftrightarrow (\phi = \psi \vee (\exists n)(\exists\chi_1)\ldots(\exists\chi_n)(\exists\sigma)(\sigma$ is an n-place sequence $\&\ (k)(k \leq \ell(\sigma) \rightarrow \sigma_k = \underline{c}) \,\&\, \phi = \sigma{*}\chi_1{*}\ldots{*}\chi_n{*}\psi))$.

We will use the notion of a conditional generalization to define the three conditional logics we will study in much the same way we used the notion of a modal generalization to define the four modal logics discussed in the last chapter. But first we need to say what a conditional logic is in the most general case.

DEFINITION 144. Σ is a *conditional logic* $\leftrightarrow$ (Σ is a logistic system $\&\ L_\Sigma = L_>$).

In this chapter we will use 'Σ', etc., as special variables which range over conditional logics.

EXERCISES

62.1 Prove Theorem 119.

62.2 Rewrite ' ϕ' using only '$\sim$', '$>$', and 'ϕ'.

EXERCISES

63.1 Show that $(A)(w)(w \varepsilon U_A \rightarrow (w(\Box\phi) = 1 \leftrightarrow f_A(\sim\phi,w) =$
.

63.2 Show that $\phi > \phi$ is true in A.

63.3 Show that $(\phi > (\psi \supset \chi)) \supset ((\phi > \psi) \supset (\phi > \chi))$ is
e in A.

63.4 Show that $\phi \supset \psi$ is true in A $\rightarrow$ $\phi > \psi$ is true in A.

63.5 Show that ϕ is true in A $\rightarrow$ $\psi > \phi$ is true in A.

63.6 Show that $\sim\phi$ is true in A $\rightarrow$ $\phi > \psi$ is true in A.

63.7 Show that $(\phi > \sim\phi) \supset (\phi \supset \psi)$ is true in A.

§64. The Very Weak Conditional Logic C. We noted in the ceding section the analogy between modal logics and condinal logics when interpreted in terms of RWS's and FWS's rectively. This analogy gives us some clues concerning the tures of the conditional logic we seek. We should expect h a logic to incorporate in some way counterparts for the oms for modal logic. When the modal logic we start with is weak logic Kr, we get a very weak conditional logic. First see that the axioms of Kr include all modal generalizations modal sentences of certain forms. This suggests that the oms of the logic we seek should include all conditional genlizations of conditional sentences of the appropriate forms. only special axioms of Kr involve distribution of the mooperator over material implications. The corresponding uirement for conditionals involves distribution of any exssion of the form 'ϕ >' over material implications. We l incorporate these suggestions into the conditional logic hich we are about to construct.

There is a special feature of FWS's, however, which we l miss if we only try to mimic Kr in our construction of Notice Definition 146 requires that where <U;f> is an FWS,)(w' ε f(ϕ,w) $\rightarrow$ w'(ϕ) = 1). Put in terms of the sententi-

§63. The Functional World System Interpretation of the Conditional Language. The interpretation of the conditional language which will be developed here uses a modification of the notion of a world which was defined in the last chapter. We will also need a new semantical notion which we shall call a selection function. When we consider whether a conditional is true or false, we consider various ways things might have been in which the antecedent of the conditional would have been true. But we do not usually consider all possible situations in which the antecedent would have been true. We are more selective and we only consider situations which are fairly similar to the way things actually are. For example, if we consider what would have happened if President Kennedy had not been assassinated, we consider situations which are much like the actual situation but in which Kennedy was not assassinated. We would not consider situations in which Kennedy was not assassinated but in which he committed suicide since we think that Kennedy would have had to have been a very different man to have committed suicide. Nevertheless, we could ask ourselves what would have happened if Kennedy had committed suicide. Of course he would not have been assassinated if he had committed suicide, so all the situations which we consider in this latter case will be situations in which Kennedy was not assassinated. Yet the situations we would consider if we were evaluating a conditional with the antecedent 'If Kennedy had not been assassinated' and the situations we would consider if we were evaluating a conditional with the antecedent 'If Kennedy had committed suicide' are totally different and include no common situations. So when we consider what would have happened if Kennedy had not been assassinated, we can't just look at all logically or physically possible situations in which Kennedy was not assassinated since these would include those situations in which he committed suicide. (If we did this, we would in fact be interpreting the conditional as a strict implication and we already have seen that we do not want to interpret conditionals in this way.) We need to restrict the situations at which we look differently in the case of each different antecedent.

Of course the situations we look at when we evaluate a conditional will also depend on the way things actually are. For example, if we consider what would happen if a man were to fall from a certain airplane at a certain time, the result of his falling from the plane will depend on whether the plane is sitting on the runway or is in the air, on whether the man is wearing a parachute (if the plane is in the air), etc. The results will also depend on the physical laws which govern the world. We don't list all of the factors which affect the truth value of our conditionals. Instead we look, in the case of a particular man and a particular set of circumstances, at alternative situations in which the man falls from the plane and which are otherwise reasonably similar to the way things actually are. The situations we look at will therefore be a function both of the antecedent of the conditional and of a world (i.e., of a function which says that some sentences are true and others are not) which serves as a description of the way the world might be.

Many of the important definitions of the last chapter were formulated in terms of the language $L_{\Box}$ and we must now reformulate new but similar definitions in terms of the language $L_{>}$.

DEFINITION 145. w is a c-world $\leftrightarrow$ $(w:ST_{>} \longrightarrow \{0,1\}$ & $(\phi)(\psi)((w(\sim\phi) = 1 \leftrightarrow w(\phi) = 0)$ & $(w(\phi \supset \psi) = 1 \leftrightarrow (w(\phi) = 0 \vee w(\psi) = 1))))$.

DEFINITION 146. $\mathcal{A}$ is a functional world system (FWS) $\leftrightarrow (\exists U)(\exists f)(\mathcal{A} = \langle U;f\rangle$ & $U \neq \emptyset$ & $(w)(w \in U \rightarrow$ w is a c-world) & $f:\{\langle\phi;w\rangle: w \in U\} \longrightarrow Power(U)$ & $(w)(w')(\phi)(w'$

$\in f(\phi,w) \rightarrow w'(\phi) = 1)$ & $(w)(\phi)(\psi)($

$(w')(w' \in f(\phi,w) \rightarrow w'(\psi) = 1)))$.

Where $\mathcal{A} = \langle U;f\rangle$ is an FWS we will often den as $f_{\mathcal{A}}$. An FWS, then, consists of a set of lection function for that set of c-worlds. ther $\phi > \psi$ is true at a c-world w in $U_{\mathcal{A}}$, we true in all c-worlds in $f_{\mathcal{A}}(\phi,w)$. Intuitivel that set of c-worlds in $U_{\mathcal{A}}$ in which ϕ is tru enough like w for our consideration in evalu with ϕ as antecedent if w is the actual worl the capital script letter '$\mathcal{A}$' as a special v over FWS's in the rest of this chapter, and etc., as special variables ranging over c-wo

DEFINITION 147. ϕ is true in $\mathcal{A} \leftrightarrow$ ($= 1)$.

A conditional sentence is true in an FWS if tence is true in every c-world in that FWS.

We can think of an FWS simply as an RWS infinitely many different accessibility rela just one. A selection function in effect pr unique) accessibility relation for each possi To see this, let $\langle U;f\rangle$ be an FWS and let ϕ be sentence. We can define an accessibility rel $\{\langle w;w'\rangle: w' \in f(\phi,w)\}$. Then $w(\phi > \psi) = 1$ if $(w')(\langle w;w'\rangle \in R_{\phi} \rightarrow w'(\psi) = 1)$. This way of l makes the role played by an expression in our the form '$\phi >$' resemble that of an expression when used with regard to a modal logic. We m of a conditional logic as what some logicians sententially indexed modal logic.

ally indexed accessibility relations discussed in the last section, this means that $(w')(\langle w;w'\rangle \in R_{\phi} \rightarrow w'(\phi) = 1)$. We have no similar requirement for RWS's and we should expect to have to do something special to accommodate this feature in our axiomatization of C. The way we accommodate it is by including all conditional generalizations of sentences of the form $\phi > \phi$.

DEFINITION 148. $AX_C = \{\phi: (\exists\psi)(\psi \in BAX_{L_>}$ & ϕ is a conditional generalization of $\psi) \vee (\exists\psi)(\exists\chi)(\exists\theta)(\phi$ is a conditional generalization of either $\psi > \psi$ or $(\psi > (\chi \supset \theta)) \supset ((\psi > \chi) \supset (\psi > \theta)))\}$.

DEFINITION 149. $K\vdash_C\phi \leftrightarrow (\exists\sigma)(\sigma$ is an MP-derivation of ϕ from $K \cup AX_C)$.

DEFINITION 150. $C = \langle L_>;\emptyset;ST_>;AX_C;\vdash_C\rangle$.

THEOREM 120. C is a conditional logic.

THEOREM 121. $\vdash_C\phi \rightarrow \vdash_C\psi > \phi$.

THEOREM 122. $\vdash_C\phi \rightarrow \vdash_C\Box\phi$.

Theorem 122 is an obvious corollary of Theorem 121. Note that a modal logic for which the analog of Theorem 122 holds is called normal. We will define a new notion of c-normality in terms of the condition given in Theorem 121.

DEFINITION 151. Σ is c-normal $\leftrightarrow (\phi)(\psi)(\vdash_C\phi \rightarrow \vdash_C\psi > \phi)$.

No one has suggested that C might be the proper logic for conditionals as we use them in every day thought and speech. It is generally agreed that C is much too weak to serve this purpose. Among other things, C is not closed under substitution of provable equivalents; in particular we do not have $\vdash_C\phi \equiv \psi \rightarrow \vdash_C(\phi > \chi) \equiv (\psi > \chi)$. In subsequent sections we will develop two stronger conditional logics, VW and VC, which show more promise for achieving our goal. Both of these logics will be extensions of our weak logic C.

EXERCISES

64.1 Prove Theorems 120-122. Hint: To prove Theorem 121, let σ be an MP-derivation of ϕ from AX_C and use mathematical induction to show that for each $n \leq \ell(\sigma)$, $\vdash_C \psi > \sigma_n$.

64.2 Show each of the following.

a. $\vdash_C \phi \supset \psi \rightarrow \vdash_C \phi > \psi$.

b. $\vdash_C (\phi > \sim\phi) \supset (\phi > \psi)$.

c. $\vdash_C \phi \supset \psi \rightarrow \vdash_C (\chi > \phi) \supset (\chi > \psi)$.

d. $(\vdash_C \phi > \psi_1 \ \& \ \ldots \ \& \vdash_C \phi > \psi_n) \rightarrow \vdash_C \phi > (\psi_1 \wedge \ldots \wedge \psi_n)$.

§65. Canonical Functional World Systems. In this section we will show that for every consistent, c-normal extension Σ of C, there is some FWS A_Σ such that $(\phi)(\vdash_\Sigma \phi \leftrightarrow \phi$ is true in $A_\Sigma)$.

DEFINITION 152. K is maximally Σ-consistent $\rightarrow$ $(w_K = f \leftrightarrow (f{:}ST_> \longrightarrow \{0,1\} \ \& \ (\phi)(f(\phi) = 1 \leftrightarrow \phi \in K)))$.

THEOREM 123. K is maximally Σ-consistent $\rightarrow$ w_K is a c-world.

DEFINITION 153. $U_A = \{w_K$: K is maximally Σ-consistent$\}$.

DEFINITION 154. $f_A = \{<<\phi;w_K>;\Delta>: \Delta \cup \{w_K\} \subseteq U_A \ \& \ (w_\Gamma)(w_\Gamma \in \Delta \rightarrow \{\psi: \phi > \psi \in K\} \subseteq \Gamma)\}$.

DEFINITION 155. $A_\Sigma = <U_A;f_A>$.

THEOREM 124. Σ is a consistent, c-normal extension of C $\rightarrow$ A_Σ is an FWS.

Proof. Suppose Σ is a consistent, c-normal extension of C. Then AX_Σ is Σ-consistent by Definitions 112 and 144, and we can let K be maximally Σ-consistent such that $AX_\Sigma \subseteq K$. Then $w_K \in U_\Sigma \ \& \ U_\Sigma \neq \emptyset$. By Theorem 123, $(w_K)(w_K \in U_\Sigma \rightarrow w_K$ is a c-world).

Let $w_K \in U_\Sigma \ \& \ w_\Gamma \in U_\Sigma$ such that $w_\Gamma \in f_\Sigma(\phi,w_K)$. $\phi > \phi \in K$ by Theorems 92 and 77 and Definition 148. But then $\phi \in \Gamma$ by Definition 154 and $w_\Gamma(\phi) = 1$ by Definition 152. So $f_\Sigma{:}\{<\psi;w_K>:$

$w_K \in U_\Sigma\} \longrightarrow \text{Power}(U_\Sigma)$ & $(w_\Gamma)(w_\Gamma \in U_\Sigma \rightarrow w_\Gamma(\phi) = 1)$.

Let $w_\Gamma \in f_\Sigma(\phi, w_K)$ and suppose $w_K(\phi > \psi) = 1$. Then $\phi > \psi \in K$ by Definition 152, $\psi \in \Gamma$ by Definition 154, and $w_\Gamma(\psi) = 1$ by Definition 152. Next suppose $(w_\Gamma)(w_\Gamma \in f_\Sigma(\phi, w_K) \rightarrow w_\Gamma(\psi) = 1)$. Then $(w_\Gamma)(w_\Gamma \in f_\Sigma(\phi, w_K) \rightarrow \psi \in \Gamma)$ by Definition 152, and $(\Gamma)((\Gamma$ is maximally Σ-consistent & $\{\chi: \phi > \chi \in K\} \subseteq \Gamma) \rightarrow \psi \in \Gamma)$ by Definition 154. But then $\sim(\exists\Gamma)(\Gamma$ is maximally Σ-consistent & $\{\chi: \phi > \chi \in K\} \cup \{\sim\psi\} \subseteq \Gamma)$, and $\{\chi: \phi > \chi \in K\} \cup \{\sim\psi\}$ is not Σ-consistent by Theorem 94. So $\{\chi: \phi > \chi \in K\} \vdash_\Sigma \psi$ by Theorem 86 and Definition 144. By Theorem 80 we can pick $\{\chi_1, \ldots, \chi_n\} \subseteq \{\chi: \phi > \chi \in K\}$ such that $\{\chi_1, \ldots, \chi_n\} \vdash_\Sigma \psi$, and $\vdash_\Sigma (\chi_1 \wedge \ldots \wedge \chi_n) \supset \psi$ by the Deduction Theorem (and other obvious results). Since Σ is c-normal, $\vdash_\Sigma \phi > ((\chi_1 \wedge \ldots \wedge \chi_n) \supset \psi)$. But $\vdash_\Sigma (\phi > ((\chi_1 \wedge \ldots \wedge \chi_n) \supset \psi)) \supset ((\phi > (\chi_1 \wedge \ldots \wedge \chi_n)) \supset (\phi > \psi))$ by Definition 148, and $\vdash_\Sigma (\phi > (\chi_1 \wedge \ldots \wedge \chi_n)) \supset (\phi > \psi)$ by Theorem 78, so $K \vdash_\Sigma (\phi > (\chi_1 \wedge \ldots \wedge \chi_n)) \supset (\phi > \psi)$ by Theorem 81. $\{\phi > \chi_1, \ldots, \phi > \chi_n\} \vdash_\Sigma \phi > (\chi_1 \wedge \ldots \wedge \chi_n)$ by Exercise 64.2.d and the Deduction Theorem (since Σ is an extension of C), and $\{\phi > \chi_1, \ldots, \phi > \chi_n\} \subseteq K$, so $K \vdash_\Sigma \phi > (\chi_1 \wedge \ldots \wedge \chi_n)$ by Theorem 79. Thus $K \vdash_\Sigma \phi > \psi$ by Theorem 78, $\phi > \psi \in K$ by Theorem 90, and $w_K(\phi > \psi) = 1$ by Definition 152. So $w_K(\phi > \psi) = 1 \leftrightarrow (w_\Gamma)(w_\Gamma \in f_\Sigma(\phi, w_K) \rightarrow w_\Gamma(\psi) = 1)$.

So by Definition 146, A_Σ is an FWS.

We call A_Σ the <u>canonical functional world system for</u> Σ.

<u>THEOREM 125.</u> Σ is a consistent, c-normal extension of C $\rightarrow$ ($\vdash_\Sigma \phi \leftrightarrow \phi$ is true in A_Σ).

Again we use techniques which we have used before. Our definitions of canonical relational world systems and canonical functional world systems are very similar, as are the results concerning each and the proofs of those results. We do not always have to develop new techniques to explore new formal systems we devise. We can often adapt old techniques.

EXERCISES

65.1 Prove Theorems 123 and 125.

§66. Soundness and Completeness of C.

THEOREM 126. (Soundness of C.) $\vdash_C \phi \rightarrow (A)(\phi$ is true in $A)$.

THEOREM 127. C is consistent.

THEOREM 128. (Completeness of C.) $(A)(\phi$ is true in $A) \rightarrow \vdash_C \phi$.

EXERCISES

66.1 Prove Theorems 126-128.

66.2 Show that $\sim\vdash_C (<P_1> \, > \, <P_2>) \equiv (\sim\sim<P_1> \, > \, <P_2>)$. Hint: Construct an FWS A such that $(<P_1> \, > \, <P_2>) \equiv (\sim\sim<P_1> \, > \, <P_2>)$ is not true in A. Since $\vdash_C <P_1> \equiv \sim\sim<P_1>$, this shows that C is not closed under substitution of provable equivalents.

66.3* Show that $\sim\vdash_C (<P_1> \, > \, <P_2>) \supset (<P_1> \supset <P_2>)$.

§67. The Conditional Logic VW. One logic which has been proposed as a serious candidate for the logic of ordinary conditionals is the formal system VW defined in David Lewis's *Counterfactuals*. (See the Select Bibliography.) Lewis also developed the system VC which we will consider in later sections. Lewis's axiomatizations of these two systems is quite different from the sort of axiomatizations we have been providing so far. In particular Lewis defines a derivation in his systems in terms not only of *modus ponens* but also in terms of a rule which he calls *deduction within conditionals*. The two logics to be defined here and to be called VW and VC will have exactly the same *theorems* and *derivability relations* as do the two systems Lewis defines, but the axioms and the

derivations will be defined differently from the way Lewis defines them. We depart from Lewis's development in order to maintain the similarity of structure we have already seen between the various axiomatizations of formal systems we have studied so far.

DEFINITION 156. $AX_{VW} = AX_C \cup \{\phi: (\exists\psi)(\exists\chi)(\exists\theta)(\phi$ is a conditional generalization of one of the following:

C1. $(\psi > \chi) \supset (\psi \supset \chi)$;

C2. $\Box\psi \supset (\chi > \psi)$;

C3. $(\psi > \chi) \supset (\sim(\psi > \sim\theta) \supset ((\psi \wedge \theta) > \chi))$;

C4. $((\psi \wedge \chi) > \theta) \supset (\psi > (\chi \supset \theta))$;

C5. $((\psi > \chi) \wedge (\chi > \psi)) \supset ((\psi > \theta) \equiv (\chi > \theta)))\}$.

Each of these axiom schemata has certain intuitive appeal, yet a couple of them have been questioned. C3 and C5 in particular have been rejected by some philosophers who think they may be too strong to be included in a logic which is supposed to represent the logical structure of conditionals as we ordinarily understand them. For discussions of the merits of these and other possible axioms, the reader should consult some of the works listed in the Select Bibliography. While both weaker and stronger systems have been suggested, most of the formal systems which have been proposed for conditionals have come very close to the system VW. We will consider one stronger system, VC, beginning in Section 69.

DEFINITION 157. $K \vdash_{VW} \phi \leftrightarrow (\exists\sigma)(\sigma$ is an MP-derivation of ϕ from $K \cup AX_{VW})$.

DEFINITION 158. $VW = \langle S_>; \emptyset; ST_>; AX_{VW}; \vdash_{VW}\rangle$.

THEOREM 129. VW is a conditional logic.

THEOREM 130. VW is a c-normal extension of C.

EXERCISES

67.1 Prove Theorems 129 and 130.

67.2 Show that (Σ is a c-normal extension of VW & $\vdash_{\Sigma}\phi \equiv \phi'$) → (σ)(τ)((σ is a conditional expression & τ is a conditional expression & $\psi = \sigma*\phi*\tau$) → ($\sigma*\phi'*\tau \in ST_{>}$ & $\vdash_{\Sigma}\psi \equiv \sigma*\phi'*\tau$)). Thus every c-normal extension of VW is closed under substitution of provable equivalents.

67.3 Show each of the following.

a. $\vdash_{VW} \Diamond\phi \equiv \sim(\phi > \sim\phi)$.

b. $\vdash_{VW} \Diamond\phi \supset ((\phi > \psi) \supset \sim(\phi > \sim\psi))$.

c. $\vdash_{VW} (\phi > \psi) \supset (\Diamond\phi \supset \Diamond\psi)$.

d. $\vdash_{VW} ((\phi > \psi) \wedge (\chi > \psi)) \supset ((\phi \vee \chi) > \psi)$.

e. $\vdash_{VW} ((\phi \wedge \psi) > \chi) \supset ((\phi > \psi) \supset (\phi > \chi))$.

f. $\vdash_{VW} \Box(\phi \supset \psi) \supset (\Box\phi \supset \Box\psi)$.

g. $\vdash_{VW} \Box\phi \supset \phi$.

h. $\vdash_{VW} \Box(\phi \equiv \psi) \supset ((\phi > \chi) \equiv (\psi > \chi))$.

§68. Soundness and Completeness of VW. We must further restrict our selection functions before we can provide a soundness result for VW.

DEFINITION 159. f_A is regulated ↔ (f_A satisfies the following four conditions:

1. $(w)(\phi)((w \in U_A \ \&\ w(\phi) = 1) \rightarrow w \in f_A(\phi,w))$;

2. $(w)(\phi)(\psi)(f_A(\phi,w) = \emptyset \rightarrow (w')(w' \in f_A(\psi,w) \rightarrow w'(\phi) = 0))$;

3. $(w)(\phi)(\psi)((\exists w')(w' \in f_A(\phi,w) \ \&\ w'(\psi) = 1) \rightarrow f_A(\phi \wedge \psi,w) \subseteq f_A(\phi,w))$;

4. $(w)(\phi)(\psi)(((w')(w' \in f_A(\phi,w) \rightarrow w'(\psi) = 1) \ \&\ (w')(w' \in f_A(\psi,w) \rightarrow w'(\phi) = 1)) \rightarrow f_A(\phi,w) = f_A(\psi,w)))$.

Let's consider the informal import of the four conditions which define a regulated selection function. Remember that a selection function picks out for φ and w the set of c-worlds which we should consider in evaluating conditionals with φ as antecedent, provided that w accurately describes the world. When φ is true, then we should certainly consider what actually happens in deciding whether a conditional with ϕ as antecedent is true. This is what the first condition in Definition 159 says. Now suppose that there just aren't _any_ situations which we think are reasonable enough to even _consider_ in which ϕ is true. This might be the case if ϕ were physically impossible, and would certainly be the case if ϕ were logically impossible. In this case our selection function will pick out $\emptyset$ for ϕ and w. But then what about conditionals with ψ as antecedent? Would we be willing to consider any situation in which ϕ is true in evaluating these? The answer must be that we would not, and this is what the second condition in Definition 159 says. Next suppose some of the situations we consider in evaluating conditionals with ϕ as antecedent are situations in which ψ is also true. It seems that these would be the situations which we should consider in evaluating conditionals which have the conjunction of ϕ and ψ as antecedent. After all, they were reasonable enough to consider when we evaluated conditionals with ϕ as antecedent, and they are situations in which $\phi \wedge \psi$ is true. If there were any other situations which we should consider in evaluating conditionals with $\phi \wedge \psi$ as antecedent, then it seems that these should also have been reasonable enough to consider when we evaluated conditionals with ϕ as antecedent. This gives us our third condition. Finally, suppose every situation we consider in evaluating a conditional with ϕ as antecedent is a situation in which ψ is true, and _vice versa_. It seems reasonable to suppose that in a case like this we should look at exactly the same situations in evaluating conditionals with ϕ as antecedent as we do when we evaluate a conditional with ψ as antecedent, and this is what the fourth condition requires.

THEOREM 131. (Soundness of VW.) $\vdash_{VW}\phi \rightarrow (A)(f_A$ is regulated $\rightarrow \phi$ is true in A).

THEOREM 132. VW is consistent.

THEOREM 133. (Completeness of VW.) $(A)(f_A$ is regulated $\rightarrow \phi$ is true in $A) \rightarrow \vdash_{VW}\phi$.

EXERCISES

68.1 Prove Theorems 131-133.

68.2 Show that $\sim\vdash_{VW}(\langle P_1\rangle \wedge \langle P_2\rangle) \supset (\langle P_1\rangle > \langle P_2\rangle)$.

68.3 Let $R_A = \{\langle w;w'\rangle : (\exists\phi)(w' \in f_A(\phi,w))\}$. Show that $(w)(w \in U_A \rightarrow (w(\Box\phi) = 1 \leftrightarrow (w')(\langle w;w'\rangle \in R_A \rightarrow w'(\phi) = 1)))$. Thus for every regulated FWS A we can define an "RWS" $\langle U_A;R_A\rangle$ which we can use to interpret the "modal" sentences in $L_>$. Look at Theorem 122 and Exercises 67.8 and 67.9. What can we conclude concerning the "modal" logic contained in VW?

68.4 Show that VW $\neq$ C.

§69. The Conditional Logic VC.

DEFINITION 160. $AX_{VC} = AX_{VW} \cup \{\phi: (\exists\psi)(\exists\chi)(\phi$ is a conditional generalization of $(\psi \wedge \chi) \supset (\psi > \chi))\}$.

DEFINITION 161. $K\vdash_{VC}\phi \leftrightarrow (\exists\sigma)(\sigma$ is an MP-derivation of ϕ from $K \cup AX_{VC})$.

DEFINITION 162. $VC = \langle S_>;\emptyset;ST_>;AX_{VC};\vdash_{VC}\rangle$.

THEOREM 134. VC is a conditional logic.

THEOREM 135. VC is a c-normal extension of both C and VW.

In fact VC is a proper extension of each of C and VW by Exercise 68.2.

The special axioms of VC are perhaps even more controversial than are the special axioms of VW. At least, more people seem to have proposed that they are not acceptable as part of an analysis of ordinary language conditionals. A putative counterexample would be 'If dogs were fish or mammals, then they would nurse their young'. Both the antecedent and the consequent of this conditional are true, and yet we are very hesitant to accept the conditional itself.

Part of the appeal of the special axioms of VC must be that if the consequent of a conditional is true, and if the antecedent wouldn't make it false, then the conditional must be true. We add to this the observation that if the antecedent and the consequent are both true, then the antecedent obviously didn't make the consequent false. However, even when both antecedent and consequent are true, if the antecedent poses a kind of situation which very well could make the consequent false, then we tend to reject the conditional. This is what we find in apparent counterexamples to these axioms.

Putative counterexamples to the special axioms of VC usually involve conditionals in the subjunctive mood. These axioms may be quite acceptable for conditionals in the indicative mood. For example, 'If dogs are fish or mammals, then they nurse their young' doesn't sound nearly so odd or counterintuitive as does our earlier example. We may need to adopt different logics for subjunctive conditionals and indicative conditionals.

We can even more clearly see the difference between subjunctive conditionals and indicative conditionals when we consider examples like 'If Shakespeare hadn't written Hamlet, someone else would have' and 'If Shakespeare didn't write Hamlet, someone else did'. We can probably all agree that the first of these conditionals is false while the second is true.

EXERCISES

69.1 Prove Theorems 134 and 135.

69.2 Try to devise some additional apparent counterexamples for the special axioms of VC. Can you find a persuasive counterexample in the indicative mood?

69.3 Show each of the following.

a. $\vdash_{VC} \phi \supset ((\phi \supset \psi) \equiv (\phi > \psi))$.

b. $\vdash_{VC} \phi \supset ((\phi > \psi) \vee (\phi > {\sim}\psi))$.

c. $\vdash_{VC} (\phi \wedge \psi) \supset ((\phi > \chi) \equiv (\psi > \chi))$.

§70. Soundness and Completeness of VC. We noted in Section 68 that if ϕ is actually true, then the way things actually are is one of the situations we will want to consider in evaluating conditionals with ϕ as antecedent. This is reflected in our axiomatization of the conditional logic VW by the inclusion of all conditional generalizations of sentences of the form $(\phi > \psi) \supset (\phi \supset \psi)$. Now the conditional logic VC implicitly suggests that we restrict our attention in evaluating conditionals with true antecedents even further. In effect, the special axioms of VC tell us that if the antecedent of a conditional is true, then the only situation we have to consider in evaluating that conditional is the actual situation.

DEFINITION 163. f_A is centered $\leftrightarrow (w)(\phi)(w(\phi) = 1 \rightarrow f_A(\phi,w) = \{w\})$.

THEOREM 136. (Soundness of VC.) $\vdash_{VC} \phi \rightarrow (A)((f_A$ is regulated & f_A is centered) $\rightarrow \phi$ is true in A).

THEOREM 137. VC is consistent.

THEOREM 138. (Completeness of VC.) $(A)((f_A$ is regulated & f_A is centered) $\rightarrow \phi$ is true in $A) \rightarrow \vdash_{VC} \phi$.

Since VC is an extension of both C and VW, we see from Exercises 70.2-70.5 below that we can use any of the three conditional logics we have developed in this chapter to represent the conditionals we use in our ordinary conversation without committing ourselves to the paradoxes of implication or the other difficulties which were mentioned in the opening section of this chapter. To this extent at least, any of these conditional logics provides a way of representing ordinary language conditionals which is superior to either material implication or strict implication. But the exact formulation of an adequate conditional logic remains an open question. No conditional logic has yet gained general acceptance. This is but one illustration of the character of axiomatization and formal semantics as a continuing philosophical and linguistic endeavor rather than as a static, sanctified body of theory.

EXERCISES

70.1 Prove Theorems 136-138.

70.2 Show that $\sim(\{\phi\} \vdash_{VC} \psi > \phi)$.

70.3 Show that $\sim(\{\sim\phi\} \vdash_{VC} \phi > \psi)$.

70.4 Show that $\sim(\{\phi > \psi, \psi > \chi\} \vdash_{VC} \phi > \chi)$.

70.5 Show that $\sim(\{\phi > \psi\} \vdash_{VC} (\phi \wedge \chi) > \psi)$.

Answers to Starred Exercise Items

4.2 $(x)(y)((x \varepsilon N \,\&\, y \varepsilon N) \rightarrow (x + (y + 1) = (x + y) = 1))$.

4.3 Eliminating the special variable, we write $A \neq \emptyset \rightarrow (\exists x)$ $x \varepsilon A$ as y is a set $\rightarrow (y \neq \emptyset \supset (\exists x)x \varepsilon y)$. Suppose y is a set $\&\ y \neq \emptyset$. Then $(\exists x)x \varepsilon y \vee y = \emptyset$ by Definition 1, and $(\exists x)x \varepsilon y$ by disjunctive syllogism.

5.1 According to Definition 2, $(x)(y)(\{x\} = y \leftrightarrow (z)(z \varepsilon y \leftrightarrow z = x))$. By instantiation we have $\{x\} = \{x\} \leftrightarrow (z)(z \varepsilon \{x\} \leftrightarrow z = x)$. Since $\{x\} = \{x\}$, $(z)(z \varepsilon \{x\} \leftrightarrow z = x)$. Instantiating once again, $y \varepsilon \{x\} \leftrightarrow y = x$.

5.3 Suppose $\{x\} = \{y\}$. Then $x \varepsilon \{x\} \leftrightarrow x \varepsilon \{y\}$. $x \varepsilon \{x\}$ by Exercise 5.2, so $x \varepsilon \{y\}$. $x \varepsilon \{y\} \leftrightarrow x = y$ by Exercise 5.1, so $x = y$. Thus $\{x\} = \{y\} \rightarrow x = y$.

6.3 $w \varepsilon \{x,y,x\} \leftrightarrow w \varepsilon \{x,y\} \cup \{x\}$ by Definition 4, $w \varepsilon \{x,y\} \cup \{x\} \leftrightarrow (w \varepsilon \{x,y\} \vee w \varepsilon \{x\})$ by Exercise 6.1, $(w \varepsilon \{x,y\} \vee w \varepsilon \{x\}) \leftrightarrow (w \varepsilon \{x\} \cup \{y\} \vee w \varepsilon \{x\})$ by Definition 4, $(w \varepsilon \{x\} \cup \{y\} \vee w \varepsilon \{x\}) \leftrightarrow (w \varepsilon \{x\} \vee w \varepsilon \{y\} \vee w \varepsilon \{x\})$ by Exercise 6.1, $(w \varepsilon \{x\} \vee w \varepsilon \{y\} \vee w \varepsilon \{x\}) \leftrightarrow (w \varepsilon \{x\} \vee w \varepsilon \{y\})$, $(w \varepsilon \{x\} \vee w \varepsilon \{y\}) \leftrightarrow w \varepsilon \{x\} \cup \{y\}$ by Exercise 6.1, and $w \varepsilon \{x\} \cup \{y\} \leftrightarrow w \varepsilon \{x,y\}$ by Definition 4. So by the Extensionality Axiom, $\{x,y,z\} = \{x,y\}$.

8.8 Suppose $A \subseteq B$. $(x)(x \in A \rightarrow x \in B)$ by Definition 5. If $x \in A \cap B$, then $x \in A$ by Exercise 8.1; so $x \in A \cap B \rightarrow x \in A$. If $x \in A$, then $x \in B$ since $x \in A \rightarrow x \in B$, $x \in A \,\&\, x \in B$, and $x \in A \cap B$ by Exercise 8.1. So $x \in A \rightarrow x \in A \cap B$. Then by the Extensionality Axiom, $A \cap B = A$. So $A \subseteq B \rightarrow A \cap B = A$.

9.1 We will do an indirect proof. Suppose $\{x\colon x \notin x\} \neq \emptyset$. By Definitional Schema 9, $\{x\colon x \notin x\} = \{x\colon x \notin x\} \leftrightarrow (((y)(y \in \{x\colon x \notin x\} \leftrightarrow y \notin y) \,\&\, \{x\colon x \notin x\}$ is a set) $\vee$ $(\{x\colon x \notin x\} = \emptyset \,\&\, {\sim}(\exists A)\,(y)(y \in A \leftrightarrow y \notin y)))$. But $\{x\colon x \notin x\} = \{x\colon x \notin x\}$, and we have assumed that $\{x\colon x \notin x\} \neq \emptyset$, so $(y)(y \in \{x\colon x \notin x\} \leftrightarrow y \notin y) \,\&\, \{x\colon x \notin x\}$ is a set. Instantiating the first conjunct, we have $\{x\colon x \notin x\} \in \{x\colon x \notin x\} \leftrightarrow \{x\colon x \notin x\} \notin \{x\colon x \notin x\}$, which is a contradiction. So after all, $\{x\colon x \notin x\} = \emptyset$.

10.1 Suppose $\langle w,x\rangle = \langle y,z\rangle$. $\{w\} \in \{\{w\}\}$ and $\{w,x\} \in \{\{w,x\}\}$ by Exercise 5.2, $\{w\} \in \{\{w\}\} \vee \{w\} \in \{\{w,x\}\}$ and $\{w,x\} \in \{\{w\}\} \vee \{w,x\} \in \{\{w,x\}\}$, $\{w\} \in \{\{w\}\} \cup \{\{w,x\}\}$ and $\{w,x\} \in \{\{w\}\} \cup \{\{w,x\}\}$ by Exercise 6.1, $\{w\} \in \langle w,x\rangle$ and $\{w,x\} \in \langle w,x\rangle$ by Definitions 4 and 10, $\{w\} \in \langle y,z\rangle$ and $\{w,x\} \in \langle y,z\rangle$ since $\langle w,x\rangle = \langle y,z\rangle$, $\{w\} \in \{\{y\}\} \cup \{\{y,z\}\}$ and $\{w,x\} \in \{\{y\}\} \cup \{\{y,z\}\}$ by Definitions 10 and 4, and $\{w\} \in \{\{y\}\} \vee \{w\} \in \{\{y,z\}\}$ and $\{w,x\} \in \{\{y\}\} \vee \{w,x\} \in \{\{y,z\}\}$ by Exercise 6.1. If $\{w\} \in \{\{y\}\}$, then $\{w\} = \{y\}$ by Exercise 5.1, and $w = y$ by Exercise 5.3. If $\{w\} \in \{\{y,z\}\}$, then $\{w\} = \{y,z\}$ by Exercise 5.1, $\{w\} = \{y\} \cup \{z\}$ by Definition 4, $y \in \{w\} \leftrightarrow (y \in \{y\} \vee y \in \{z\})$ by Definition 3, $y \in \{w\}$ since $y \in \{y\}$ by Exercise 5.2, and $w = y$ by Exercise 5.1. So whether $\{w\} \in \{\{y\}\}$ or $\{w\} \in \{\{y,z\}\}$, $w = y$. We leave it to the reader to show that $x = z$.

13.2 Basis step. $3(3^1 - 1)/2 = 3(2)/2 = 6/2 = 3$.

Induction step. Suppose $k > 1$ & $(n)(n < k \rightarrow (3 + 3^2 + \ldots + 3^n) = 3(3^n - 1)/2)$. Then $3 + 3^2 + \ldots + 3^{k-1} = 3(3^{k-1} - 1)/2$. Adding 3^k to both sides we have $3 + 3^2 + \ldots + 3^{k-1} + 3^k = 3(3^{k-1} - 1)/2 + 3^k$. But $3(3^{k-1} - 1)/2 + 3^k = 3(3^{k-1} - 1)/2 + 2(3^k)/2 = (3(3^{k-1} - 1) + 2(3^k))/2 = (3(3^{k-1} - 1) + 3(2(3^{k-1})))/2 = 3(3^{k-1} - 1 + 2(3^{k-1}))/2 = 3(3(3^{k-1}) - 1)/2 = 3(3^k - 1)/2$. So $(n)(n < k \rightarrow (3 + 3^2 + \ldots + 3^n) = 3(3^n - 1)/2) \rightarrow 3 + 3^2 + \ldots + 3^k = 3(3^k - 1)/2$.

Then by mathematical induction, $(n)(3 + 3^2 + \ldots + 3^n = 3(3^n - 1)/2)$.

16.3 $D'(\emptyset) = \{<1>\}$ & $D'(\{<2>\}) = \{<2>\}$; so $\emptyset \subseteq \{<2>\}$ but $\sim(D'(\emptyset) \subseteq D'(\{<2>\}))$. Therefore $<S;T;F;A;D'>$ violates condition 3.c of Definition 29 and is not a formal system.

18.3 This is not an SL-expression because P_1 is not an SL-expression. We know P_1 is not an SL-expression because of our distinctness assumption that no sentence letter is a sequence of SL-symbols.

19.2 $<\underline{i},\underline{n},\underline{i},P_1,P_2,\underline{i},P_3,\underline{n},P_4,\underline{n}> \notin ST_{SL}$ because the last member of an SL-sentence can never be $\underline{n}$. To show this, let σ be an SL-construction and use mathematical induction to show that $(n)(n \leq \ell(\sigma) \rightarrow (\sigma_n)_{\ell(\sigma_n)} \neq \underline{n})$.

20.4 Let $K = \{\phi: (\sigma)(\phi * \sigma \in ST_{SL} \rightarrow \sigma = \emptyset)\}$. We shall use mathematical induction on the length of ϕ to show that $ST_{SL} \subseteq K$. This is a different technique from that of using Theorem 1.

Basis step. Suppose $\ell(\phi) = 1$ & $\phi * \sigma \in ST_{SL}$. Then $\phi = <P_k>$ for some $k \in N$, and $<P_k> * \sigma \in AT_{SL} \vee P_k = \underline{n} \vee P_k = \underline{i}$ by Exercise 20.2. But $P_k \neq \underline{n}$ & $P_k \neq \underline{i}$ by our distinctness assumptions, so $<P_k> * \sigma \in AT_{SL}$ and $\sigma = \emptyset$.

Induction step. Let $k > 1$ and suppose $(\phi)((\ell(\phi) < k$ & $\phi * \sigma \in ST_{SL}) \rightarrow \sigma = \emptyset)$. Suppose $\ell(\phi) = k$ & $\phi * \sigma \in ST_{SL}$. Since

$k > 1$, $\phi \notin AT_{SL}$. Therefore $(\exists\psi)(\phi = {\sim}\psi) \vee (\exists\psi)(\exists\chi)(\phi = \psi \supset \chi)$.

Case 1. $\phi = {\sim}\psi$. Then ${\sim}\psi{*}\sigma \in ST_{SL}$; but ${\sim}\psi{*}\sigma = \langle\underline{n}\rangle{*}\psi{*}\sigma = {\sim}(\psi{*}\sigma)$, so $\psi{*}\sigma \in ST_{SL}$. Then since $\ell(\psi) < \ell(\phi) = k$, $\sigma = \emptyset$ by our inductive hypothesis.

Case 2. $\phi = \psi \supset \chi$. Then $(\psi \supset \chi){*}\sigma \in ST_{SL}$; but $(\psi \supset \chi){*}\sigma = \langle\underline{i}\rangle{*}\psi{*}\chi{*}\sigma$, so there exists ρ and π such that $\rho \in ST_{SL}$ and $\pi \in ST_{SL}$ and $(\psi \supset \chi){*}\sigma = \rho \supset \pi = \langle\underline{i}\rangle{*}\rho{*}\pi$. Either $\ell(\rho) \leq \ell(\psi)$ or $\ell(\psi) < \ell(\rho)$.

Case 2a. $\ell(\rho) \leq \ell(\psi)$. Then $\rho = \langle\psi_1;\ldots;\psi_{\ell(\rho)}\rangle$. Since $\rho{*}\langle\psi_{\ell(\rho)+1};\ldots;\psi_{\ell(\psi)}\rangle = \psi$ and $\ell(\psi) < \ell(\phi) = k$, $\langle\psi_{\ell(\rho)+1};\ldots;\psi_{\ell(\psi)}\rangle = \emptyset$ by our inductive hypothesis and $\ell(\psi) = \ell(\rho)$. But then $\chi{*}\sigma = \pi$, $\ell(\chi) < \ell(\phi) = k$, and $\sigma = \emptyset$ by our inductive hypothesis.

Case 2b. $\ell(\psi) < \ell(\rho)$. Then $\rho = \psi{*}\langle(\chi{*}\sigma)_1;\ldots;(\chi{*}\sigma)_{\ell(\rho) - \ell(\psi)}\rangle \in ST_{SL}$, $\ell(\psi) < \ell(\phi) = k$, and $\langle(\chi{*}\sigma)_1;\ldots;(\chi{*}\sigma)_{\ell(\rho) - \ell(\psi)}\rangle = \emptyset$. So $\ell(\rho) = \ell(\psi)$ contradicting our assumption, and this case is impossible.

Therefore in case 2a, which is the only case possible, $\sigma = \emptyset$.

Then by mathematical induction, $(n)((\ell(\phi) = n \,\&\, \phi{*}\sigma \in ST_{SL}) \to \sigma = \emptyset)$. But $(\phi)(\exists n)(\ell(\phi) = n)$, so $ST_{SL} \subseteq K$.

20.5 Let $K = \{\phi\colon \sigma{*}\langle\underline{i}\rangle{*}\tau = \phi \to (\exists\psi)(\exists\chi)(\exists\rho)(\tau = \psi{*}\chi{*}\rho)\}$.

Basis step. $\sigma{*}\langle\underline{i}\rangle{*}\tau \in AT_{SL}$. This is impossible, so $\sigma{*}\langle\underline{i}\rangle{*}\tau \in AT_{SL} \to (\exists\psi)(\exists\chi)(\exists\rho)(\tau = \psi{*}\chi{*}\rho)$ is vacuously true and $AT_{SL} \subseteq K$.

Induction step. Suppose $\phi \in K \,\&\, \psi \in K$.

Suppose $\sigma{*}\langle\underline{i}\rangle{*}\tau = {\sim}\phi$. If $\sigma = \emptyset$, then $\underline{n} = ({\sim}\phi)_1 = \underline{i}$ which violates our distinctness assumptions; so $\sigma \neq \emptyset$. Then $\sigma_1 = \underline{n}$, ${\sim}\phi = {\sim}(\langle\sigma_2;\ldots;\sigma_{\ell(\sigma)}\rangle{*}\langle\underline{i}\rangle{*}\tau)$, $\langle\sigma_2;\ldots;\sigma_{\ell(\sigma)}\rangle{*}\langle\underline{i}\rangle{*}\tau = \phi \in ST_{SL}$, and since $\phi \in K$, $(\exists\chi')(\exists\chi'')(\exists\rho)(\tau = \chi'{*}\chi''{*}\rho)$. So ${\sim}\phi \in K$.

Suppose $\sigma{*}\langle\underline{i}\rangle{*}\tau = \phi \supset \psi$.

Case 1. $\sigma = \emptyset$. Then $\langle\underline{i}\rangle{*}\tau = \langle\underline{i}\rangle{*}\phi{*}\psi$ and $\tau = \phi{*}\psi{*}\emptyset$.

Case 2. $\sigma \neq \emptyset$. Then $\sigma_1 = \underline{i} \,\&\, \phi{*}\psi = \langle\sigma_2;\ldots;\sigma_{\ell(\sigma)}\rangle{*}\langle\underline{i}\rangle{*}\tau$, and $\ell(\phi) < \ell(\sigma) \vee \ell(\phi) = \ell(\sigma) \vee \ell(\sigma) < \ell(\phi)$.

Case 2a. $\ell(\phi) < \ell(\sigma)$. Then $\phi = <\sigma_2;\ldots;\sigma_{\ell(\phi)+1}>$, $\psi = <\sigma_{\ell(\phi)+2};\ldots;\sigma_{\ell(\sigma)}>*<\underline{i}>*\tau$, and $(\exists\chi')(\exists\chi'')(\exists\rho)(\tau = \chi'*\chi''*\rho)$ since $\psi \in K$.

Case 2b. $\ell(\phi) = \ell(\sigma)$. Then $\phi_{\ell(\phi)} = \underline{i}$, which is impossible according to Exercise 20.3.

Case 2c. $\ell(\sigma) < \ell(\phi)$. Then $\phi = <\sigma_2;\ldots;\sigma_{\ell(\sigma)}>*<\underline{i}>*<\tau_1;\ldots;\tau_{\ell(\phi)-\ell(\sigma)}>$. Since $\phi \in K$, we can select χ', χ'', and ρ such that $<\tau_1;\ldots;\tau_{\ell(\sigma)-\ell(\sigma)}> = \chi'*\chi''*\rho$ by our induction hypothesis. But then $\tau = \chi'*\chi''*(\rho*<\tau_{\ell(\phi)-\ell(\sigma)+1};\ldots;\tau_{\ell(\tau)}>)$.

In every possible case, then, $(\exists\chi')(\exists\chi'')(\exists\rho)(\tau = \chi'*\chi''*\rho)$. So $\phi \supset \psi \in K$.

Then $ST_{SL} \subseteq K$ by Theorem 1.

22.1 Proof of Theorem 5. Suppose $K \models \phi$. If v is a valuation and $(\psi)(\psi \in K \cup \{\sim\phi\} \rightarrow I_v(\psi) = 1)$, then $(\psi)(\psi \in K \rightarrow I_v(\psi) = 1)$, $I_v(\phi) = 1$ by Definition 38 since $K \models \phi$, and $I_v(\sim\phi) = 1$ since $\sim\phi \in K \cup \{\sim\phi\}$. But this is impossible, so $\sim(\exists v)(\psi)(\psi \in K \cup \{\sim\phi\} \rightarrow I_v(\psi) = 1)$, and $K \cup \{\sim\phi\}$ is semantically inconsistent by Definition 40.

Now suppose $K \cup \{\sim\phi\}$ is semantically inconsistent. If v is a valuation and $(\psi)(\psi \in K \rightarrow I_v(\psi) = 1)$, then $I_v(\sim\phi) \neq 1$; otherwise, $(\psi)(\psi \in K \cup \{\sim\phi\} \rightarrow I_v(\psi) = 1)$ and $K \cup \{\sim\phi\}$ is semantically consistent contrary to our hypothesis. But then by Definition 37, $I_v(\sim\phi) = 0$ and $I_v(\phi) = 1$. So $(v)((\psi)(\psi \in K \rightarrow I_v(\psi) = 1) \rightarrow I_v(\phi) = 1)$, and $K \models \phi$ by Definiton 38.

Thus $K \models \phi \leftrightarrow K \cup \{\sim\phi\}$ is semantically inconsistent.

23.3 Consider the 5-place sequence σ such that

$\sigma_1 = (\phi \supset ((\phi \supset \phi) \supset \phi)) \supset ((\phi \supset (\phi \supset \phi)) \supset (\phi \supset \phi))$ AX2

$\sigma_2 = \phi \supset ((\phi \supset \phi) \supset \phi)$ AX1

$\sigma_3 = (\phi \supset (\phi \supset \phi)) \supset (\phi \supset \phi)$ σ_1, σ_2, modus ponens

$\sigma_4 = \phi \supset (\phi \supset \phi)$ AX1

$\sigma_5 = \phi \supset \phi$ σ_3, σ_4, modus ponens

Then σ is an SL-derivation of $\phi \supset \phi$ from $\emptyset$ and $\vdash_{SL} \phi \supset \phi$.

26.7 $\vdash_{SL} {\sim}{\sim}\phi \supset ({\sim}{\sim}{\sim}{\sim}\phi \supset {\sim}{\sim}\phi)$ by AX1 and Theorem 8.

$\{{\sim}{\sim}\phi\} \vdash_{SL} {\sim}{\sim}{\sim}{\sim}\phi \supset {\sim}{\sim}\phi$ by Theorem 13.

$\{{\sim}{\sim}\phi\} \vdash_{SL} ({\sim}{\sim}{\sim}{\sim}\phi \supset {\sim}{\sim}\phi) \supset ({\sim}\phi \supset {\sim}{\sim}{\sim}\phi)$ by AX3 and Theorem 8.

$\{{\sim}{\sim}\phi\} \vdash_{SL} {\sim}\phi \supset {\sim}{\sim}{\sim}\phi$ by Theorem 9.

$\{{\sim}{\sim}\phi\} \vdash_{SL} ({\sim}\phi \supset {\sim}{\sim}{\sim}\phi) \supset ({\sim}{\sim}\phi \supset \phi)$ by AX3 and Theorem 8.

$\{{\sim}{\sim}\phi\} \vdash_{SL} {\sim}{\sim}\phi \supset \phi$ by Theorem 9.

$\{{\sim}{\sim}\phi\} \vdash_{SL} {\sim}{\sim}\phi$ by Theorem 7.

$\{{\sim}{\sim}\phi\} \vdash_{SL} \phi$ by Theorem 9.

$\vdash_{SL} {\sim}{\sim}\phi \supset \phi$ by Theorem 13.

26.23 Suppose $\vdash_{SL} \phi \equiv \phi'$ and let $K = \{\psi\colon (\sigma)(\tau)(\psi = \sigma{*}\phi{*}\tau \rightarrow \vdash_{SL} \psi \equiv \sigma{*}\phi'{*}\tau)\}$.

Basis step. Suppose $\langle P_k \rangle = \sigma{*}\phi{*}\tau$. Since $\ell(\phi) \geq 1$ and $\ell(\langle P_k \rangle) = 1$, $\sigma = \emptyset$ & $\tau = \emptyset$. Then $\langle P_k \rangle = \phi$, $\sigma{*}\phi'{*}\tau = \phi'$, and $\vdash_{SL} \langle P_k \rangle \equiv \sigma{*}\phi'{*}\tau$. So $AT_{SL} \subseteq K$.

Induction step. Suppose $\psi \in K$ & $\chi \in K$.

Suppose ${\sim}\psi = \sigma{*}\phi{*}\tau$.

Case 1. $\sigma = \emptyset$. Then ${\sim}\psi = \phi{*}\tau$, $\tau = \emptyset$ by Exercise 20.4, ${\sim}\psi = \phi$, $\sigma{*}\phi'{*}\tau = \phi'$, and $\vdash_{SL} {\sim}\psi \equiv \sigma{*}\phi'{*}\tau$.

Case 2. $\sigma \neq \emptyset$. Then $\sigma_1 = \underline{n}$, $\psi = \langle \sigma_2;\ldots;\sigma_{\ell(\sigma)} \rangle{*}\phi{*}\tau$, and $\vdash_{SL} \psi \equiv \langle \sigma_2;\ldots;\sigma_{\ell(\sigma)} \rangle{*}\phi'{*}\tau$ since $\psi \in K$. $\vdash_{SL} (\psi \equiv \langle \sigma_2;\ldots;\sigma_{\ell(\sigma)} \rangle{*}\phi'{*}\tau) \supset ({\sim}\psi \equiv \langle \underline{n} \rangle{*}\langle \sigma_2;\ldots;\sigma_{\ell(\sigma)} \rangle{*}\phi'{*}\tau)$ by Exercise 26.20, and $\vdash_{SL} {\sim}\psi \equiv \sigma{*}\phi'{*}\tau$ by Theorem 9.

So in either case, $\vdash_{SL} {\sim}\phi \equiv \sigma{*}\phi'{*}\tau$ and ${\sim}\phi \in K$.

Next suppose $\psi \supset \chi = \sigma{*}\phi{*}\tau$.

Case 1. $\sigma = \emptyset$. Then $\psi \supset \chi = \phi{*}\tau$, $\tau = \emptyset$ by Exercise 20.4, $\phi = \psi \supset \chi$, $\phi' = \sigma{*}\phi'{*}\tau$, and $\vdash_{SL} (\psi \supset \chi) \equiv \sigma{*}\phi'{*}\tau$.

Case 2. $\sigma \neq \emptyset$. Then $\sigma_1 = \underline{i}$ & $\psi{*}\chi = \langle \sigma_2;\ldots;\sigma_{\ell(\sigma)} \rangle{*}\phi{*}\tau$.

Now $\ell(\psi) \leq \ell(\sigma) - 1 \vee \ell(\sigma) - 1 < \ell(\psi) < \ell(\sigma) + \ell(\phi) - 1 \vee \ell(\sigma) + \ell(\phi) - 1 \leq \ell(\psi)$.

Case 2a. $\ell(\psi) \leq \ell(\sigma) - 1$. Then $\psi = \langle\sigma_2;\ldots;\sigma_{\ell(\psi)+1}\rangle$ & $\chi = \langle\sigma_{\ell(\psi)+2};\ldots;\sigma_{\ell(\sigma)}\rangle*\phi*\tau$. $\vdash_{SL}\chi \equiv \langle\sigma_{\ell(\psi)+2};\ldots;\sigma_{\ell(\sigma)}\rangle*\phi'*\tau$ since $\chi \in K$, and $\vdash_{SL}(\chi \equiv \langle\sigma_{\ell(\psi)+2};\ldots;\sigma_{\ell(\sigma)}\rangle*\phi'*\tau) \supset ((\psi \supset \chi) \equiv (\psi \supset \langle\sigma_{\ell(\psi)+2};\ldots;\sigma_{\ell(\sigma)}\rangle*\phi'*\tau))$ by Exerxise 26.21; so $\vdash_{SL}(\psi \supset \chi) \equiv (\psi \supset \langle\sigma_{\ell(\psi)+2};\ldots;\sigma_{\ell(\sigma)}\rangle*\phi'*\tau)$ by Theorem 9. But $\psi \supset \langle\sigma_{\ell(\psi)+2};\ldots;\sigma_{\ell(\sigma)}\rangle*\phi'*\tau = \sigma*\phi'*\tau$, so $\vdash_{SL}(\psi \supset \chi) \equiv \sigma*\phi'*\tau$.

Case 2b. $\ell(\sigma) - 1 < \ell(\psi) < \ell(\sigma) + \ell(\phi) - 1$. Then $\psi = \langle\sigma_2;\ldots;\sigma_{\ell(\sigma)};\phi_1;\ldots;\phi_{\ell(\psi)-\ell(\sigma)+1}\rangle$, $\langle\phi_1;\ldots;\phi_{\ell(\psi)-\ell(\sigma)+1}\rangle*\langle\phi_{\ell(\psi)-\ell(\sigma)+2};\ldots;\phi_{\ell(\phi)}\rangle \in ST_{SL}$, and $\langle\sigma_2;\ldots;\sigma_{\ell(\sigma)}\rangle = \emptyset \vee \langle\phi_1;\ldots;\phi_{\ell(\psi)-\ell(\sigma)+1}\rangle = \emptyset \vee \langle\phi_{\ell(\psi)-\ell(\sigma)+2};\ldots;\phi_{\ell(\phi)}\rangle = \emptyset$ by Exercise 20.6. Since $\ell(\sigma) - 1 < \ell(\psi) < \ell(\sigma) + \ell(\phi) - 1$, $\langle\phi_1;\ldots;\phi_{\ell(\psi)-\ell(\sigma)+1}\rangle \neq \emptyset$ & $\langle\phi_{\ell(\psi)-\ell(\sigma)+2};\ldots;\phi_{\ell(\phi)}\rangle \neq \emptyset$. So $\langle\sigma_2;\ldots;\sigma_{\ell(\sigma)}\rangle = \emptyset$, $\psi = \langle\phi_1;\ldots;\phi_{\ell(\psi)-\ell(\sigma)+1}\rangle$, $\psi*\langle\phi_{\ell(\psi)-\ell(\sigma)+2};\ldots;\phi_{\ell(\phi)}\rangle \in ST_{SL}$, and $\langle\phi_{\ell(\psi)-\ell(\sigma)+2};\ldots;\phi_{\ell(\phi)}\rangle = \emptyset$ by Exercise 20.4. But this is impossible.

Case 2c. $\ell(\sigma) + \ell(\phi) - 1 \leq \ell(\psi)$. Then $\psi = \langle\sigma_2;\ldots;\sigma_{\ell(\sigma)}\rangle*\phi*\langle\tau_1;\ldots;\tau_{\ell(\psi)-\ell(\sigma)-\ell(\phi)+1}\rangle$ & $\chi = \langle\tau_{\ell(\psi)-\ell(\sigma)-\ell(\phi)+2};\ldots;\tau_{\ell(\tau)}\rangle$. $\vdash_{SL}\psi \equiv \langle\sigma_2;\ldots;\sigma_{\ell(\sigma)}\rangle*\phi'*\langle\tau_1;\ldots;\tau_{\ell(\psi)-\ell(\sigma)-\ell(\phi)+1}\rangle$ since $\psi \in K$, and $\vdash_{SL}(\psi \equiv \langle\sigma_2;\ldots;\sigma_{\ell(\sigma)}\rangle*\phi'*\langle\tau_1;\ldots;\tau_{\ell(\psi)-\ell(\sigma)-\ell(\phi)+1}\rangle) \supset ((\psi \supset \chi) \equiv (\langle\sigma_2;\ldots;\sigma_{\ell(\sigma)}\rangle*\phi'*\langle\tau_1;\ldots;\tau_{\ell(\psi)-\ell(\sigma)-\ell(\phi)+1}\rangle \supset \chi))$ by Exercise 26.22; so $\vdash_{SL}(\psi \supset \chi) \equiv (\langle\sigma_2;\ldots;\sigma_{\ell(\sigma)}\rangle*\phi'*\langle\tau_1;\ldots;\tau_{\ell(\psi)-\ell(\sigma)-\ell(\phi)+1}\rangle \supset \chi)$ by Theorem 9. But $\langle\sigma_2;\ldots;\sigma_{\ell(\sigma)}\rangle*\phi'*\langle\tau_1;\ldots;\tau_{\ell(\psi)-\ell(\sigma)-\ell(\phi)+1}\rangle \supset \chi = \sigma*\phi'*\tau$, so $\vdash_{SL}(\psi \supset \chi) \equiv \sigma*\phi'*\tau$.

So in every possible case, $\vdash_{SL}(\psi \supset \chi) \equiv \sigma*\phi'*\tau$. Therefore, $\psi \supset \chi \in K$.

Then $ST_{SL} \subseteq K$ by Theorem 1.

<u>30.1</u> All of them.

<u>34.5</u> Suppose t is a PL-term. By Definition 56, $t \in VR \vee t$ is

a constant expression. Therefore by Definitions 50 and 53, we let x be a variable symbol or a constant such that t = <x>. If x is a variable symbol, let A = $\emptyset$; if x is a constant, let A = {x}. In either case, (x)(x ε A $\rightarrow$ x is a constant). So by Exercise 34.4, we can let L be a PL-language such that L_B = A. Then TM_L = VR $\cup$ {<x>} = VR $\cup$ {t} and t ε TM_L.

35.2 We will use Theorem 36. Let K = {ϕ: ϕ ε FM_L & ($\exists$t)(t TM_L & $<\phi_{\ell(\phi)}>$ = t)}.

Basis step. Let ϕ ε AT_L. Then ($\exists$n)($\exists$F)($\exists t_1$)...($\exists t_n$)(ϕ = $Ft_1...t_n$ & F is an n-place predicate expression of L & t_1 ε TM_L & ... & t_n ε TM_L). But then $<\phi_{\ell(\phi)}> = t_n$, ϕ ε K, and $AT_L \subseteq K$.

Induction step. Suppose ϕ ε K & ψ ε K. Then $<(\sim\phi)_{\ell(\sim\phi)}>$ = $<(\psi \supset \phi)_{\ell(\psi \supset \phi)}>$ = $<(\Lambda\alpha\phi)_{\ell(\Lambda\alpha\phi)}>$ = $<\phi_{\ell(\phi)}>$. But $<\phi_{\ell(\phi)}>$ ε TM_L since ϕ ε K, so $\sim\phi$ ε K & $\psi \supset \phi$ ε K & $\Lambda\alpha\phi$ ε K.

So $FM_L \subseteq K$ by Theorem 36.

36.6 We begin by assuming that $<(\Lambda\alpha\phi)_n>$ = β.

Suppose OB(β,n, $\Lambda\alpha\phi$). We are finished if $\alpha = \beta$, so suppose $\alpha \neq \beta$. By Definition 61, we let ψ be a PL-formula and let x ε N $\cup$ {0} such that $<(\Lambda\alpha\phi)_n>$ = β & ψ_1 = $\underline{u}$ & $<\psi_2>$ = β & x < n $\leq$ x + $\ell(\psi)$ & (j)(j $\leq$ $\ell(\psi)$ $\rightarrow$ ψ_j = $(\Lambda\alpha\phi)_{j+x}$). Now n $\neq$ 1 by Exercise 36.5 and n $\neq$ 2 by Exercise 36.3, since $\alpha \neq \beta$. Similarly, x $\neq$ 0 & x $\neq$ 1. So n > 2 & $<\phi_{n-2}>$ = $<(\Lambda\alpha\phi)_n>$ = β & ψ_1 = $\underline{u}$ & $<\psi_2>$ = β & x - 2 ε N $\cup$ {0} & x - 2 < n - 2 $\leq$ x - 2 + $\ell(\psi)$ & (j)(j $\leq$ $\ell(\psi)$ $\rightarrow$ ψ_j = $(\Lambda\alpha\phi)_{j+x}$ = ϕ_{j+x+2}). Then by Definition 61, OB(β,n - 2,ϕ), and OB(β,n, $\Lambda\alpha\phi$) $\rightarrow$ ($\alpha = \beta$ v (n > 2 & OB(β,n - 2,ϕ))).

Now suppose $\alpha = \beta$ v (n > 2 & OB(β,n - 2,ϕ)).

Case 1. $\alpha = \beta$. Then $<(\Lambda\alpha\phi)_n>$ = β & $(\Lambda\alpha\phi)_1$ = $\underline{u}$ & $<(\Lambda\alpha\phi)_2>$ = β & 0 < n $\leq$ $\ell(\Lambda\alpha\phi)$ + 0 & (j)(j $\leq$ $\ell(\Lambda\alpha\phi)$ $\rightarrow$ $(\Lambda\alpha\phi)_j$ = $(\Lambda\alpha\phi)_{j+0}$). So OB($\beta$,n, $\Lambda\alpha\phi$).

Case 2. n > 2 & OB(β,n - 2,ϕ). Let ψ be a PL-formula and let x ε N $\cup$ {0} such that $<\phi_{n-2}>$ = β & ψ_1 = $\underline{u}$ & $<\psi_2>$ =

β & $x < n - 2 \leq \ell(\psi) + x$ & $(j)(j \leq \ell(\psi) \to \psi_j = \phi_{j + x})$. Then $<(\bigwedge \alpha\phi)_n> = \beta$ & $\psi_1 = \underline{u}$ & $<\psi_2> = \beta$ & $x + 2 < n - 2 + 2 = n \leq \ell(\psi) + x + 2$ & $(j)(j \leq \ell(\psi) \to \psi_j = \phi_{j + x} = (\bigwedge \alpha\phi)_{j + x + 2})$, and $OB(\beta, n, \bigwedge \alpha\phi)$.

So in either case we see that $(\alpha = \beta \vee (n > 2$ & $OB(\beta, n - 2, \phi))) \to OB(\beta, n, \bigwedge \alpha\phi)$.

Therefore $<(\bigwedge \alpha\phi)_n> = \beta \to (OB(\beta, n, \bigwedge \alpha\phi) \leftrightarrow (\alpha = \beta \vee (n > 2$ & $OB(\beta, n - 2, \phi))))$.

37.3 Let ϕ be a PL-formula, let c be a constant expression, and let L be a PL-language such that $\phi \in FM_L$ & $c \in TM_L$. We will show that $\alpha \notin FV(|\alpha/c|\phi)$ by using Theorem 36 to show that $FM_L \subseteq K$ where $K = \{\psi\colon \psi \in FM_L$ & $\alpha \notin FV(|\alpha/c|\psi)\}$.

First we show that $t \in TM_L \to |\alpha/c|t \neq \alpha$. Let $t \in TM_L$. Then $t = \alpha \vee t \neq \alpha$. If $t = \alpha$, then $|\alpha/c|t = c$ by Definition 69; but then since no variable symbol is a constant by our distinctness assumptions, $|\alpha/c|t \neq \alpha$. If $t \neq \alpha$, then $|\alpha/c|t = t$ by Definition 69 and $|\alpha/c|t \neq \alpha$. So in either case, $|\alpha/c|t \neq \alpha$.

Basis step. Let $Ft_1 \ldots t_n \in AT_L$. $|\alpha/c|(Ft_1 \ldots t_n) = F|\alpha/c|t_1 \ldots |\alpha/c|t_n$ by Definition 69. Then $(k)(k \leq \ell(|\alpha/c|(Ft_1 \ldots t_n) \to (<(|\alpha/c|(Ft_1 \ldots t_n))_k> = F \vee <(|\alpha/c|(Ft_1 \ldots t_n))_k> = |\alpha/c|t_{k - 1}))$. By our distinctness assumptions, no variable symbol is a predicate and hence $F \neq \alpha$. Therefore, since we have already seen that $(k)(k \leq n \to |\alpha/c|t_k \neq \alpha)$, we conclude that $(k)(k \leq \ell(|\alpha/c|(Ft_1 \ldots t_n)) \to <(|\alpha/c|(Ft_1 \ldots t_n))_k> \neq \alpha)$. Then $\sim(\exists k)(OF(\alpha, k, |\alpha/c|(Ft_1 \ldots t_n)))$ by Definition 64, and $\alpha \notin FV(|\alpha/c|(Ft_1 \ldots t_n))$ by Definition 66. So $AT_L \subseteq K$.

Induction step. Suppose $\psi \in K$ & $\chi \in K$. $|\alpha/c|(\sim\psi) = \sim|\alpha/c|\psi$ by Definition 69, and $FV(\sim|\alpha/c|\psi) = FV(|\alpha/c|\psi)$ by Exercise 36.3; so $FV(|\alpha/c|(\sim\psi)) = FV(|\alpha/c|\psi)$. But $\psi \in K$ and hence $\alpha \notin FV(|\alpha/c|\psi)$; so $\alpha \notin FV(|\alpha/c|(\sim\psi))$ and $\sim\psi \in K$.

Similarly we can use Exercise 36.4 to show that $\psi \supset \chi \in K$.

By Definition 69, $(\alpha = \beta$ & $|\alpha/c|(\bigwedge \beta\psi) = \bigwedge \beta\psi) \vee (\alpha \neq \beta$ & $|\alpha/c|(\bigwedge \beta\psi) = \bigwedge \beta|\alpha/c|\psi)$.

Case 1. Suppose $\alpha = \beta$ & $|\alpha/c|(\bigwedge\beta\psi) = \bigwedge\beta\psi$. By Exercise 36.8, $FV(\bigwedge\beta\psi) = FV(\psi) - \{\beta\}$. Since $\alpha = \beta$, it follows that $\alpha \notin FV(|\alpha/c|(\bigwedge\beta\psi))$ & $\bigwedge\beta\psi \in K$.

Case 2. Suppose $\alpha \neq \beta$ & $|\alpha/c|(\bigwedge\beta\psi) = \bigwedge\beta|\alpha/c|\psi$. By Exercise 36.8, $FV(\bigwedge\beta|\alpha/c|\psi) = FV(|\alpha/c|\psi) - \{\beta\}$. But $\psi \in K$, so $\alpha \notin FV(|\alpha/c|\psi)$, $\alpha \notin FV(|\alpha/c|(\bigwedge\beta\psi))$, and $\bigwedge\beta\psi \in K$.

Therefore $FM_L \subseteq K$.

37.12 Suppose $c \notin OC(|c/\alpha||\beta/c|\phi)$ and let L be a PL-language such that $\phi \in FM_L$ & $c \in TM_L$.

A. Suppose $t \in TM_L$. If $t = \beta$, then $|c/\alpha||\beta/c|t = |c/\alpha|c = \alpha = |c/\alpha|\alpha = |c/\alpha||\beta/\alpha|t$. If $t \neq \beta$, then $|\beta/c|t = t = |\beta/\alpha|t$ and $|c/\alpha||\beta/c|t = |c/\alpha||\beta/\alpha|t$. So in any case, $|c/\alpha||\beta/c|t = |c/\alpha||\beta/\alpha|t$.

B. Let $K = \{\psi: \psi \in FM_L$ & $(|\beta/c|\psi \neq \psi \rightarrow c \in OC(|\beta/c|\psi))\}$. We will show that $FM_L \subseteq K$.

Basis step. Suppose $Ft_1 \ldots t_n \in AT_L$ & $|\beta/c|(Ft_1 \ldots t_n) \neq Ft_1 \ldots t_n$. Then $|\beta/c|(Ft_1 \ldots t_n) = F|\beta/c|t_1 \ldots |\beta/c|t_n$ and $F = F$, so there is a $k \leq n$ such that $|\beta/c|t_k \neq t_k$. But if $t_k \neq \beta$, then $|\beta/c|t_k = t_k$; so $t_k = \beta$, $|\beta/c|t_k = c$, and $c \in OC(|\beta/c|(Ft_1 \ldots t_n))$. So $AT_L \subseteq K$.

Induction step. Suppose $\psi \in K$ & $\chi \in K$.

Suppose $|\beta/c|(\sim\psi) \neq \sim\psi$. Then $|\beta/c|(\sim\psi) = \sim|\beta/c|\psi$, $|\beta/c|\psi \neq \psi$, $c \in OC(|\beta/c|\psi)$ since $\psi \in K$, $c \in OC(|\beta/c|(\sim\psi))$ by Exercise 37.6, and $\sim\psi \in K$. Similarly, we can show that $\psi \supset \chi \in K$.

Suppose $|\beta/c|(\bigwedge\gamma\psi) \neq \bigwedge\gamma\psi$. Then $\gamma \neq \beta$ by Definition 69, $|\beta/c|(\bigwedge\gamma\psi) = \bigwedge\gamma|\beta/c|\psi$, $|\beta/c|\psi \neq \psi$, $c \in OC(|\beta/c|\psi)$ since $\psi \in K$, and $c \in OC(|\beta/c|(\bigwedge\gamma\psi))$ by Exercise 37.6. So $\bigwedge\gamma\psi \in K$.

Then $FM_L \subseteq K$ by Theorem 36.

C. Next let $\Gamma = \{\psi: \psi \in FM_L$ & $(c \notin OC(|c/\alpha||\beta/c|\psi) \rightarrow |c/\alpha||\beta/c|\psi = |c/\alpha||\beta/\alpha|\psi)\}$. We will show that $FM_L \subseteq \Gamma$.

Basis step. Suppose $Ft_1 \ldots t_n \in AT_L$ & $c \notin OC(|c/\alpha||\beta/c|(Ft_1 \ldots t_n))$. Then $|c/\alpha||\beta/c|(Ft_1 \ldots t_n) = F|c/\alpha||\beta/c|t_1 \ldots$

$|c/\alpha||\beta/c|t_n = F|c/\alpha||\beta/\alpha|t_1 \ldots |c/\alpha||\beta/\alpha|t_n$ (from our result A above) $= |c/\alpha||\beta/\alpha|(Ft_1 \ldots t_n)$, and $AT_L \subseteq \Gamma$.

Induction step. Suppose $\psi \in \Gamma$ & $\chi \in \Gamma$.

Suppose $c \notin OC(|c/\alpha||\beta/c|(\sim\psi))$ $(= OC(\sim|c/\alpha||\beta/c|\psi))$. Then $c \notin OC(|c/\alpha||\beta/c|\psi)$ by Exercise 37.6, $|c/\alpha||\beta/c|\psi = |c/\alpha||\beta/\alpha|\psi$ since $\psi \in \Gamma$, $|c/\alpha||\beta/c|(\sim\psi) = \sim|c/\alpha||\beta/c|\psi = \sim|c/\alpha||\beta/\alpha|\psi = |c/\alpha||\beta/\alpha|(\sim\psi)$, and $\sim\psi \in \Gamma$. Similarly, we can show that $\psi \supset \chi \in \Gamma$.

Suppose $c \notin OC(|c/\alpha||\beta/c|(\bigwedge\gamma\psi))$.

Case 1. $\gamma = \beta$. Then $|c/\alpha||\beta/c|(\bigwedge\gamma\psi) = |c/\alpha|(\bigwedge\gamma\psi) = |c/\alpha||\beta/\alpha|(\bigwedge\gamma\psi)$.

Case 2. $\gamma = \alpha$ & $\gamma \neq \beta$. Then $|c/\alpha||\beta/c|(\bigwedge\gamma\psi) = |c/\alpha|\bigwedge\gamma|\beta/c|\psi = \bigwedge\gamma|\beta/c|\psi$ and $|c/\alpha||\beta/\alpha|(\bigwedge\gamma\psi) = \bigwedge\gamma\psi$. Since $c \notin OC(|c/\alpha||\beta/c|(\bigwedge\gamma\psi))$, $c \notin OC(\bigwedge\gamma|\beta/c|\psi)$, and $c \notin OC(|\beta/c|\psi)$ by Exercise 37.6. Then by our result B above, $|\beta/c|\psi = \psi$. So $|c/\alpha||\beta/c|(\bigwedge\gamma\psi) = |c/\alpha||\beta/\alpha|(\bigwedge\gamma\psi)$.

Case 3. $\gamma \neq \alpha$ & $\gamma \neq \beta$. Then $|c/\alpha||\beta/c|(\bigwedge\gamma\psi) = \bigwedge\gamma|c/\alpha||\beta/c|\psi$, $c \notin OC(|c/\alpha||\beta/c|\psi)$ by Exercise 37.6 since $c \notin OC(\bigwedge\gamma|c/\alpha||\beta/c|\psi)$, $|c/\alpha||\beta/c|\psi = |c/\alpha||\beta/\alpha|\psi$ since $\psi \in \Gamma$, and $|c/\alpha||\beta/c|(\bigwedge\gamma\psi) = \bigwedge\gamma|c/\alpha||\beta/c|\psi = \bigwedge\gamma|c/\alpha||\beta/\alpha|\psi = |c/\alpha||\beta/\alpha|(\bigwedge\gamma\psi)$.

So in any case, $|c/\alpha||\beta/c|(\bigwedge\gamma\psi) = |c/\alpha||\beta/\alpha|(\bigwedge\gamma\psi)$ and $\bigwedge\gamma\psi \in \Gamma$.

Therefore $FM_L \subseteq \Gamma$ by Theorem 36. Since $\phi \in FM_L$ & $c \notin OC(|c/\alpha||\beta/c|\phi)$, $|c/\alpha||\beta/c|\phi = |c/\alpha||\beta/\alpha|\phi$.

Now that we have completed our proof, let's look at its structure. Although it may not be obvious that this is what we have done, we have here an induction on FM_L <u>within</u> an induction on FM_L. Our construction of the proof really begins with part C. When we try to do the basis step, we find that we need to show that certain combinations of substitutions in the terms of L produce the same results. So we do part A of our proof. Then in the induction step we run into another problem when we reach case 2 in trying to show that $\bigwedge\gamma\psi \in \Gamma$.

We solve this problem by providing part B of our proof. The proof would be very messy if we tried to insert parts A and B into the middle of part C at the points at which they are needed. That is why we pull them out and put them at the front end of our proof. Results of this sort which are needed in order to establish a different, major result are often called lemmas. Thus the Lindenbaum Lemma is a result which we establish on our way to proving completeness.

39.1 Proof of Theorem 48. Suppose $\alpha \notin FV(\phi)$ & $\beta \notin FV(|\beta/\alpha|\phi)$. We leave it to the reader to show that $\alpha \notin FV(\phi) \rightarrow |\alpha/\beta||\beta/\alpha|\phi = \phi$, and thus $\alpha \notin FV(|\alpha/\beta||\beta/\alpha|\phi)$. Therefore,

$\vdash_L \Lambda\beta(\Lambda\alpha|\beta/\alpha|\phi \supset |\alpha/\beta||\beta/\alpha|\phi)$ by AX5 and Theorem 39.

$\vdash_L \Lambda\beta(\Lambda\alpha|\beta/\alpha|\phi \supset \phi)$ since $|\alpha/\beta||\beta/\alpha|\phi = \phi$.

$\vdash_L \Lambda\beta(\Lambda\alpha|\beta/\alpha|\phi \supset \phi) \supset (\Lambda\beta\Lambda\alpha|\beta/\alpha|\phi \supset \Lambda\beta\phi)$ by Ax4 and Theorem 39.

$\vdash_L \Lambda\beta\Lambda\alpha|\beta/\alpha|\phi \supset \Lambda\beta\phi$ by Theorem 40.

$\vdash_L \Lambda\alpha|\beta/\alpha|\phi \supset \Lambda\beta\Lambda\alpha|\beta/\alpha|\phi$ by Exercise 36.8, AX6, and Theorem 39.

$\vdash_L \Lambda\alpha|\beta/\alpha|\phi \supset \Lambda\beta\phi$ by Hypothetical Syllogism.

(By AX1-AX3 and Theorem 40, we can in effect show that any SL-theorem has an L-counterpart for any PL-language L. Because of this, we can abbreviate some of our proofs by listing such results as the exercises at the end of Section 26 as justifications in our arguments concerning L-derivations. More accurately, we can say that a proof that $\phi \in FM_L \rightarrow \vdash_L \phi \supset \phi$, for example, exactly parallels a proof that $\phi \in ST_{SL} \rightarrow \vdash_{SL} \phi \supset \phi$. Hypothetical Syllogism falls into this category as well. To complete our present proof, then, all we need to show is the converse of our last line above since this together with the last line will imply our result in "sentential logic". See Section 50 on logistic systems.)

$\vdash_L \Lambda\alpha(\Lambda\beta\phi \supset |\beta/\alpha|\phi)$ by AX5 and Theorem 39.

$\vdash_L \Lambda\alpha(\Lambda\beta\phi \supset |\beta/\alpha|\phi) \supset (\Lambda\alpha\Lambda\beta\phi \supset \Lambda\alpha|\beta/\alpha|\phi)$ by AX4, Theorem 39.

$\vdash_L \bigwedge\alpha \bigwedge\beta\phi \supset \bigwedge\alpha|\beta/\alpha|\phi$ by Theorem 40.

$\vdash_L \bigwedge\beta\phi \supset \bigwedge\alpha \bigwedge\beta\phi$ by Exercise 36.8, AX6, and Theorem 39, since $\alpha \notin FV(\phi)$.

$\vdash_L \bigwedge\beta\phi \supset \bigwedge\alpha|\beta/\alpha|\phi$ by Hypothetical Syllogism.

<u>39.2.b</u> $\vdash_L \bigwedge\beta G\alpha\beta \supset G\alpha\beta$ by AX5 and Theorem 39.

$\vdash_L (\bigwedge\beta G\alpha\beta \supset G\alpha\beta) \supset ({\sim}G\alpha\beta \supset {\sim}\bigwedge\beta G\alpha\beta)$ by Exercise 26.11.

$\vdash_L {\sim}G\alpha\beta \supset {\sim}\bigwedge\beta G\alpha\beta$ by Theorem 40.

$\vdash_L \bigwedge\alpha({\sim}G\alpha\beta \supset {\sim}\bigwedge\beta G\alpha\beta)$ by Theorem 46.

$\vdash_L \bigwedge\alpha({\sim}G\alpha\beta \supset {\sim}\bigwedge\beta G\alpha\beta) \supset (\bigwedge\alpha{\sim}G\alpha\beta \supset \bigwedge\alpha{\sim}\bigwedge\beta G\alpha\beta)$ by AX4 and Theorem 39.

$\vdash_L \bigwedge\alpha{\sim}G\alpha\beta \supset \bigwedge\alpha{\sim}\bigwedge\beta G\alpha\beta)$ by Theorem 40.

$\vdash_L (\bigwedge\alpha{\sim}G\alpha\beta \supset \bigwedge\alpha{\sim}\bigwedge\beta G\alpha\beta) \supset ({\sim}\bigwedge\alpha{\sim}\bigwedge\beta G\alpha\beta \supset {\sim}\bigwedge\alpha{\sim}G\alpha\beta)$ by Exercise 26.11.

$\vdash_L \bigvee\alpha \bigwedge\beta G\alpha\beta \supset \bigvee\alpha G\alpha\beta$ by Theorem 40 and Definition 55.

$\vdash_L \bigwedge\beta(\bigvee\alpha \bigwedge\beta G\alpha\beta \supset \bigvee\alpha G\alpha\beta)$ by Theorem 46.

$\vdash_L \bigwedge\beta(\bigvee\alpha \bigwedge\beta G\alpha\beta \supset \bigvee\alpha G\alpha\beta) \supset (\bigwedge\beta\bigvee\alpha \bigwedge\beta G\alpha\beta \supset \bigwedge\beta\bigvee\alpha G\alpha\beta)$ by AX4 and Theorem 39.

$\vdash_L \bigwedge\beta\bigvee\alpha \bigwedge\beta G\alpha\beta \supset \bigwedge\beta\bigvee\alpha G\alpha\beta$ by Theorem 40.

$\vdash_L \bigvee\alpha \bigwedge\beta G\alpha\beta \supset \bigwedge\beta\bigvee\alpha \bigwedge\beta G\alpha\beta$ by AX6 and Theorem 39.

$\vdash_L \bigvee\alpha \bigwedge\beta G\alpha\beta \supset \bigwedge\beta\bigvee\alpha G\alpha\beta$ by Hypothetical Syllogism.

<u>39.3</u> Here is a sketch of a proof for this result. Suppose $\phi \in FM_L$ & $\alpha \notin OC(\phi)$. Let $K = \{\bigwedge\alpha{\sim}(\bigvee\beta\phi \supset |\beta/\alpha|\phi)\}$ and show that $K \vdash_L {\sim}\bigwedge\beta{\sim}\phi$ and $K \vdash_L |\beta/\alpha|({\sim}\phi)$. Then $K \vdash_L \bigwedge\alpha|\beta/\alpha|({\sim}\phi)$ by Theorem 47, $K \vdash_L \bigwedge\beta{\sim}\phi \equiv \bigwedge\alpha|\beta/\alpha|({\sim}\phi)$ by Theorem 48, and $K \vdash_L \bigwedge\beta{\sim}\phi$. But $K \vdash_L \bigwedge\beta{\sim}\phi \supset ({\sim}\bigwedge\beta{\sim}\phi \supset {\sim}(\phi \supset \phi))$, so $K \vdash_L {\sim}(\phi \supset \phi)$, and $\vdash_L \bigwedge\alpha{\sim}(\bigvee\beta\phi \supset |\beta/\alpha|\phi) \supset {\sim}(\phi \supset \phi)$ by Theorem 43. Then we can show that $\vdash_L (\phi \supset \phi) \supset \bigvee\alpha(\bigvee\beta\phi \supset |\beta/\alpha|\phi)$, and since $\vdash_L (\phi \supset \phi)$, we are done.

<u>42.4</u> Let $A = \{x,y,z\}$ such that $c = \langle x\rangle$, $F = \langle y\rangle$, and $G = \langle z\rangle$, and let L be the PL-language such that $L_B = A$. Let $U = \{1\}$, let $R(c) = 1$, let $R(F) = \{\langle 1\rangle\}$, let $R(G) = \{\langle 1;1\rangle\}$, and let

$a(\beta) = 1$ for each $\beta \in VR$. Then $\langle U;R\rangle$ is an L-model and a is an assignment for $\langle U;R\rangle$ such that a sim-sat $\{Gc\alpha, Fc, F\alpha\}$ in $\langle U;R\rangle$. Then $\{Gc\alpha, Fc, F\alpha\}$ is semantically consistent by Definitions 85 and 86.

54.4 Define $w{:}ST_{\Box} \longrightarrow \{0,1\}$ recursively as follows.

1. For each $n \in N$, let $w(\langle P_n\rangle) = 0$.
2. Let $w(\sim\phi) = 1$ if and only if $w(\phi) = 0$.
3. Let $w(\phi \supset \psi) = 0$ if and only if $w(\phi) = 1$ & $w(\psi) = 0$.
4. Let $w(\Box\phi) = 1$.

Clearly w is a world. Let $U = \{w\}$ and let $R = \emptyset$. Then $w(\Box\phi) = 1$ if and only if $(w')(\langle w;w'\rangle \in R \rightarrow w'(\phi) = 1)$, and $\langle U;R\rangle$ is an RWS by Definition 104. But $w(\Box\langle P_1\rangle) = 1$ & $w(\langle P_1\rangle) = 0$, so $\Box\langle P_1\rangle \supset \langle P_1\rangle$ is not true in $\langle U;R\rangle$ by Definition 105 and $\sim\vdash_{Kr} \Box\langle P_1\rangle \supset \langle P_1\rangle$ by Theorem 101.

56.2 Let $R^* = \{\langle 1;1\rangle, \langle 2;2\rangle, \langle 3;3\rangle, \langle 1;2\rangle, \langle 2;3\rangle\}$. We will define three worlds w_1, w_2, and w_3 simultaneously as follows.

1. Let $w_1(\langle P_1\rangle) = w_2(\langle P_1\rangle) = 1$ and $w_3(\langle P_1\rangle) = 0$.
2. For $n > 1$, let $w_1(\langle P_n\rangle) = w_2(\langle P_n\rangle) = w_3(\langle P_n\rangle) = 1$.
3. For $n \leq 3$, let $w_n(\sim\phi) = 1$ if and only if $w_n(\phi) = 0$.
4. For $n \leq 3$, let $w_n(\phi \supset \psi) = 0$ if and only if $w_n(\phi) = 1$ & $w_n(\psi) = 0$.
5. For $n \leq 3$, let $w_n(\Box\phi) = 1$ if and only if $(k)(\langle n;k\rangle \in R^* \rightarrow w_k(\phi) = 1)$.

Let $U = \{w_1, w_2, w_3\}$ and let $R = \{\langle w_i;w_j\rangle : \langle i;j\rangle \in R^*\}$. Then examination of all cases shows that $\langle U;R\rangle$ is an RWS and R is reflexive. But $w_1(\Box\langle P_1\rangle) = 1$, $w_2(\Box\langle P_1\rangle) = 0$, and $w_1(\Box\Box\langle P_1\rangle) = 0$. So $w_1(\Box\langle P_1\rangle \supset \Box\Box\langle P_1\rangle) = 0$, $\Box\langle P_1\rangle \supset \Box\Box\langle P_1\rangle$ is not true in $\langle U;R\rangle$, and $\sim\vdash_{T} \Box\langle P_1\rangle \supset \Box\Box\langle P_1\rangle$ by Theorem 105.

57.2 The difficult part of this proof is to show that $\vdash_{S4'} \Box\phi \supset \Box\Box\phi$. Assume that we have shown that S4 is a normal extension of T and hence a logistic system.

$\vdash_{S4'} \phi \supset ((\phi \supset \phi) \supset \phi)$ since S4' is a logistic system.

$\vdash_{S4'} \Box(\phi \supset ((\phi \supset \phi) \supset \phi))$ since S4' is normal.

$\vdash_{S4'} \Box(\phi \supset ((\phi \supset \phi) \supset \phi)) \supset (\Box\phi \supset \Box((\phi \supset \phi) \supset \phi))$ since S4' is an extension of T.

$\vdash_{S4'} \Box\phi \supset \Box((\phi \supset \phi) \supset \phi)$ since S4' is a logistic system.

$\vdash_{S4'} \Box((\phi \supset \phi) \supset \phi) \supset \Box(\Box(\phi \supset \phi) \supset \Box\phi)$ by the Definition of $AX_{S4'}$.

$\vdash_{S4'} \Box\phi \supset \Box(\Box(\phi \supset \phi) \supset \Box\phi)$ since S4' is a logistic system (Hypothetical Syllogism).

$\vdash_{S4'} \Box(\Box(\phi \supset \phi) \supset \Box\phi) \supset (\Box\Box(\phi \supset \phi) \supset \Box\Box\phi)$ since S4' is an extension of T.

$\vdash_{S4'} \Box\phi \supset (\Box\Box(\phi \supset \phi) \supset \Box\Box\phi)$ by Hypothetical Syllogism again.

$\vdash_{S4'} \phi \supset \phi$ since S4' is a logistic system.

$\vdash_{S4'} \Box(\phi \supset \phi)$ & $\vdash_{S4'} \Box\Box(\phi \supset \phi)$ since S4' is normal.

$\vdash_{S4'} \Box\phi \supset \Box\Box\phi$ since S4' is a logistic system.

<u>59.2</u> Let $K = \{\phi\colon \phi$ is modally closed $\rightarrow \vdash_{S5} \phi \supset \Box\phi\}$.

Basis step. $\phi \in AT_{SL}$. Then ϕ is not modally closed, so $\phi \in K$. Thus $AT_{SL} \subseteq K$.

Induction step. Suppose $\phi \in K$ & $\psi \in K$. We need to show that ($\sim\phi$ is modally closed $\rightarrow$ ϕ is modally closed) and that ($\phi \supset \psi$ is modally closed $\rightarrow$ (ϕ is modally closed & ψ is modally closed)). Here we show the first of these results and leave the other to the reader.

Suppose that $\sim\phi$ is modally closed and that $\phi = \sigma * \langle P_n \rangle * \tau$. Then $\sim\phi = \langle \underline{n} \rangle * \sigma * \langle P_n \rangle * \tau$ and since $\sim\phi$ is modally closed we choose σ', σ'', τ', τ'', and χ such that $\langle \underline{n} \rangle * \sigma = \sigma' * \sigma''$, $\tau = \tau' * \tau''$, and $\Box\chi = \sigma'' * \langle P_n \rangle * \tau'$. Then $\sigma''_1 = \underline{1}$, $\sigma''_1 \neq \underline{n}$ by our distinctness assumptions for modal symbols, $\ell(\sigma') \geq 1$, and $\phi = \langle \sigma'_2; \ldots; \sigma'_{\ell(\sigma')} \rangle * \sigma'' * \langle P_n \rangle * \tau$. Then ϕ is modally closed by Definition 135.

Now we will show that $\sim\phi \in K$ & $\phi \supset \psi \in K$.

Suppose $\sim\phi$ is modally closed. Then ϕ is modally closed, and $\vdash_{S5} \phi \supset \Box\phi$ since $\phi \in K$. Then $\vdash_{S5} \sim\Box\phi \supset \sim\phi$, $\vdash_{S5} \Box(\sim\Box\phi \supset \sim\phi)$ since S5 is normal, and $\vdash_{S5} \Box\sim\Box\phi \supset \Box\sim\phi$. Now $\vdash_{S5} \sim\Box\sim\Box\phi \supset \Box\phi$ by

Exercise 59.5.a, so $\vdash_{S5} \sim\Box\phi \supset \Box\sim\Box\phi$, and $\vdash_{S5} \sim\Box\phi \supset \Box\sim\phi$ by Hypothetical Syllogism. But $\vdash_{S5} \Box\phi \supset \phi$, so $\vdash_{S5} \sim\phi \supset \sim\Box\phi$, and $\vdash_{S5} \sim\phi \supset \Box\sim\phi$ by Hypothetical Syllogism. Therefore $\sim\phi \in K$.

Suppose $\phi \supset \psi$ is modally closed. Then ϕ and ψ are modally closed, and $\vdash_{S5} \phi \supset \Box\phi$ & $\vdash_{S5} \psi \supset \Box\psi$ since $\phi \in K$ & $\psi \in K$. Then $\vdash_{S5} \psi \supset (\phi \supset \psi)$, $\vdash_{S5} \Box(\psi \supset (\phi \supset \psi))$ since S5 is normal, $\vdash_{S5} \Box\psi \supset \Box(\phi \supset \psi)$, and $\vdash_{S5} \psi \supset \Box(\phi \supset \psi)$ by Hypothetical Syllogism. Furthermore, $\vdash_{S5} \sim\phi \supset (\phi \supset \psi)$, $\vdash_{S5} \Box(\sim\phi \supset (\phi \supset \psi))$, and $\vdash_{S5} \Box\sim\phi \supset \Box(\phi \supset \psi)$. But $\sim\phi \in K$, so $\vdash_{S5} \sim\phi \supset \Box\sim\phi$ since $\sim\phi$ is clearly modally closed if ϕ is, and $\vdash_{S5} \sim\phi \supset \Box(\phi \supset \psi)$. Using Exercise 26.22, we conclude that $\vdash_{S5} (\phi \supset \psi) \supset \Box(\phi \supset \psi)$. So $\phi \supset \psi \in K$.

Since $\vdash_{S5} \Box\phi \supset \Box\Box\phi$, $\Box\phi \in K$.

Therefore $ST_{\Box} \subseteq K$ by Theorem 74.

66.3 Define $f^*:\{<\phi;i> : i = 1 \vee i = 2\} \longrightarrow \text{Power}(\{1,2\})$ as follows.

1. $f^*(<P_1>,1) = \{2\}$.
2. If $\phi \neq <P_1>$, then $f^*(\phi,1) = \{1,2\}$.
3. $f^*(\phi,2) = \{2\}$.

We simultaneously define two c-worlds w_1 and w_2 as follows.

1. $w_1(<P_2>) = 0$ & $w_2(<P_2>) = 1$.
2. If $n \neq 2$, $w_1(<P_n>) = w_2(<P_n>) = 1$.
3. For $n \leq 2$, $w_n(\sim\phi) = 1$ if and only if $w_n(\phi) = 0$.
4. For $n \leq 2$, $w_n(\phi \supset \psi) = 0$ if and only if $w_n(\phi) = 1$ & $w_n(\psi) = 0$.
5. For $n \leq 2$, $w_n(\phi > \psi) = 1$ if and only if $(j)(j \in f^*(\phi,n) \rightarrow w_j(\phi \supset \psi) = 1)$.

Let $U = \{w_1,w_2\}$, and for each $w_n \in U$ and each ϕ, let $f(\phi,w_n) = \{w_j: j \in f^*(\phi,n)$ & $w_j(\phi) = 1\}$. Examination of all cases shows that $<U;f>$ is an FWS. But $w_1(<P_1> > <P_2>) = 1$ & $w_1(<P_1> \supset <P_2>) = 0$; so $(<P_1> > <P_2>) \supset (<P_1> \supset <P_2>)$ is not true in $<U;f>$ and $\sim\vdash_{C} (<P_1> > <P_2>) \supset (<P_1> \supset <P_2>)$ by Theorem 126.